Anymore for Anymore

The
RONNIE LANE
Story

Anymore for Anymore

The
RONNIE LANE
Story

Caroline & David Stafford

OMNIBUS PRESS

London / New York / Paris / Sydney / Copenhagen / Berlin / Madrid / Tokyo

Copyright © 2023 Omnibus Press
(A division of the Wise Music Group
14–15 Berners Street, London, W1T 3LJ)

Cover designed by Amazing15
Picture research by the author

ISBN 978-1-913172-53-4

Every effort has been made to trace the copyright holders of the
photographs in this book but one or two were unreachable. We would
be grateful if the photographers concerned would contact us.

A catalogue record for this book is available from the British Library.

Typeset in Bembo by Palimpsest Book Production Ltd, Falkirk, Stirlingshire

Printed in the Czech Republic

www.omnibuspress.com

Dedicated to Kate Lane and her children
Alana, Luke and Reuben Lane – Rock on, Katie!

Contents

Prologue   1

1 Bronco Lane   3

2 Some Experience in Pubs   12

3 Mod   24

4 Maurice the Monster and Terry the Egg   31

5 The Jewish Teddy Bear   38

6 'Sort of Leader of the Small Faces'   48

7 The Rigours of the Road   55

8 The Seeker   63

9 Ungrateful Bastards   73

10 We Are Stardust   82

11 The Small Faces Transcend Pop   91

12 Things Fall Apart   101

13 Keep Playing, We'll Try and Bring Him Back   113

14 The Best Place to Be on the Planet   125

15 Raffish Incorrigibles   139

16 The Healing Power of Good Rock'n'roll   148

17 What the Fuck's Happened to Ronnie Lane?   162

18 I'm Leaving the Group   174

19 Wanting Leads Inevitably to Suffering   187

20 Melodious Winos   205

21 Well, Hello   218

22 We Used to Roam So Freely   228

23 As Many Custard Creams as You Can Eat   238

24 Oh Mate, Oh Mate   247

25 Arms and the Man   256

26 Something Can Be Done and You Can Do It   262

27 An Uncommon Amount of Courage   277

    Selected Bibliography   293

    UK Discography   296

    Acknowledgements   299

    Picture Credits   301

    Index   303

Prologue

It is 1974. There is a convoy of assorted vehicles coming down the road – the M4, say, or the A1. Some of them had not been fully roadworthy for 30 years. Many are belching smoke and there is a lot of towing going on – a lorry towing a lorry towing a caravan; a Range Rover towing a bus towing a caravan. Traffic cops bring the procession to a stop and ask questions. A huge red-bearded man called Captain Hill emerges from one of the trucks. He confuses the police with might and reason until, eventually, they back down and, stammering face-saving warnings, drive away to wonder.

This was Ronnie Lane's Passing Show, a rock'n'roll circus that, for a few glorious weeks, toured the country and within the confines of a moth-eaten tent presented entertainment – music, fire-eating, clowns, can-can dancing and comedy – that was shared with grateful audiences who, on a good night, almost half-filled the available seating.

'It looked perfect on paper,' said Bruce Rowland, the drummer with the band.

Everyone, artistes and crew, lived in a selection of defective caravans.

Ronnie Lane, formerly of the Small Faces and the Faces and the presiding genius of the enterprise, and his partner Kate, shared a proper old Romany vardo – travelling on a transporter lest the wheels should crumble at the touch of asphalt – which was 'a bizarre world of tiny knick-knacks, drapes and mementos, with a large bed for Master Lane and his good lady. It looked like the 19th century in miniature.'

For a short time, Viv Stanshall, formerly of the Bonzo Dog Doo-Dah Band, had been hired as ringmaster but, having drunkenly mistaken a guitar player's wardrobe for some sort of caravan toilet – 'Terribly sorry, old bean!' – had disappeared into the night.

Jimmy Jewell, the sax player – travelling with his wife and child, trying to keep them vaguely healthy and dry (God, it rained that summer) on £30 a week (less than the starting salary of a junior schoolteacher) and deeply disenchanted by the romance of it all – jumped ship too, leaving a note that said, 'Goodbye cruel circus, I'm off to join the world.'

Wherever they pitched their tent, the ladies and gentlemen of the Passing Show broke every fire, health and safety regulation on the statute books. They stole electricity. They got wonderfully drunk. They contracted curious illnesses. But their three-hour show brought great joy and, if only they'd got a bit of pre-publicity together so that people knew they were coming and were safe to approach, it would have been a storming success.

Instead, 'Of course it went tits up,' Kate said, 'but I was glad it did. Added to the fun.'

And all the money that Ronnie Lane had made with the Faces – big money, American money – had gone.

So . . . why the fuck did he do it?

1

Bronco Lane

Stanley Lane was a lorry driver who worked for his Uncle Charlie out of a yard in the East End of London. One day, sometime in the early 1930s, he took his motorbike for a run out to Epping Forest and stopped off for a drink at the Wake Arms on the Epping Road.

Elsie May worked on the jam roll conveyor belt at the huge Kearley and Tonge cake and biscuit factory on the Bethnal Green Road. She'd been infected by the interwar craze for rambling and other healthy outdoor pursuits. With her knapsack on her back, she'd set off at weekends and go camping in Epping Forest. By coincidence, she popped into the Wake Arms at the same time as Stan did.

Presumably eyes met across a crowded room and Stanley moved in with his best line – the exact details are lost to history, but one way or another a romance kindled.

Technically Elsie was a bit out of Stanley's league. He was from Stratford, London E15. She'd been born in Highgate, north London – not as posh then as it is now, but still a cut or two above E15 – and was now living on Old Street, a busy commercial district close to the City of London.

They were married in 1935 at St Luke's Church on the City Road and moved into a flat on Bonner Road in Bethnal Green. Their first child, named Stanley after his dad, was born in 1938 and the following year, Hitler invaded Poland.

Stanley Snr didn't have to go to war because he was a lorry driver, a reserved occupation. But the war came to them. In the space of two weeks, in September 1940, 95 high explosive bombs, two parachute mines and thousands of incendiary bombs were dropped on Bethnal Green. On the night of the 7th/8th the Columbia Market Shelter took a direct hit. Thirty-eight people were killed.

Death and destruction came to Grove Road, Braintree Street and Roman Road, too – none of them more than a brisk ten-minute stroll from Stanley and Elsie's flat.

To get out of the firing line, they moved out to Forest Gate, just north of Stanley's old stomping ground in Stratford. It was only four miles from Bethnal Green, so not quite the same as evacuating to rural Somerset or getting on a liner to America, but all the same it was a good bit safer. Being a bit further away from the docks and industry meant that the only bombs that did fall were those dropped by particularly cack-handed Bombenschützen. The new place was a two-bedroom upstairs flat on 385 Romford Road, busy and noisy. This became home and remained so for the next 25 years.

On a side note, Romford Road found its place in the legends of rock'n'roll when, 25 years after Stanley and Elsie moved there, three of The Rolling Stones, Mick, Bill and Brian, were arrested for pissing against the wall of a garage at number 175. When apprehended, Mick allegedly remarked, 'We piss anywhere, man', a line that was taken up by Bill and Brian, who repeated it in 'a kind of chant' while 'dancing'. In their defence, Mr Dale Parkinson pointed out that the Stones were not 'morons', which was how they'd been described elsewhere. 'These are not three young men from Hoxton,' he said (the exact nature of his prejudice against young men from Hoxton being unreported). 'They are world famous artists.' ('Satisfaction' was riding high in the charts at the time and nobody was immune to the thrill of fuzztone.)

They were fined £5. After the trial, police had to help them fight their way through the hundreds of fans who'd assembled outside. But they'd learned their lesson and were never caught pissing again. Just the drugs. And the women.

Hitler died in his bunker on 30 April 1945 and just under a year later, on 1 April 1946, April Fool's Day, Ronald Frederick Lane was born at the Plaistow Maternity Hospital.

It was, it had to be said, not the most propitious year in which to be born. The war had left the country nearly bankrupt. Most foodstuffs were still rationed and, thanks to the wet summer that destroyed the wheat crops, for the first time bread had to be rationed, too. The rain all summer followed by one of the coldest, cruellest winters in living memory meant that kids like Ronnie barely saw sunshine for a year. And, since the NHS was still two years off being created, neither were their vitamins boosted with the government-supplied orange juice and cod liver oil that made '49-ers bounce with health.

He bore the signs for the rest of his life: 5ft 5in tall (at the most generous estimate), pasty face, bad teeth. Nevertheless . . . you know . . . clichés about being poor but happy, making their own entertainment, smiling through, gorblimey Mrs Jones how's your Bert's lumbago?

Dad was the centre of Ronnie's world. Mum tended to be cold and distant. She had her reasons – the first inklings of multiple sclerosis, the disease that would blight Ronnie's life later. Often, she took to her bed and stayed there all day.

Stanley senior was the family's primary source of love, warmth, affection and encouragement. He loved a market. On Sunday mornings he'd take the two boys down Petticoat Lane or Brick Lane or, best of all, Club Row, the animal market in Shoreditch. Unlike the zoo, you could touch the animals in Club Row, even take them home if you had the inclination and the money and, even better, it was free to get in. Mostly it was dogs, cats and caged birds, but more exotic tastes were catered for, too. You could buy monkeys in Club Row, and even, if you were there on the right day, lions and tigers. The enterprise was, of course, immeasurably cruel and after years of protests from the RSPCA, it was closed down in the sixties.

Next to the animal market was a bomb site that Ronnie remembered was called The Debris. 'People came out there with all their chuck-outs and flotsam and jetsam and spread it out on The Debris,' he said. 'Every Sunday morning, my dad would take me down there and he'd root around for hours in all this shit.'

Sometimes Dad would take the lads to see their grandparents. Mum's dad worked as a bookbinder. Dad's dad had a French polishing shop in Bethnal Green. And on Saturdays, Stanley Jnr, eight years older, would take Ronnie roller skating or to the Saturday morning pictures at the Odeon just up the Romford Road. Here you got cartoons, maybe a Batman or a Flash Gordon or a Tarzan, and almost certainly a cowboy film featuring Roy Rogers, Gene Autry or Hopalong Cassidy.

One must never underestimate the importance of cowboys in the lives of boomer kids – boys anyway, and some girls, too. They were everywhere. And when telly came along the schedules were dominated by the aforementioned Rogers and Cassidy, the Cisco Kid, the Lone Ranger, *Rawhide*, *Wagon Train*, *Sugarfoot*, *Maverick*, *Gun Law*, *Cheyenne*, *Tales of Wells Fargo* and on and on. Most of them had theme songs. Go into a pub, or more promisingly some sort of sheltered accommodation – anywhere you can guarantee a decent supply of people born in the forties and fifties. Start singing, as loud as you can, 'Cheyenne, Cheyenne, where will you be camping tonight?' The reply will come back immediately, a thousand happy voices singing, 'Lonely man, Cheyenne, will your heart stay breezy and bright?' The lyrics of those songs, you see, 60 years ago and more, lit fires in their brains sometimes hot enough to burn even through the Alzheimer's.

'Who is the tall dark stranger, there?'

'Maverick is his name!'

Rationing, the weather and the NHS made your body, but cowboy films made your mind. And it would be in Trinidad, Colorado – in sight of the Rocky Mountains – that Ronnie Lane would be buried, in his favourite cowboy shirt.

Cowboys – particularly Roy Rogers and Gene Autry – arguably had a more profound influence on British pop between 1960 and 1980 than the entire Sun Records catalogue.

First of all, cowboys were cool. They walked cool, they rode cool, they talked cool.

Second, they dressed impeccably. In the late sixties, when neat suits and Chelsea boots had had their day, pop groups and their fans adopted coloured shirts, blue jeans, leather waistcoats, moccasins or tooled boots, fringed jackets, sometimes even Stetsons.

Third, they lived free. In practical terms, this was always more difficult in Plaistow, Wallsend or Dingle than it was in New Mexico, but one might argue that really it was more to do with a state of mind than a blanket under the stars. Once you had the right mentality, nobody could tell you what to do. Except Mr Pickering (French and RE); the park keeper, Geoffrey Prentice, who could give nasty Chinese burns; your mum; and the lady at the bacon counter who passed remarks about the state of your trousers.

And fourth – perhaps the most significant point – these movie cowboys, Gene Autry and Roy Rogers anyway, were not just cowboys, they were *singing* cowboys. They played the guitar. Sometimes on horseback. Davy Crockett – a frontiersman who had killed him a bear (pronounced, for some reason, 'bar') when he was only three and thus not strictly a cowboy – played the guitar too. He wore it on his back. When canoeing down a river, he used it as a paddle. It must have been a bugger to tune afterwards with all the tuners rusted up, but that difficulty would have lapsed into insignificance once he got to the Alamo.

Thus, the guitar, like the six-gun, the Stetson and the fringed jacket became an object of desire, a fetish. From the forties onwards, the drool of cowboy fans could be seen on the windows of music stores from Thurso to Penzance. And when Elvis, Lonnie Donegan, Buddy Holly, Hank B. Marvin (Brian Rankin from Newcastle, who'd blessed himself with a cowboy name) and Eric Clapton came along, there were waterfalls of drool gumming up the windows and all but concealing the Fender Mustangs, the Gretsch Roundups (with the 'G' branded on the upper bout) and the Eko Rangers.

When Ronnie was six, his dad gave him a ukulele. Mum was outraged. Money was short, and here was Stanley squandering it on frivolous extravagance. But Stan Snr had music in him. He'd been known to sing and play drums at the local pub. And far from being a frivolous extravagance, Ronnie made that uke pay. Dressed up in his cowboy hat and fringed waistcoat, he'd go three houses down Romford Road to the bus stop and busk for the passengers and conductors. Runtish he may have been, but there was always a twinkle in his eye, and he had the cheek of the devil. Half an hour at the bus stop was enough to fill his pockets with pennies. As his father said later, and continued to say quite frequently, 'Learn to play the guitar and you'll always have a friend.'

Ronnie never liked school. A lot of the kids, despite the weather and the rationing, had grown height and muscles. He never did. He was picked on, got into a lot of fights and took no interest in lessons or sport.

The 1944 Education Act had created an exam, the 11-plus. If you passed your 11-plus, you could go to a grammar school and do Latin and differential calculus. If you failed, you went to a secondary modern and did metalwork. But there was a third option. If you passed but still didn't have the right academic mindset to want to do Latin, or if you failed but showed special potential in some other area, you might get into a technical school. Basically, the grammar schools were for office and managerial staff, secondary schools were for production line workers and technical schools were for foremen and specialists. If the turret punch press was on the blink again, send for the technical school bloke.

Ronnie failed the exam, but all the same showed some talent for drawing. In the days before CAD, every factory and workshop had a drawing office where bright lads – draughtsmen – drew intricate blueprints. Maybe he could be trained for it. Or failing that, commercial art, pasting up art work with Cow Gum and applying Letraset. Or plain lettering for shop fronts and one-off adverts. There was no end of possibilities.

Accordingly, he was sent to Lister Technical School in Plaistow. He thrived.

'Ronnie was one of the best liked kids in the school by both the teachers and the other pupils,' Ron Chimes, one of the other pupils, said. 'He was called Bronco Lane after the cowboy on the telly and because he had bronco written on his bike.'

Bronco, starring Ty Hardin as Bronco Layne (with a Y), was one of the westerns on TV. It had one of the best songs (written by Mack David, big brother to Burt Bacharach's lyricist Hal David), the lyric of which suggests that when riled, Bronco makes a 'foursquare Texas twister' seem 'meek and mild' and any girl who kisses him twice immediately finds herself 'dreaming of shoes and rice', although since he was known, as well, for drinking water from his hat, he couldn't have been all that.

Perhaps hoping to make a man of him, Stanley Snr signed Ronnie up for the cadet corps of the Green Jackets Rifle Brigade. This meant going, along with hundreds of other boys, to a training camp in Aldershot. He didn't cover himself with glory. As well as many other misdemeanours, there was an incident with a grass snake in the bath. If it had been the real army, he'd probably have been shot. It was here that he first met up with Kenney Jones, later drummer with the Small Faces, the Faces and The Who, although at the time they

9

didn't bond and forgot about each other until they met again a few years later.

During the school holidays, Ronnie worked for a while at the Battersea Fun Fair – first on a roll-a-penny stall and then, more excitingly, as a brakeman on the Big Dipper. 'My last task at the end of the season was removing the bulbs from the Big Dipper's girders – I nearly fell off the top of that a few times.'

But though he was attracted by its shabby glamour – an allure to which he would return in later life – fairground work could never be a career. 'The trouble with that job was that the season used to finish in September. Y'know, a fair when it's closed is the saddest sight in the world.'

So, instead he got a job as fourth assistant at Dunn's, the elderly gentlemen's outfitters, in Stratford. This came to an end apparently when he had a row with the third assistant and hit him on the head with a window pole.

After that Ronnie worked as a bicycle courier for a dental firm. 'I kept falling off all over London. So, after 48 hours, I gave it up.' Undaunted, he took a job as a pipe fitter's mate, installing central heating, excavating floorboards. 'You'd find anything under those floorboards – I had to get right underneath. Dead cats, spiders, the lot. The spiders were the worst – I've only just got over them.' Ronnie's big asset was, of course, his size – he could fit into spaces that others couldn't.

Along the way, he'd developed an interest in girls. Steve Barrow, another regular at the Ilford Palais, knew the score.

'My first "dancehall" while I was still at school was the Ilford Palais Saturday afternoon sessions, which instead of having a band like Ray McVay's, they played records over the house PA. So, you'd hear the top chart tunes of the day, the danceable stuff rather than the ballads. Records like Dion's 'Runaround Sue', Del Shannon's 'Runaway', The Shirelles' 'Will You Love Me Tomorrow', Gary U.S. Bonds' 'Quarter

To Three', The Marcels' 'Blue Moon' The Tokens' 'The Lion Sleeps Tonight', Barbara George's 'I Know', all the "twist" records and things like The Dovells and The Orlons, all those Cameo-Parkway pop/R'n'B-type things. And my hero Ray Charles, with 'Hit The Road Jack'.

'The main thing was you could at least look at girls for three hours between 3pm and 6pm on a Saturday afternoon even if you didn't manage to get off with anyone. Sometimes, you'd end up going home to a girl's house, and get some kissing and maybe a bit more, on the doorstep before her parents called her inside. But the Ilford Palais was full of them, it was a highlight of the week, seeing as at that time I wasn't allowed out at night yet.'

Girls and twisting demanded a certain pride in the appearance. Ronnie, as soon as he started earning, invested heavily in sharp threads.

'There were shops where you got just trousers, like Harry Myers in Bethnal Green – they had tailors on the premises to take up the bottoms of the legs to fit you, or any other alterations, any kind of material, Prince of Wales check, dogtooth check, cavalry twill in three shades, various worsteds and blends.'

Everybody knew that the way to make girls fancy you – more effective than cavalry twill trousers, more effective than dancing the twist, more effective even than efficient kissing – was to stand on stage with a shiny guitar and wiggle.

2

Some Experience in Pubs

The ukulele had long been superseded.

'I learned to play a little on an acoustic guitar and my dad was so tickled with it that he went out and bought me a cheap little Broadway guitar,' Ronnie told journalist Allan Vorda in 1987. 'He brought it home and was bursting to give it to me. My mum said "Why did you buy him that? He's never going to do anything with it." She was so negative.'

'I introduced Ronnie to a guy I knew called Steve Taylor who lived near Ronnie and played guitar,' Ron Chimes, Ronnie's schoolfriend, said. 'I was playing piano and a bit of guitar too. Ronnie and Steve got on like a house on fire. They did a couple of gigs just as a duo where they played background music at a coffee bar or something [under the name The Spiders]. I said to them "What about if I join the band?" I remember our first gig was at my neighbour's local in Barking and we got paid £1 10s – 10 shillings each.'

Then – memories vary – came The Muleskinners, featuring Kenny Bennet on guitar and Alan Hutton on bass, both kids from Three Mills School in Stratford. Kenny knew more chords than Ronnie and was able to show him how to negotiate his way around the Chuck Berry playlist. They weren't a proper pop group, though, because they hadn't got a drummer.

Stan Jnr, Ronnie's big brother, found just the right bloke for the job.

In 1963, Stan had got married and bought himself a car. To pay for it, he got a second job working the bar at The British Prince in Stepney. They had live jazz at The British Prince. A fourteen-year-old kid was often seen hanging about outside the pub – too young to go in – listening to the music. When the drummer in the jazz band went off for a drink, sometimes the kid plucked up his courage, entered the forbidden territory and asked if he could take over the kit for a couple of numbers. He was all right. And he'd hold his own until the pub's landlord noticed there was a child on the premises and, fearing for his licence, chucked him out.

The lad's name was Kenney Jones. Stan introduced him to Ronnie.

'I'll never forget my first meeting with Ronnie Lane,' Kenney said. 'He walked into The British Prince, and he had a really smart suit on with a starched collar and a tie, looking very much like one of The Beatles but before The Beatles, if you know what I mean. Every time he talked, his collar and tie would stay still while his neck moved.

'He was funny, we just hit it off straight away. I knew it was meant to be. We started laughing at each other straightaway and immediately warmed to each other. He was very confident and we could look each other in the eye because we were the same size!'

More bands followed. Again, memories vary, and the written record is sketchy, but it doesn't really matter. Whether they're true or not, there's a sort of folk-poetry about the stories.

For instance, Google might lead you to a copy of an ad that Ronnie was supposed to have placed in a newsagent's window.

LEAD GUITARIST AGE 17
WOULD LIKE TO JOIN
OR START UP ROCK GROUP
SOME EXPERIENCE IN PUBS

APPLY AFTER 6P.M. TO
RON
385 ROMFORD ROAD
FOREST GATE

At the time, The Beatles weren't looking for a new lead guitarist, and even if they had been they were really too busy being the Toppermost of the Poppermost to spend time browsing in Forest Gate newsagent's windows. In fact, not even Forest Gate bands showed much interest.

Instead, Ronnie stuck with the people he knew. He formed a band with Kenney on drums, Ron Chimes on organ, Steve Taylor on second guitar, and Alan Hutton on bass. They played with several names until one night Kenney's dad was going to drive them to a gig but after they'd loaded in the drum kit there wasn't room for Kenney or Ronnie. 'What are we, then? The Outcasts?' they said. And that is what they became.

There followed a series of personnel changes with a floating pool of pals – Ronnie, Kenney, Ron Chimes, Steve Taylor, Alan Hutton, guitarist Kenny Newman, singer George Cambridge and maybe a couple of others – coming together in various configurations, usually calling themselves The Outcasts or The Muleskinners. At one point, identity confusion led to there being two bands called The Outcasts. And up and down the country, there were endless bands called The Muleskinners. Ian McLagan, later keyboard player with the Small Faces and Faces, was in one over the way in west London.

Neither The Muleskinners nor The Outcasts were professionally recorded, but in 1996 George Cambridge handed a reel of tape to John Hellier (biographer and Ronnie super fan), explaining that it had been in a drawer for 32 years and he didn't have anything to play it on.

Along with some bluesy noodlings around Bo Diddley's 'Before

You Accuse Me (Take A Look at Yourself)' it contains two takes of one of Ronnie's earliest compositions, a moody minor-key moan co-written with Terry Newman called 'Don't Talk To Me Of Love' – recorded with percussion played on what sounds like a Coke bottle and spoon and ends with a full band (personnel uncertain) playing a very credible version of 'That's What I Want', a minor hit by The Marauders from August 1963. The playing is rough around the edges and the recording diabolical but there is a sense there of a band that knows what it's doing. The drummer – presumably Kenney – is a class act.

Though they hadn't attracted any attention from management or record companies, The Outcasts were building a reputation. At a pub gig at the Albion in Rainham, they shared the bill with another local band called The Moments, who were working regularly mostly because of a magnificent lead singer called Steve Marriott. Steve was clearly impressed by The Outcasts because the following night he showed up at their next gig, bringing a mate with him to check them out.

Ronnie's big brother Stan was still driving for a living. He did regular deliveries to Selmer Electronics, manufacturers of guitar amps, on Theobalds Road behind Holborn Library and had heard they were looking for somebody to test the amps. He put in a word and Ronnie got the job. As a day job for an 18-year-old guitar player, it could not have been bettered. Tasks included spending time in a semi-soundproofed room equipped with a Fender Stratocaster and a Fender Precision Bass, plugging them in, turning them up and blasting the place apart.

Sometimes Ronnie would lock himself in the testing room with a coffee and the newspaper: if anyone banged on the door to see what he was up to, he would wriggle out of the room through a hole he'd cut in the wall, sidle up behind the person knocking, and say, 'Looking for me?'

There was other fun to be had, too. Alan Baldwin worked there not long after Ronnie had left. 'Plugging in a newly wired amp could be interesting. Sometimes the large smoothing capacitors were connected the wrong way round and exploded in your face! Bits of silver foil and wax paper would float down from the ceiling of the test room for about five minutes and the test engineer would be temporarily blinded.'

Eventually Kenney worked there, too, on the assembly lines. And it was there that Ronnie first started to realise that the Precision Bass could provide as much, if not more, fun than the Stratocaster.

'During that time, I really learned to play,' Ronnie said, 'mostly in my lunch break. I used to really dig Booker T. & The M.G.'s and fancied myself as a bass player.'

It's not hard to see why. Listen to 'Green Onions'. Steve Cropper on guitar is riding over the groove, but Duck Dunn on bass *is* the groove.

On 24 November 1964, The Who began a seven-week Thursday night residency at the Marquee Club on Wardour Street in Soho. Under the name The High Numbers, they'd released one single, 'Zoot Suit'/'I'm the Face', which, though the product had been carefully tailored for the 'mod' demographic, had sunk, leaving no more than a couple of tiny ripples.

Since then, though, they'd changed their name back to The Who and, under new management, were being recognised by those who cared as a band that mattered. Ronnie and Kenney went to the Marquee and watched them take the place apart.

Pete Townshend had already discovered the theatrical appeal of smashing his guitar.

'Really, you should have seen the audience,' Keith Moon remembered some years later. 'Mouths open, great rows of teeth showing. You could almost count the cavities.'

And if you'd told Kenney that, 15 years later, he'd be recruited to the band as Keith Moon's replacement, his mouth would have stayed open for a week.

Afterwards, Kenney told Ronnie he reckoned they must be posh because they came from Shepherd's Bush (to east Londoners, anywhere west of the City is posh).

A similar thought was shared by the many musicians who were struggling to keep up with the HP payments on their Hofner Colorados and Watkins Dominators. How rich do you have to be to smash up a hundred and seventy quid Rickenbacker?

Ronnie was paying off the HP payments on a ruinously expensive Gretsch Tennessean guitar, an impressive piece of kit that would have cost nearly as much as a Rickie, something like £150–£160 – the equivalent today of about £2,500. George Harrison sometimes played a Gretsch Tennessean, and it was the guitar that Hilton Valentine of The Animals used on 'House of the Rising Sun'.

But the bass had caught his imagination.

'We could never get a bass player,' he said. 'Everybody just wanted to play lead guitar, or they wanted to be the singer, or they wanted to play drums. Nobody wanted to play the bass. Even the advent of someone like The Beatles and Paul McCartney, it didn't make anyone want to play the bass. So, I got fed up with this. I thought, "this is stupid! I'll play the bass!" So, I went . . . I talked me dad into it, because he'd bought me a nice guitar. A Gretsch Tennessean, he'd bought me! I talked him into letting me have a bass. Well, I was gonna pay for it, but I had to kinda sweet-talk him a bit because he was still payin' for the Gretsch guitar.'

So, one day, Ronnie went bass shopping at the J60 music store in Manor Park and discovered that Steve Marriott, the singer from The Moments, was working there.

Steve was ten months younger than Ronnie and had been born premature (birth weight just 4lb 4oz) and brought up in Strone Road in Manor Park, a 15-minute saunter from Ronnie's house. He grew up small – the same height as Ronnie – and was, in the words of his Auntie Sheila, 'a very, very naughty boy. In fact, he was wicked sometimes.'

There was a bit of music in the family. His dad played piano in pubs and at parties, 'that meant he got his drinks for free.'

He was also a born performer.

The Lionel Bart musical *Oliver!* played the West End for six years, during which time it employed scores of kids who could sing a bit, dance a bit and had a general aptitude for showing off. Tony Robinson, later to be Baldrick and TV's favourite archaeologist, served time in the chorus. Phil Collins and Davy Jones (of The Monkees) were both in it at one time or another playing the Artful Dodger. Little Stephen Marriott was also a shoo-in for the Dodger and would have nabbed the part if, as his mum said, 'he hadn't been so cheeky and rude. He didn't like the matron [in charge of the youngsters backstage] because she was posh, and she didn't like him because she thought he was cocky and disrupted her boys.'

All the same he got to sing it on record – not on the Decca original cast recording, but on the knock-off World Record Club version with Ian Carmichael as Fagin and Joyce Blair (Lionel's sister) as Nancy – and it leaves nobody in any doubt that here was a boy who knew how to give a song some welly.

In 1961 he went to the Italia Conti stage school, alma mater of Noël Coward, Leslie Phillips, Bonnie Langford, Clive Dunn, Sadie Frost and scores of other notables, and this led to parts in TV series like *Mr. Pastry's Progress*, *Dixon of Dock Green*, *William* and *Taxi!* Most prestigious was a small but significant part alongside Peter Sellers, Eric Sykes and Irene Handl in the Boulting Brothers' comedy *Heavens Above!* 'I never really acted the whole time I was there,' he said. 'All the parts I got were cockney kids, which was what I was anyway.'

Acting never interested him as much as music.

By pure persistence, in 1963 he got signed to Decca Records. He had some success with his band The Moments, supporting The Nashville Teens, The Animals, Georgie Fame and John Mayall at the Crawdaddy, the Flamingo and the 100 Club on Oxford Street. Their sets included covers of Chuck Berry, Smokey Robinson and James Brown numbers.

But a year later, after their cover of The Kinks' 'You Really Got Me' went straight to landfill, The Moments fired Marriott from the band. The other members claimed he was too young to be a lead singer but there were other issues. 'They didn't want to be with him anymore,' said Bobby Cristo, who took over as lead singer. 'It's hard work – five or six hours in the back of a van – it only takes one winding everyone up . . .'

At first, his solo prospects seem good. In March 1964, *Record Mirror* had reported that four record labels were vying to sign him up for a record deal and he was being managed by Tony Calder, who later formed Immediate Records with Andrew Loog Oldham. But nothing came of the deals and Tony got too busy working for The Rolling Stones and with Marianne Faithfull, who'd just had a big hit with 'As Tears Go By', to have much time for the cheeky kid from Manor Park.

But wherever he went, whatever he did, Steve made an impression – not always a good impression but a memorable one.

Anyway, in January 1965, Steve, skint, had got himself a part-time job selling guitars at the J60 Music Bar, 445 High Street North, Manor Park (at the time of writing it's the East London Fish Bazar, with one 'A').

On 23 January 1965, Ronnie and Kenney walked in to look at basses.

Kenney Jones had recommended the shop to Ronnie. It was where he'd bought his first drum kit a few years before. Steve approached, just as if he was a proper sales assistant, and asked if they wanted any help. They recognised each other. Apart from playing on the same bill, Ronnie and Kenney had probably bought half-pints of whelks from Steve's dad's shellfish stall outside The Ruskin Arms.

Ronnie had a problem. He wanted to switch from guitar to bass but was still keeping up the HP payments on his Gretsch Tennessean. If he bought another guitar, it would have to be cheap. While Kenney wandered off to look at drums, Steve steered Ronnie towards the basses.

Kenney charts subsequent developments in his autobiography, *Let the Good Times Roll*. 'I could hear them talking over the other side of the shop. 'Nah, you don't want that one. It's fuckin' horrible. Try this.' I see Ronnie glance at the price tag and grimace . . .'

It was a Harmony, a class brand, out of Ronnie's price range, but he thought there's no harm in trying it out, so he plugged it in. Steve grabbed a guitar himself and the three of them started to jam. Guitar shop owners have a sixth sense for spotting the difference between genuine customers and kids who'll spend an hour playing 'Smoke on the Water' (or, in 1965, 'House of the Rising Sun') on the most expensive instruments in stock before buying a plectrum. Steve's boss appeared, not best pleased, his radar signalling 'time wasters', and told Ronnie either to buy the Harmony or clear off.

Ronnie couldn't afford the Harmony. Steve told him not to worry about all that. Just come back with your dad and we will sort out the hire purchase agreement.

Half an hour later, Stanley and Ronnie Lane were back at J60. Magically, the Harmony had become affordable. Steve had made up the paperwork at the price of the cheapest bass in the shop and slipped the sale through.

Under the circumstances, the very least that Ronnie could do was invite his new friend and benefactor to his gig that night in Bermondsey.

★

The day had started out sunny but got colder in the afternoon. *Doctor Who* was on telly, *Carry on Cleo* was on at the pictures, and the Earl of Derby pub in Bermondsey, London, was featuring live entertainment – a band of uncertain identity. Sometimes they were The Pioneers, sometimes The Outcasts and sometimes The Muleskinners. Opinion is divided as to what they were calling themselves on this particular night. Bog Chain & The Plastics is another possibility.

The line-up was variable, too, although on this particular night it was most probably George Cambridge on vocals, Alan Hutton on bass, Kenney Jones on drums and Ronnie Lane on guitar. Ronnie was 18. Kenney was just 16 and had no right being in a pub at all.

The Earl of Derby was a regular gig, practically a residency. And the money was all right, too. On the way to the gig, the band picked Steve Marriott up in Alan's Bedford van.

Despite the attractions of *Doctor Who*, *Carry on Cleo* and wrestling at the Grange Road Baths just up the road, there was a decent crowd at the Earl of Derby. For reasons no one can remember, Ronnie and Steve started drinking whisky, a drink Ronnie had never really tried before. Not in bulk, anyway. Within minutes, Steve had reached the horny stage of drunkenness. He rose to his full 5ft 4in (5ft 6in in Cuban heels) and started scouting the room for talent.

'I remember there was this gorgeous girl there sitting on a bar stool with a very short skirt,' he said, 'long boots and even longer legs. I was chatting her up nicely and went in for a kiss, only to discover stubble! She hadn't shaved!'

Modern notions of non-binary sexuality came early to Bermondsey.

The band got up to play. Ronnie could barely stand, but Kenney on drums, still relatively sober, managed to keep everything together. After a few numbers, Ronnie announced they had a special guest joining them to play harmonica.

Steve got on the stand and immediately owned the territory. He couldn't help it. He was born showing off and possessed a natural showmanship that could upstage a five-engine fire and easily steal attention from, say, a naked royal wedding.

George Cambridge, the vocalist, wasn't impressed.

'I got up the nose of the singer,' Steve said. 'I started taking over because I can't help it. I'm an overwhelming kind of guy.'

When he'd wailed a while on his harp, he moved over to the piano and gave a graphic demonstration of why, in theatres and concert halls everywhere, managers hid the Steinway when rock'n'roll came to town and rented something cheap and disposable. While the band tried to keep up, Steve pounded out 'Whole Lotta Shakin' and 'Great Balls of Fire', assaulting the instrument in the manner of the late Jerry Lee Lewis, first with one foot, then both, dancing up and down the keyboard until the piano's legs began to buckle and snap.

'Everything we did,' he remembered later, 'swung like Hanratty.'

Nevertheless, destruction of a pub piano was a serious offence. Plugs were pulled. The Outcasts, or Pioneers or Bog Chain & The Plastics, were kicked out and barred, their residency terminated.

George Cambridge was furious with Steve and with Ronnie for introducing this incubus into their band. But, according to Steve, George was 'a fucking miserable cunting tosspot. He looked more like a plumber or something than a singer.'

George and Alan, livid and vengeful, drove off in the Bedford leaving Steve, Ronnie, with his guitar and amp, and Kenney with his Ludwig silver glitter drum kit, sitting on the pavement outside the pub. Kenney called his dad from a phone box and asked him to come and collect them. They waited in the cold. It was two degrees centigrade, and the wind was up. All at once they began to laugh. A little at first, then unstoppably, hysterical, insensible with the joy of youth, friendship and discovery. They didn't need the others. They, the three of them, were a unit. They were a band. And they knew they'd be a fantastic band, who would enjoy fame, wealth and critical plaudits that The Beatles would envy. Well, Herman's Hermits, anyway.

This was their sweet spot.

There's a paragraph from a recent novel by Taylor Jenkins Reid called *Daisy Jones and the Six*, about a fictional group from the sixties, which sums it up.

'Let me tell you the sweet spot of being in rock'n'roll. People think it's when you're at the top but no. That's when you've got the pressure and the expectations. What's good is when everybody thinks you're headed somewhere fast, when you're all potential. Potential is pure fuckin' joy.'

They made plans for greatness. It may, of course, have been the drink talking but, if it was, in Ronnie's case at least, it didn't shut up for another 30 years.

3

Mod

'Mod' meant many things to many people. Like most social trends, it's impossible to make definitive statements about where it came from and why, although most of the definitive statements that people make are true at some level or other, even when they contradict each other. The ways in which currents and undercurrents of style and attitude intermingle are impossible to unravel. At the time, of course, nobody cared. They just wanted to dress up and dance and have sex.

In the mid-fifties, the word 'mod' was a description of a certain kind of jazz fan. Those who remained true to the sacred jazz of New Orleans (real purists sneered at anything recorded after the First World War) were called, by outsiders who could never understand, 'trads'. Those who accepted that jazz had changed and developed, who revered the music of Charlie 'Bird' Parker, Dizzy Gillespie, Miles Davis and Thelonious Monk – 'modern jazz' – were called 'mods'.

Sometimes they were, anyway.

A certain lifestyle and set of values went with being a 'trad' or a 'mod'.

'Trads' listened to their music at 78 rpm, wore duffel coats and oversized sweaters, drank beer, laughed, improvised wild dance moves, supported CND, and often studied geography at redbrick universities.

24

'Mods' listened to their music at 33 rpm, wore neat suits and ties, never danced, tried to acquire the pallor and detachment of a heroin addict, smoked Chesterfield, Camels or dope if they were really out there, and preferred cryptic utterance to opinion of any sort. And if they couldn't think of anything cryptic to say, they'd steal something from Miles Davis, who was good at that sort of thing. 'If you're not making a mistake,' they'd say, 'it's a mistake.' They also often studied geography at redbrick universities.

Anyway, then, we suppose, the Italian influence came to bear. Between 1939 and 1945, tens of thousands of British men and women, some of whose families hadn't left their immediate neighbourhood for generations, suddenly found themselves transported overseas. When they were not shooting people or dodging bullets they found odd moments to sample the culture. Some of them – particularly those who had served in Italy – came back with a taste for exotic delicacies like pasta, Bardolino, olive oil and espresso coffee.

Mocha, allegedly the first London espresso bar, was opened by Italian film star Gina Lollobrigida in 1954. By 1960, every street corner in the UK had a place, possibly with an Italian-sounding name, equipped with Formica-topped tables and a Gaggia machine, serving frothy coffee in Pyrex glass cups. There were restaurants, too, with raffia Chianti bottles hanging from the ceiling, where you could get spaghetti that didn't come out of a tin and cheese that wasn't yellow and see pepper grinders big enough for a game of rounders.

French and Italian films, previously shown only at specialist cinemas on the grounds that the words 'French' and 'Italian' were euphemisms for 'smut', began to find a wider audience. French and Italian people looked different to all the people you saw on Corporation Street. They dressed different. They talked not just in a different language but with different facial expressions and gestures. Above all, they possessed a quality that hadn't properly been seen in Britain since Charles II was on the throne. They were sexy.

Sexy was beyond the capabilities of most adolescent boys, but many reckoned they could pull off the basic look with a different haircut, a narrower tie and an Italian-style suit – with tighter trousers (but much better cut than the Teddy boy's drainpipes), and a high-buttoned jacket with dinky lapels. This, as it happens, was also the style adopted by Miles Davis, Chet Baker, Gerry Mulligan and their 'mod' (in the jazz sense) fans. And to go with the clothes, they could buy an Italian motor scooter – Vespa or Lambretta.

Many other elements were chucked into the mix.

The jazz revival had sparked an interest in other forms of black American music, particularly the blues. From the early 1950s, Big Bill Broonzy, Sonny Terry and Brownie McGhee, Muddy Waters and others had been touring in Britain, and various Brits, most notably Alexis Korner and Cyril Davies, had been trying to imitate the sounds of the Mississippi Delta and the South Side of Chicago.

Interest extended from the blues to other sorts of African-American music: The Miracles, The Marvelettes, Mary Wells, Ray Charles, Sam Cooke, Etta James, Nappy Brown, Dakota Staton, Damita Jo and a thousand others.

The visual arts were influential, too. Art colleges were notable breeding grounds for future rock stars. Pete Townshend and Ronnie Wood were both at Ealing Art College at the time when pop art was making exciting rumbles. In 1958, pop artist Jasper Johns produced a work called *Target*, which was simply an archery target rendered in a painterly way. Six years later, it was standard decoration for anything labelled 'mod'.

Perhaps it's also worth mentioning that during the war, soldiers on both sides had frequently made use of the drug Benzedrine, brand name for amphetamine sulphate, to keep themselves awake and alert. After the war, refined versions and compounds thereof were prescribed for weight loss, anxiety and depression, and, under names like 'dexys', 'blues' and 'purple hearts', were found to be just the thing to keep youngsters daisy-fresh during an all-nighter at the Flamingo.

Whatever 'mod' had signified, by 1965, the term had only two applications. The first was as a synonym for moral degeneracy. This derived from the usual 'youth in crisis' panic that had featured on the news agenda at least since the days of Socrates. Its latest manifestation was focused on the ritual battles on the beaches of Kent and Sussex (and lots of other places too far away for the London papers to bother with) where 'mods' in parkas, fought with 'rockers' in leather jackets. The *Birmingham Post* reckoned that this would bring about the 'disintegration of the nation's character' and to fogies and everywhere 'mod' had become synonymous with anything considered an evil of the modern world – sex, socialism, racial tolerance, noise, swearing, speed limits, pointed shoes, lack of deference shown by tradesman and general decline in the quality of bacon.

The second was as replacement for 'contemporary' – the buzz word of the late fifties and a synonym for up-to-date and desirable, which could be applied to pretty much anything. By mid-1965, Blacklers, the Liverpool department store, was advertising 'mod-style coats' for £6 19s 11d, as well as 'mod-style shoes' for 39s 11d. And, ever competitively priced, Farnons, in Newcastle, was doing similar 'mod-style shoes' for ten bob cheaper.

A year or two earlier 'mod style' was a matter of imagination and improvisation. It required in-depth knowledge of specialist boutiques and a keen eye for cut and colour. Now it – or a nonsense version of it – was available over the counter in your local department store, so obviously there was no point anymore.

A couple of days after the wonderfully disastrous Bermondsey gig, Ronnie and Kenney went round to Steve's flat.

'He had some great records,' Ronnie said. 'Stax, Motown, American R&B records, James Brown, Otis Redding and all those great black singers. So I said, 'Why don't you take my guitar and I'll take the bass and we'll start a group?' He was very enthusiastic. I liked him.'

Steve, now best friends with Ronnie, turned up at his workplace, Selmer Electronics, to try to blag a free amp. Neither of them was very subtle about it: the entire factory heard Ronnie testing it by announcing, 'Testing, testing, free PA for Marriott, testing, testing.' This resulted in Ronnie getting the sack. Which seemed only fair because Steve had been sacked from his job in J60, presumably for fiddling the price on Ronnie's bass.

It was the sixties. Jobs – so long as you weren't too fussy – were easy to come by. Ronnie and Steve landed up at a Lyons Corner House restaurant in Baker Street.

'I used to have to wash the plates,' Steve said, 'and Ronnie would rack them and push them through a shower. It was a nightmare – a conveyor of eggs and bacon.' It paid £8 a week. Steve packed it in after a couple of days. Ronnie stuck at it for a week, then started working as a courier for the Ministry of Defence.

Every chance they got, they rehearsed at the Ruskin Arms in East Ham. Steve was well in there. The landlord was his mate Jimmy Langwith's dad. Eventually Jimmy, though a good bit older than Steve, Ronnie and Kenney, joined them on keyboards and guitar.

They settled into a routine, with days spent around Denmark Street and nights rehearsing at the Ruskin or listening to records and smoking spliffs at Jimmy's little house in Stratford, or in the flat Steve shared up in Loughton, towards Epping. After a while, Ronnie moved in with Steve.

Along with the soul and R&B, their favourite listening was the American comedian Lord Buckley. Everybody was into Buckley. Dylan adored him. Lenny Bruce stole his material. Tom Waits, Frank Zappa, The Beatles, Robin Williams – they all knew the Buckley routines, sometimes by heart.

Though he looked like an English colonial governor complete with solar topee and waxed moustache, his schtick was hipster jive talk, which occasionally slipped into scat singing and just plain noise-making. His stories slipped into the unconscious, especially if you were high at the time of listening, and informed, sometimes in elliptical ways, lyrics, dialogue, slang and attitude.

'The Nazz' is essentially the New Testament in translation. 'Here come The Nazz, cool as anyone you ever see, right across the water . . . walkin'. And The Nazz . . . there's a little boy on board – I think his name was Jude on board the boat – he say: 'Hey, Nazz! Can I make it out there with you? Nazz say, 'Make it, Jude!'

They started gigging: church halls, the Three Puddings in Stratford, the Bridge House in Canning Town. Initially Ronnie's brother Stan drove them in his van, then Jimmy's brother started roadying in earnest.

'He bought a brand new van and we gave him a percentage of our money: we even signed a piece of paper to that effect.'

Annabella, or Annabelle, one of Jimmy's girlfriends – others remember her as being Steve's girlfriend – suggested a name. 'You've all got such small faces, you should call yourself that.'

The Small Faces.

'The term "face" was a top mod,' Steve said, 'a face about town, a respected chap!'

'I'm the Face' was the B-side of The Who/High Numbers' first single. In the 1979 remember-the-mods film *Quadrophenia*, Sting's character, with the chiselled features, blond hair and Gestapo-style leather coat, was called simply 'Ace Face'. Steve considered himself a face, in a small way, and neither he, Kenney nor Ronnie could reach things on high shelves.

But Ronnie wasn't sure. 'I didn't like the "small" bit. I was really a bit bitter about being the Small Faces because I was uptight about being little.'

But all the same, it stuck. And at around the same time, Jimmy Langwith decided he'd rather be Jimmy Winston, and that stuck too.

As well as coming up with the name, Annabelle, or Annabella, signed the HP agreement on Steve's amp. There should be some sort of plaque, or maybe a statue to Annabelle. Or Annabella.

4

Maurice the Monster and Terry the Egg

There's a general consensus that the first gig the Small Faces played under that name was on Thursday 6 May in 1965, at the Kensington Youth Centre in East Ham.

They got the gig through Steve's friend (he had ever such a lot of friends) Stuart Tuck, who organised gigs for the youth centre. That weekend he was getting married, and he booked the band to play at his reception. A setback emerged when Jimmy's brother said that neither he nor his van would be available to transport the band's gear, so Steve, being Steve, persuaded the bride and groom to hold the reception at his flat in Loughton. Drink was taken. At one point the bride threw herself off a balcony, but seemed to survive long enough to manage the honeymoon.

After that, the gigs got more regular. Two at the Ruskin Arms, then, on Sunday 16 May, again largely thanks to Stuart, they played the Starlite Club.

This was a shithole. A nicotine-parched, beer-sodden, after-hours drinking den off Oxford Street. It attracted a certain kind of celeb and a lot of crims. The place was run by Maurice King, a scary, scary man who also ran Capable Management with Barry Clayman. At one time or another they handled Van Morrison, Shirley Bassey and The

Walker Brothers. According to Anthony Reynolds, The Walker Brothers' biographer, Scott Walker used to call King 'Boris', or sometimes 'Karloff', or, more frequently, 'The Monster'.

The singer Elkie Brooks, who at that time had built a fine critical reputation on the back of a series of singles, none of which had done much business, was at that Starlite gig. She told King he should jump in there. The band was hot.

And thus, Maurice the Monster became the Small Faces' first manager.

He arranged a mini-tour of the north of England, unknown territory for lads for whom Shepherds Bush counted as 'abroad'. A chap called Terry the Egg – actually, his name was Terry Lucas, but he was bald – was hired as roadie, and they headed off to *terra incognita*.

The Twisted Wheel in Manchester had been started in 1963 by three brothers, Jack, Phillip and Ivor Abadi. This was the original Twisted Wheel in Brazenose Street rather than the proper one in Whitworth Street or one of the later manifestations, a coffee bar with a cellar beneath where the bands played. Thanks to Roger Eagle, the resident DJ who also booked most of the acts, it had already developed a reputation for playing the best R&B and soul, including import rarities unavailable at your local HMV, and had progressed from beatnik hangout to Manchester's mod central.

Memories of how that first gig went vary wildly. In fact, the whole story of how the Small Faces came to be is beset by conflicting accounts and false-memory syndrome. Unless diaries and records are kept, memories of touring are inevitably muddled or blank. Drink and drugs are often consumed, and the musicians rarely see much of the venue itself, just the backstage dressing room, or lavs. They end up with a vague impression of a room with maybe some people in it who may or may not be responsive to what they're doing. After a bit, they all merge into one.

'We were living in the back of an old Black Maria, playing for nothing, living on brown sauce rolls,' Ronnie said. 'We used to wake up in the morning, look around and think, "My God!". All the windows would be steamed up and there'd be heaps of old socks.'

There's sometimes a standout – 'That place where they dragged us off stage and stole all our clothes' – but it's rare if anybody can remember whether that was The Toxic Liver in Pitlochry or Pop-a-Doodle-Doo in Prestatyn.

In the case of the Small Faces, the problem is exacerbated by the fact that at least two of the principals involved – Steve Marriott and Don Arden (more of whom in a moment) – liked to abandon banal accuracy in favour of making stuff up, sometimes different stuff every time.

So, according to Kenney, the gig at the Twisted Wheel was a success.

'Did we have an audience outside London? Would we relate to them? Recognise them? After that session, we knew the answer. Yes. We could see ourselves out there in the crowd, dancing, kissing, smoking, posing.'

The *Torbay Express* and the *South Devon Echo*, who mentioned the gig in a general bit about the Small Faces, also reported that they 'brought the house down', but it's a long way from South Devon to Manchester, so they were probably just going off a press release issued by Maurice King.

The club's co-owner, on the other hand, reckoned that they were 'the worst band we had ever seen at the Wheel.'

Steve Marriott reckoned they failed their audition and weren't even given the chance to play. But much more vividly than the gig, he remembered that, while they were at the Twisted Wheel, Terry the Egg had used the van to nick a load of leather coats from a nearby factory.

'Me and Ronnie and Kenney all got leather coats out of it,' Steve said. 'He'd done the job while we were playing. I think it was Terry who suggested that these people used our van. I think he was driving it – said he wouldn't be gone long. Probably got paid a bit of whack. Anyway, we finished the set and the van still wasn't back and we were out there waiting for it when it screeches round the corner and someone yells, "Get in!" So, we pile in the back and it's up to here in leather coats. We screamed round to some bird's house and they were getting out the coats and bundling them up. They said, "Take a coat, anything you want." I remember mine – it was a great coat, had a belt and buttons.'

So, even if they did fail the audition, at least some good came of their trip to Manchester.

A reminder: Steve loved a story.

After that, they may have played a working men's club in Leeds before an audience of hard drinkers and anachronistic Teddy boys, who didn't warm to four tiny East End teenagers sporting sculptured bouffant-style haircuts, window-pane check button-down shirts, and white trousers. Neither were they moved when the waif-like lead singer opened his mouth and started belting out the blues. They managed to motor through Jimmy Reed's 'Baby What You Want Me to Do', but the management pulled the plug on them halfway through their version of James Brown's 'Please, Please, Please' for their own safety.

On the other hand, that club might have been in Sheffield. Or there might have been a separate but similar shambles in Sheffield, at the Gatefield Social Club, where the plug was pulled because they were too loud. Then, possibly, there was a visit to the Esquire Club, Sheffield, that nobody seems to remember anything about.

But everybody remembers what happened next.

The Mojo club was run by Peter Stringfellow and his brother Geoff. This was years before the advent of Stringfellow's club in Covent Garden, where overexcited businessmen with easily abused expense accounts were served by young women in need of proper warm clothing. This was back in the days when Peter's hair was brown and nicely cut rather than blond and mulletted, and his skin the colour and texture of pastry dough rather than aged mahogany.

Before becoming the Mojo, the venue, off Pitsmoor Road, had been a little Irish dance club. Now you had to weave your way through a maze of Lambrettas and Vespas to get to the place, all emblazoned with lamps, mirrors and fox tails flying from oversized aerials. Inside, you caught that distinct bouquet of mod – a combination of parka, mohair, bri-nylon, plastic mac, desert boot, Old Spice and Aqua Manda, together with a cool-as-a-mountain-stream undernote of menthol-fresh Consulate. Wilson Pickett had played the Mojo, as had The Who, John Mayall, The Yardbirds, Rufus Thomas, Charlie and Inez Foxx and most of the other acts that mods dug.

How the Small Faces got to play there is again a matter of mild controversy.

Most sources agree that it was done the easy way. Maurice King phoned Peter Stringfellow and secured an engagement.

Jimmy Winston remembers it different. After the fracas at the Leeds working men's club, 'All doom and gloom, we drove off, trying to find our way out of Leeds. We were at this roundabout and there was a bunch of birds there and we asked them the way and they started talking to us.

'We told them what had happened and how fed up we were, and they said, "You should go up the road to the Mojo." Peter Stringfellow ran it with his brother. Pete opened the door. We said, "We'd play for nothing," and he said, "OK, play tonight," and it was a good gig. The band that was booked that night was The Birds – Ronnie Wood was in it – and we supported them.'

Like the Twisted Wheel, the Mojo didn't have a drinks licence. This sometimes caused upset among the artists.

'Sonny Boy Williamson came over and I remember going to his dressing room and he said, "Where's the booze?" Peter Stringfellow said. 'And I said we didn't have any and he said, "I don't go on stage without no booze." He wanted a bottle of whisky so we went to the off licence across the road, brought it back and gave it to him. And he said, "Is this it?" And I said, "What, you want two?" So, he glugged half the bottle down in front of us and said, "That's better," and went on stage and drank the rest of the bottle during his show.'

The regular clientele didn't need booze anyway. Blues were readily available and those who didn't have the money for drugs happily got off on what the Small Faces had to offer.

'They went down an absolute storm,' Stringfellow said. 'And that night I put in three bookings on them at pretty low prices.'

The train-crash gigs were forgotten when the band returned to London in triumph.

Terry the Egg and Steve went to see the manager of the Cavern. This was the Leicester Square Cavern, underneath the Notre Dame Church, rather than the more famous one in Liverpool.

After some argy-bargy about the length of their set (they only had five numbers and the management said they needed a bare minimum of seven), they secured the gig – perhaps leather coats changed hands, who knows? – and they were booked to play five consecutive Saturdays, starting 29 May.

'We played there for three or four weeks and even though we were kind of busking we got very popular,' Ronnie said. 'It was a chaotic lesson in bullshitting the audience. Fuck, we had some front! We used to take about an hour and a half to play four numbers. Steve had my Gretsch off me and he only knew about three chords and I'd only just bought this bass and we used to bullshit our way through. But he had such a lot of front, Steve did. That's how we got away with it.'

'Ronnie got a blackboard,' said Steve, 'and drew a picture of a mod in a parka with "The Small Faces" on the back, like it was on Kenney's kit, which Ronnie had also painted. We put it outside the gig and it bought all these mods in. We got the following straight away down the Cavern because we were mods.'

One night, a man called Pat Meehan showed up to check them out. He ran his own management company that later looked after, among others, Black Sabbath.

'Pat Meehan, who did some of the legwork for Don Arden, came down,' said Jimmy Winston. (It should be mentioned that, if Maurice King was 'The Monster', Don Arden was – at least by reputation – 'The Ancient Serpent', 'The Great Dragon' and the 'Prince of All Demons'.) 'The cavern was a big place with a massive stage. The kids were the kind of audience where you could get a good reaction: everybody was slightly off their heads! Pat Meehan reported back to Don and in a week or two, we had the first invite up to see him.'

Don must already have been aware of Steve. The Moments had supported The Nashville Teens, whom he represented.

'That was the quantum leap – all of a sudden you're walking down Carnaby Street to the Don's office.'

'We were all very excited,' said Ronnie, 'because Don Arden had had Gene Vincent. And when I say had, I really mean had.'

5

The Jewish Teddy Bear

The relationship between artiste and management has rarely been blessed by mutual affection and shared hobbies. In 1965 (and little changes) the journey towards Management Mistrust went something like.

STAGE ONE: The artiste is pitifully grateful to the manager for noticing them, for taking them out of the factory or fast-food outlet, for getting them a record deal, studio time, maybe a hit. They're on TV. Their aunties treat them with new respect. They even have a fancy new name.

STAGE TWO: The artiste discovers that the studio time and TV appearances are short-lived holidays between endless days spent sitting in the back of a van smelling the farts of bandmates, then sitting in a dressing room (if the venue runs to such luxury) smelling the farts of bandmates, before briefly appearing on stage to play (in 1965) the same six songs every night that nobody can hear, least of all you, while smelling the farts of 1,000 adoring fans. Meanwhile the aunties, and even some respected journalists, seem to believe that three consecutive Top 10 hits should make the artiste rich beyond the dreams of Croesus and the artiste wonders how they could be so mistaken.

STAGE THREE: The artiste notices that the manager has traded his 1963 Jag for a 1965 Silver Cloud III with personalised number plates and moved his offices from Edgware to Mayfair. A sense of injustice begins to fester.

STAGE FOUR: The artiste tries to recoup some small fraction of what's owing and discovers the terrible cost of showbiz lawyers.

Mistrust is not helped by the complexity of music business accounting. The income streams are many and varied – PRS, MCPS, TV and radio fees, merchandise and so on and so on. A PRS statement is a list of numbers that maybe tell you that your latest B-side was played 756 times on Radio Norge Slamfest for which you were paid £0.08, while slightly fewer plays on Argentina's Nucleo Duro FM made a hefty £0.12. No real sense is to be made of this, and anyway a percentage of the money will have already gone to a publisher and the management will deduct their percentage from the total.

Then there are the expenses. All that studio time, the clothes, the chauffeur-driven cars, the champagne that the management 'gave' you, was being deducted from those fees. The manager would take his cut 'from the top' – before expenses. Sometimes, this meant that by the time all those clothes and limos were paid for, there's nothing left for the artiste at all. Sometimes they would even find themselves in debt and had to do yet another tour for nothing.

In short, trying to follow a paper trail to figure out whether the management is on the fiddle is a fool's errand, but it's rarely necessary. Usually, it becomes fairly obvious that something's amiss when the manager takes a private jet to a private island and the artiste can't even afford a few basic drugs.

It can rankle, that sort of thing.

Ronnie, from Romford Road, knew right when he saw it and wrong when he saw it and eventually came to the conclusion that you could and should bypass the entire filthy business and as far as possible do it all yourself. But that was a few years down the road yet, and only after he'd had his fingers really badly burned by one of the most notorious of all the finger-burners.

Don Arden had started his career at 13 as a singer touring with a show called *Ladies on Revue*. During the war he had done time in ENSA, the entertainment division of the Army.

In the fifties, he worked for a while as an impressionist. His Elvis impersonation was used by Embassy. This was the label that did knock-off versions of the latest hits and sold them at low-low prices in Woolworths, where well-meaning aunties would buy them for their nieces and nephews, not realising it wasn't the real thing. Oh, the disappointment. Don's stage career, however, floundered. 'I was too aggressive to become a star, I argued too much, and I didn't please the right people.'

But he had a brain for business. He started to come up with his own promotions.

'I saw there was a market for Hebrew folk songs at that time, so from Monday to Saturday I'd be touring the variety theatres and on Sunday I'd be doing my own Hebrew folk song concerts. And from then on, I started to put together my own shows.'

Then he jumped on the rock'n'roll bandwagon, arranging tours for imported American heroes, and ended up managing Gene Vincent, from Norfolk, Virginia, the most perfect rock'n'roll star ever invented. Don liked his artistes to stand on stage and perform nicely for the people. Gene liked to drink. And he was a mean drunk, prone to threatening anybody who came near him with a knife or a gun, whichever was the more readily available.

'The first time I saw him,' Joe Brown, the lovable British singer/guitarist/ukuleleist, said, 'he was drunk in a corner with a gun in his hand.'

On 16 April 1960, a mini-cab carrying Gene, Eddie Cochran, Eddie's girlfriend Sharon Sheeley and their roadie blew a tyre and hit a tree. The driver and roadie suffered only minor injuries. Sharon and

Gene were badly injured. Eddie was killed. Gene got even meaner after that.

In 1963, he was arrested for threatening his British wife, Margaret, with a loaded Luger pistol at their flat in Notting Hill. 'I pointed the gun at her just to scare her,' he said in court. 'I'm a crack shot and I've won medals for shooting. But I don't think I could shoot a person.' He got a slap on the wrist and a £20 fine. Margaret forgave him.

By 1965, Gene had split with Don in a blaze of arguments and recriminations. Knives were, apparently, displayed but not deployed.

By this time, Don was managing The Nashville Teens and The Animals. Stories about his swindles, his threats and his violence are now legion. Half of them might even be true. He was a committed fabulist who loved to burnish his own reputation as a canny business-man who did not always play by the rules and a tough guy. In general, he liked to foster the impression that his acts were all in the gutter when he first encountered them and owed their success entirely to his brilliant management. For this reason, he behaved as if – and possibly believed – the money they earned was his by right. From time to time he might, out of the goodness of his heart, let the artistes have a few quid – but that was only because he was a soft-hearted fool who let generosity get the better of him.

Don arranged for the Small Faces to play as support to The Nashville Teens and The Pretty Things at the Winter Gardens in Margate on 3 June and went with his son, Dave (who had been at stage school with Steve) to see them perform.

'To me they had an image of their own,' Dave said. 'They looked like four little Oliver Twists – street urchins . . . When they came out they looked like four half-grown kids and when they opened up the sound it was so powerful – that was the impact . . . I thought, "They can't fail".'

So, the band was called into Don's office at 55 Carnaby Street.

'As we knocked on the door, Eric Burdon and The Animals were walking out,' Jimmy Winston said. 'It was, "Hi man, what you doing?" "We're just going up to see Don Arden," all that sort of enthusiastic stuff. And Eric Burdon looked at me, and laughed, "You're fucking crazy. It's just taken us a year to get out of that deal." They walked up the road laughing, but by then, we were on the flow. Couldn't stop ourselves.'

Again, accounts of that first meeting vary wildly. Mr Arden's version (one of them, anyway) says that when he asked Steve where he was living, Steve replied that he had a mud hut in Finsbury Park. It was how Steve liked to describe the vile flat he was living in at the time, but, since it suited the 'they were in the gutter narrative', Don chose to believe it. He claimed his staff complained that the four young mods stank and had shit on their trousers.

Regardless, he signed them up to a three-year contract and asked whether they wanted a wage or royalties. They asked for both and got £20 a week and 1.5 per cent on all record sales. With a great show of magnanimity, Don also opened accounts for them in all the best shops in Carnaby Street so that they could kit themselves out in non-shitty trousers. Eventually they would learn that they were paying for all this out of future earnings, but not for a while.

For the time being he was their saviour.

'He was kind of a Jewish teddy bear I suppose,' Kenney said. 'You liked him immediately because he was enthusiastic and he talked about what he could do and what he couldn't do and whenever he said – "I'll do this, I'll do that" – he did and it came true.'

Within days, Don had negotiated a record deal with Decca. He had a song already lined up for them; a bluesy number called 'Whatcha Gonna Do About It' by Ian Samwell and Brian Potter, who Arden described as 'two guys that worked for me for £25 a week'.

Actually, Samwell had written 'Move It', arguably the first credible British rock'n'roll song, which Cliff Richard took to number two, as well as other hits for Cliff and other artistes including The Isley Brothers. Brian Potter was relatively unknown at the time, but would go on to produce records for Tavares, Glenn Campbell, Dusty Springfield and many other worthies.

According to Don, the song was a hard sell. 'We tried about 20 times and couldn't get any artists to take it, but on this occasion I insisted. The boys had a great image but I didn't think they knew a good song from a bad song, so I fucking told them to keep their mouths shut! "You're going to do this song and this guy's going to record it for you." I admit I bullied them into doing it, but it doesn't matter because I was proved right.'

Nobody else, not Ronnie, Kenney, Steve or Jimmy, has ever suggested that they needed to be coerced or bullied into recording the song.

'We loved it,' says Kenney. 'It had a great groove, was soulful, and each of us was given a starring moment.'

And, rather than taking a 'hard sell' off the shelf, most people agree that Ronnie and Steve in fact half wrote 'Whatcha'. The riff was a rip-off from Solomon Burke's 'Everybody Needs Somebody to Love', a song that had been covered by The Rolling Stones and featured on the setlists of many, many bands, because it was easy to play and infinitely extendable. Ronnie and Steve had been messing around with the riff and had come up with a melody. Samwell and Potter were brought in to provide lyrics and, in Kenney's words, 'sand down the edges.' Ian Samwell produced the record and it was released on 6 August 1965.

Steve's guitar skills had progressed well beyond the three-chord stage, but still didn't stretch to the sort of thing Eric Clapton and Jeff Beck were turning out. On the other hand, he knew that showmanship could trump technical ability, and he knew how to turn up his amp and hold his guitar in the right place to make it scream, howl and holler. It's a trick Pete Townshend had been employing for a while. The Beatles, too, had used it – in a much more controlled way

– at the start of 'I Feel Fine'. Later, Jimi Hendrix would turn feedback into a whole new art form.

The next day the single received coverage on an ITV offshoot from the long-running pop show *Thank Your Lucky Stars*, called *Lucky Stars – Summer Spin*. The mighty Vicki Wickham (assistant producer on ITV's much better pop show *Ready Steady Go!*, Dusty Springfield's manager, and an acknowledged expert on all things mod) was the producer. 'They were a mod group,' she said. 'They were cute, they had great music, they were right up our street.'

Joe Brown and his Bruvvers were on the same bill, along with the German ex-Tornado Heinz, US country singer Sue Thompson, and Sonny & Cher, promoting their first hit 'I Got You Babe'. Cher surprised the Small Faces by telling them that they had caught their act in Sheffield and even asking for copies of the single to take home. 'Sonny and Cher gave us a tremendous boost,' Steve said, 'offering advice and encouragement. We never forgot that.'

Mick Jagger and Keith Richards were impressed by them too. Annie Nightingale, later to become BBC Radio 1's first female DJ, remembers Jagger telling her around this time, 'if you don't like the Small Faces you must be getting old.'

She was 25.

On 23 August, the band did their first session for BBC Radio on *Saturday Club*. Steve introduced the members, 'This is James our organist and Kenney our drummer. And this is Plonk, our bass. He's called that cos he plonks away. We've been together for nearly 11 weeks. We met in a pub in the East End, sort of, over a beer. [The record] . . . has been out about three weeks and was written by our recording manager, Ian Samwell. I think he did a good job on it.'

Ronnie's nickname, Plonk, was said to be a reflection of his style of playing. Although there is another more salacious interpretation.

The TV and radio exposure meant gigs were easy to come by. Don Arden owned a healthy slice of Galaxy Entertainments, run by Ron

King, who initially organised a week's mini-tour around the country, ending at the Cavern in London on 11 September.

Meanwhile, Don got busy 'promoting' the record.

In *The Music Moguls: Masters of Pop – Money Makers*, a BBC TV documentary from 2016, Don claimed, 'I employed a technique I had done before – which was perfectly legal. I hired housewives to go out and buy the record for us. To legitimately go into a shop and buy, instead of one record, let's say, two or three records. Perfectly legal.

'With the Small Faces, I only had to do it for a few weeks because they took off. But if they want to say Don Arden spent thousands on hyping the record, if they want to say that – fine. So what? So what?

'I had a saying, "you can't polish a turd". In other words, if the record's no good to begin with, it still won't be any good after you've wasted your time and money getting it played.'

Whatever, it worked. The song entered the chart at number 42 before they'd finished their mini-tour. A week later it went up to number 33.

On 16 September (Kenney Jones' 17th birthday), the Small Faces made their first appearance on *Top of the Pops* alongside The Walker Brothers singing 'Make It Easy on Yourself' and The Rolling Stones who had the number one spot with 'Satisfaction'.

The day after, they did *Ready Steady Go!* alongside The Hollies and Dusty Springfield.

Jimmy Page was a session musician when he first met them during that performance for *Ready Steady Go!* in 1965. 'They invited me to have something to eat at this Italian restaurant after the show, which I thought was really sweet. They all had this generosity and warmth – a bunch of really good guys.'

Don Arden, of course, claimed full credit for their popularity.

'I used to phone up *Ready Steady Go!* and *Top of the Pops*,' he said, 'and get artists on television just bosh, like that, through the fact that I was the number one promoter in Europe. If I phoned them up, they were on.'

A week or so later, George Melly, journalist, blues singer and surrealist, interviewed them for *The Observer* under the headline 'Life's A Gas For The Latest Pop Sensations'.

'I love to hear someone singing like a coloured feller [sic]. If they mean it, that is. You can always tell,' said one of them they called Plonk.

'We're useless instrumentalists.'

In consequence they keep their music simple. They use an organ, bass and lead guitars, and drums. What they aim at is an original sound based on unusual rhythm. They improvise at rehearsal until something develops. 'Modern soul' is how they describe what they're after. The Small Faces know their audience. 'Little Mods,' they call them affectionately. They're less certain of themselves, 'in the sticks, where it's a bit rockier, where they're, well . . . slightly backward.'

On 30 September, they did *Top of the Pops* for a second time, with The Hollies, again, Sandie Shaw, The Searchers and Ken Dodd singing 'Tears for Souvenirs'.

Four days later, they did another gig at the Mojo club up in Sheffield.

'The second time they played they had a record at near number one and they packed the place solid,' Peter Stringfellow said. 'Then as they became massive they kept this friendliness about them, which is why everyone loved them.'

On 7 October, the band appeared for a third time on *Top of the Pops*, this time with P. J. Proby, The Everly Brothers, Wilson Pickett, The Supremes and, of course, the ever-popular Ken Dodd.

Gradually, the record had eased its way into the Top 20. Despite Peter Stringfellow's claims, it never got close to number one, but peaked, on 20 October, at a respectable number 14.

In order to cut a dash on TV, they all took full advantage of the accounts Mr Arden had set them up with at the Carnaby Street boutiques. 'We were like a bunch of old women at a jumble sale, when we walked into a shop: some of the stuff we never even wore,' said Ronnie. 'We'd get home and think, what did I buy that for? . . . We often had money left over from that twenty quid and we were out of our boxes most of the time. In the beginning I trusted him. I thought Don was a wonderful guy.'

Ha.

6

'Sort of Leader of the Small Faces'

For the second single, Ronnie and Steve convinced Don to let them record one of their own compositions called 'I've Got Mine' – all moody minor key verses exploding into major key chorus.

'We'd had a hit after being in the business for about five minutes,' Kenney said, 'so we thought, "Well . . . we've written a song." I loved it 'cos it was more expressive on the drums and had this guitar line through a Leslie amp. Stunning. It's underestimated and still one of my favourite Small Faces songs. But because it wasn't a hit . . . that was it.'

A massive opportunity to publicise the song came via film producer Harold Shampan, an upright gent with a beautifully trimmed moustache. He had previously worked on the film *Band of Thieves* (1962), in which Acker Bilk and His Paramount Jazz Band play ex-cons who revert to their old bad ways, and *Be My Guest* (1965), which starred David Hemmings and the young Steve Marriott in his acting days and featured The Nashville Teens – another of Mr Arden's charges.

Shampan's new masterpiece, *Dateline Diamonds*, was a thriller with music in which Kenneth Cope, a pop manager with a seedy past, is blackmailed by a gentleman diamond thief into smuggling stolen diamonds to Amsterdam via the ship MV *Galaxy*, which is anchored in international waters three miles off Frinton, home to the pirate station Radio London. The Small Faces would be one of Kenneth Cope's charges, along with The Caravelles, a girl group who'd had a hit a couple of years earlier with 'You Don't Have to Be a Baby to Cry', and an 18-year-old session singer from Bradford called Kiki Dee.

The script for the film was provided by the extravagantly named Tudor Gates, whose finest hour came later with 1970's *The Vampire Lovers*, a Hammer horror classic starring Ingrid Pitt and Peter Cushing, uncontestably the finest naked lesbian vampire film ever made.

In the film, the Small Faces perform 'I've Got Mine' (at the Rank Ballroom, Watford) to an audience of about 30 extras, who try hard to look like adoring masses.

As it turned out, a brief appearance in a dud movie that would probably have gone straight to DVD, if DVDs had been invented, didn't do much for the band. The film's release was delayed by a year – too late to do any good for 'I've Got Mine' – so, although the record picked up a couple of nice reviews, it never came within sight of the Top 50.

The film did, however, do terrific business for the Ford Transit van, then new to the world, which featured heavily. The van went on, of course, to become the standard vehicle in which bands schlepped their gear from gig to gig, hid their stash, slept and fucked. It was also robust enough to take a good kicking when it broke down at three in the morning on some godforsaken B-road in the Scottish Highlands.

Meanwhile, personnel problems were emerging. Steve and Ronnie had had enough of Jimmy Winston.

'Jimmy went off his rocker every now and then,' Steve said, 'plus we didn't get on too well personally.'

'Jimmy was a big head,' Ronnie said, 'and I don't think Steve could take any more.'

Val Weedon, Don Arden's receptionist at the time, thought that 'the conflict was more Ronnie and Jimmy . . . Ronnie and Jimmy had fisticuffs in the office arguing over women . . . [Jimmy] loved being in the limelight at that time and he would compete with Steve onstage and show off and that got up Ronnie's nose.'

Jimmy, it also has to be said, was taller than the others and insisted on remaining so.

Jimmy himself, in a 1999 interview with John Hellier, said the core problem was money, specifically the band's agreement to pay Jimmy's brother 10 per cent of anything they earned touring for the use of his van.

'The rest of the band got a bit grumpy about this, dunno why. It was one of those incidents where I got stuck in the middle and I did get into conflict with Steve and Ronnie over this. I'd always been close to my brother and they weren't being fair to him.'

Don, however, saw the problem as Ronnie Lane. He was one of the very few people in the music business ever to badmouth Ronnie (the other being Andrew Loog Oldham). He didn't hold back.

'The first thing he did after the hit record came out was to demand the keyboard player be replaced. He was the nicest one in the group . . . I never got over the fact that Ronnie pointed the finger at him when he thought the time was right – "I can't play with him, he's no fucking good." I asked, "Why don't you give him a chance? We've only just started, you're in the charts, you're stars, give him a fucking break." . . . He didn't want to know, so they just kicked him out. The guy they kicked out was ten times better than this Scottish cunt they got in.'

Ian McLagan isn't even all that Scottish. He's from Hounslow.

At the end of October, after a three-week tour, Jimmy Winston played his last gig with the Small Faces at the Manor Lounge, Stockport.

On 1 November, Don called Ian McLagan into his office in Carnaby Street. He'd previously been playing with a band called Boz People and before that The Muleskinners.

Ian said in a radio interview in 2013 that he had no idea what Don wanted to talk to him about. He remembered that while he was waiting to go in to see the man, he noticed four pictures on the wall – 'The first was the Small Faces – and I thought "No chance!" He'd seen them on *Ready Steady Go!* His dad was a fan.

'I was getting ready to go out on a date and he shouted up the stairs, "Ian! Come and look at this band. They're great!"

'The second picture on the stairs was The Animals but I knew that they had just got a new organ player, then there was The Nashville Teens but I knew that their pianist was great and then the fourth picture was this band called Clayton Squares that I'd never heard of. So, I thought it must be something to do with them.'

After Don had offered Ian the job, he bought the other three in to meet him.

'There were some funny little things about the four of us coming together that it almost sounds fictional,' Ronnie said. 'I think the four of us definitely had it in our destiny, it was no accident.'

'When I met the other Faces,' Ian said, 'it was like looking at a mirror of myself – I couldn't believe it. We all looked alike – Plonk and Steve might have been my brothers. It was about the first time that I've ever counted myself lucky to be small because, apart from needing a new organist, I fitted the group image of being little.'

A Ph.D. thesis needs to be written on the contribution made to the success of a band by all its members being of a similar height. The front line of The Beatles were all within half an inch of each other. Ringo was two inches shorter, but he was sitting down. Similarly, Mick, Keith, Ronnie Wood and Charlie of The Rolling Stones are all within an inch of each other. Brian Jones and Bill Wyman were both shorter, which is presumably why they had to go.

Ian's first task was to buy a guitar so that he could mime Jimmy Winston's part on 'I've Got Mine' when the track got airplay on *Ready Steady Go!* and the BBC children's programme *Crackerjack!*

Then it was off for a gruelling two-month tour, starting – with barely time for rehearsal – at the Locarno, Swindon, then criss-crossing the country from Cleethorpes to Plymouth, taking in the RAF Flying Fox Club at Cottesmore, the Leyton Baths, the Marine Ballroom in Morecambe and, on Christmas Eve, the Wilton Hall in Bletchley.

Ian settled right in.

'We'd always hang out together, we were always smoking dope and taking pills, there wasn't any time we weren't stoned, unless you ran out of dope and that was the worst part. We'd be touring up in Manchester or whatever and after four or five days it'd be like, "This is it, the last joint. Fuck it, we'll try and score". And I'm telling you it was very difficult to score in fucking Barnsley in 1965. So, when we got back to London at two or three in the morning, the first thing I'd do was get in a cab to score the dope. But on the road we'd be constantly writing songs, and they had it down, they figured, like John [Lennon] and Paul [McCartney], that's what we're here for, and the songs would just fly out. Some were Steve's, some were Ronnie's, some were both.'

After 'I've Got Mine' flopped, the boss wasn't interested in their own compositions.

'I remember Don Arden,' said Kenney, 'telling us he was getting in Kenny Lynch and Mort Schuman to write the next single as he couldn't afford another flop.'

Mort Schuman was a veteran of the Brill Building, the song factory in New York where, among many others, Carole King and Gerry Goffin, Ellie Greenwich and Jeff Barry, Neil Diamond, Barry Mann and Cynthia Weill, Jerry Leiber and Mike Stoller, Burt Bacharach and Hal David had served time churning out songs for the music machine. With Doc Pomus, Schuman was responsible for a string of hits including 'Little Sister', '(Marie's the Name) His Latest Flame' and 'Viva Las Vegas' for Elvis, 'Save the Last Dance for Me' for The Drifters and 'Can't Get Used to Losing You' for Andy

Williams. When the British invaded the US, Pomus and Schuman relocated to the UK.

Kenny Lynch was an actor/singer/songwriter, who'd had a couple of hits in the early sixties. He knew everybody and had earned the distinction of being the first non-Beatle to record a Lennon and McCartney song when he did 'Misery' – a tune they'd originally written for Helen Shapiro. The Beatles subsequently nicked Lynch's arrangement for their own version on their first LP.

Don wanted something like 'Do Wah Diddy Diddy', the Jeff Barry/Ellie Greenwich song that Manfred Mann had taken to number one on both sides of the Atlantic. Shuman and Lynch came up with 'Sha-La-La-La-Lee', which is similar inasmuch as it espouses the notion that true love can be fully expressed only through the medium of nonsense baby babble.

Ronnie didn't like it.

'The problem was,' he said, 'Arden knew what he wanted from us before he'd even heard of us . . . but he just didn't get the black thing. If he'd had it all his way, we'd have been doing 'Sha-La-La-La-Lee' forever.'

Don put his foot down. 'The band hated it, but it brought them massive success. Then they were all kissing my feet.'

It was a story that was heard a lot in the 1960s. Bands wanted the credibility of Dylan or Otis Redding; management wanted the money-making potential of Herman's Hermits.

Along with the nonsense lyrics, the band found their Booker T. ambitions travestied in the pop comics – a typical example being Dawn James' breathless piece for *Rave* magazine.

Plonk (Ronnie Lane) collapsed on to a chair so surely that it crunched even under his featherweight.

'I'm late because I went shopping,' he gasped. 'So sorry, but I can't keep away from Carnaby Street.'

Plonk has enormous hazel eyes, dark brown hair, and a skinny body. He is a sort of leader of the Small Faces (Steve Marriott, vocal and lead guitar; Ian McLagan, organ and rhythm guitar; Kenney Jones, drums.)

'We call him Plonk because he plonks instead of plinks on his bass,' said Kenney, helpfully.

They hail from the East End of London and bring into the world of Soho and Mayfair a fresh honesty, a cockney sense of humour, and the ability to stand outside themselves and laugh.

'We do some crazy things onstage,' Plonk said, 'and they are never planned, they just happen.'

The boys have nice manners, are quietly spoken, and seem to know exactly what they are, what they want to be, and what they consider important to them.

To bring them a little nearer to the world of Soho and Mayfair – a bit nearer than Loughton, anyway – Don rehoused them in a beautiful stucco house at 22 Westmoreland Terrace, Pimlico.

'At that time, they didn't have anything at all, no clothes, no furniture,' Don said. 'Within three months they had a house, a Mark 10 Jaguar with a chauffeur, a maid to serve them with breakfasts, get their dinners at night and clean their clothes. And after 12 months they had 500 pairs of shoes between them and more clothes than they knew what to do with.'

7

The Rigours of the Road

Few bands have a lifespan longer than two or three years. Some expire after a few weeks. The usual reasons are money, love, management and drugs – most likely a combination of them all. The band loses all its money to bent managers and dodgy coke dealers, then one day the bass player finds the drummer in bed with his wife, or the lead singer finds the keyboard player in bed with her husband, or everybody finds everybody else in bed with members of Fleetwood Mac and the whole thing explodes. These events are usually described as 'musical differences'.

With such a limited lifespan, there is an urgent need to make as much cash as possible before you become no more than a trick question in a pub quiz after which there is no more cash to be had. A night (and wherever possible a morning or afternoon) without a gig, a day without a record on the rise, is money down the drain. Mr Arden liked to work his bands hard.

On 5 January 1966, the Small Faces flew off to Europe for seven gigs around the Netherlands, Belgium and Germany followed by months spent slogging round the UK playing every ballroom, university, town hall and club that Mr Arden and Gaiety Entertainments could get them into.

'For the next three years we were a top teeny scream band,' Ronnie said. 'We worked seven nights a week. The Small Faces were very much a band to go and wet your knickers at. For three years we never heard a thing we played, literally, because of the screaming.'

Between 1 May 1966 and the end of June they clocked up 52 live performances including shows in Iceland, France and all over the UK. Only very, very occasionally did they get the chance to break the teeny scream mould. On 22 March, the band got to play at the Marquee in London, where Ronnie and Kenney had gone a year before to see The Who. It made a change. Many of the punters were taller than they were. They did not scream, wet their knickers or mob the stage. They didn't even dance. They watched and listened thought-fully. The band, looking out at the audience, saw people like them and they tailored their setlist to please them, with classics like Joe Williams' 'Baby Please Don't Go', Muddy Waters' 'You Need Love' and Booker T. & The M.G.'s' 'Plum Nellie'. This, they felt, was the real essence of the band.

The teeny screamers thought otherwise.

Don Arden had hired The Beatles' ex-driver Bill Corbet to drive them around. He was a man no one would mess with – a 6ft 6in former boxer. He didn't appreciate the band smoking dope in the car. Ronnie, Steve and Mac apparently used to put up a blanket between the front and the back seats so they could smoke in peace: Kenney, who didn't like dope (he preferred pills), would travel in the front seat next to Bill.

'We played at a northern venue recently,' Mac said. 'Bill had phoned the manager earlier in the day to tell him to put crash barriers round the stage. We knew they'd be needed, because we'd only just escaped with our lives at a show the night before!

'I don't think this manager really knew what it was all about, because when we got there, there were no crash barriers and he said: "Don't worry, I can handle this."

'We found we had to walk backwards and forwards from our dressing room through the wildest crowd you ever saw! We were all being pulled to the ground and dragged about, all in fear of instant death!'

Ronnie was treated for concussion after being knocked unconscious when fans besieged the group outside their hotel in Scotland.

At a skating rink in Streatham, the fans marauded again. Kenney had his shoulder dislocated. Steve was knocked unconscious. 'Thank goodness they didn't wreck my camel hair jacket,' he said, when he woke up. 'I only bought it the other day. Cost 40 quid.'

In Glasgow, Mac spent the night in a police cell when he was locked out of his hotel room, 'For his own safety.'

It was unrelenting – a year later, at Oldham Athletic football stadium, as they were driven onto the field, the fans laid siege to the car.

'The ground was pretty soft and the car just wouldn't move,' Mac said. 'It was right in the middle of the pitch, and it just started to go down and down and down. The four of us and the driver were getting the real horrors. The kids' faces were getting mashed up against the windows and I remember seeing one little kid being pushed down and her head disappearing out of sight. We were shouting, 'Look out for that kid', and then the roof of the car started to bow inward under the sheer weight of the kids on top. We were holding the roof up which was really starting to cave in and there wasn't much air in the car 'cos we couldn't open the windows, which really set a panic in.'

The band eventually left the football ground in shock and told the driver to keep going for five miles, when they got out of the car and ran crazily over the moors, screaming their heads off in shock.

Pills, booze, youth and adrenalin can only keep you going for so long. Eventually the body rebels. On 10 June 1966, Steve collapsed in front of the *Ready Steady Go!* cameras, suffering from nervous exhaustion.

Glyn Johns, their producer, once found Ronnie passed out backstage.

'They had been on the road solidly for weeks, sometimes doing two shows a night with long distances to travel in between. This had taken its toll on them and they were pretty wiped out. I put Ronnie in my car and drove him back to the house I shared with Stu (Ian Stewart, the 'sixth' member of The Rolling Stones and all-round good guy). He stayed a couple of nights with no one knowing where he was and got to rest and recover.'

Mac noticed the effect the constant onslaught was having on Ronnie. 'There were a few times on long journeys when Ronnie would say something a bit weird and I'd say, "What do you mean?" and he'd just say, "Well I'm mad, ain't I? I'm going mad." And we had a few tough times with each other then, a definite feeling that we were going round the twist.

'Thinking about those touring days, travelling up and down Britain and across Europe it's the friendship that sits most prominently in my memory. Four young blokes footloose and carefree, mates who were always watching each other's backs . . .

'But Steve was hard work to be around. Working within a band it's like you're an enabler, and Ronnie was Steve's enabler and I was Ronnie's. The three of us also used to do all the drugs together, laugh at the same things.'

Kenney felt he had drawn the short straw if he had to share a hotel room with Steve. Steve would talk incessantly, pacing around, looking for girls to bring back to the room. He much preferred to share with Ronnie.

'Ronnie,' he said, 'instead of pacing, spent his time slowly wandering around, shirt hanging out, wondering where he'd put something.'

Their status as a teeny screamer band made a fan club obligatory.

Pauline Corcoran was 16 when Don Arden hired her to become the official Small Faces Fan Club secretary (she was initially disappointed because she had hoped that the pop group Don was talking about was her favourite, The Who). As well as dealing with member-ship and correspondence, she made it her business to accompany the band to gigs and TV appearances.

'Ronnie was always so stoned,' Pauline said, 'more so than the other three. He was always away with the fairies.

'Once on a trip to Birmingham with Don Arden and the Small Faces, Ronnie invited me to his hotel room. Don had told all the boys very firmly, "If any one of you goes near her room tonight, I'll break your legs!" Don was very protective of me. I was a 16-year-old virgin and he looked after me. Ronnie would ring my room, about half past 12 when I was in bed, and say, "Do you wanna come over?" I'd say, "Do you know what time it is?" He'd say, "You don't have to get changed, come as you are!" He was a lovable character but defi-nitely not boyfriend material.'

Sometimes the demands of the job got weird. 'Ronnie said in a magazine that he would like an alligator as a pet,' Pauline said. 'Then one day a special delivery guy came into the office with a big box, addressed to the fan club. When we first opened the box we thought that they were stuffed alligators or toy ones. I went to pick one up and they all moved. Everybody screamed! We didn't expect them to be real. Kenney ran out first and Don came in to see what all the fuss was about. He took one look but he didn't look surprised. He was laughing. Next thing I know, Don's on the phone to a photog-rapher and he took the boys up the road for some pictures. It's funny how all the alligators had leads! Once the photos were taken, they were all put back into the box and he got somebody from the RSPCA to come and take them away. It was almost certainly one big publicity stunt although we were never told that. The official story was that they were from a group of fans, but what fans would think to do that?'

By the time 'Sha-La-La-La-Lee' disappeared from the Top 40 at the end of April, the new product was ready to be shipped.

'Hey Girl', written by Steve and Ronnie, had a relentlessly catchy call-and-response chorus. For a magic few weeks if you went anywhere that young people were likely to assemble and shouted 'Hey, hey', the young people would reply, 'It's all right!' They couldn't help it.

An album was released at around the same time. Called *Small Faces*, it included 'Whatcha Gonna Do About It' and 'Sha-La-La-La-Lee', covers of Sam Cooke's 'Shake', sung by Ronnie, and Willie Dixon and Muddy Waters' 'You Need Love' (retitled 'You Need Loving' and credited to Marriott/Lane). There were a couple of songs in which Kenny Lynch had a hand and the rest were either by Ronnie and Steve or the whole band. Some of the tracks, recorded before Mac came on board, shared the writing credit with Jimmy Winston.

With the album, Steve proves his right to be crowned Best Young White Male British Blues Singer (or at least to contest the title with Steve Winwood), and Ian McLagan demonstrates his right to be crowned Best Young White Male British Blues Hammond Organ Player (or at least to contest the title with Steve Winwood, Graham Bond and a couple of other people), and the band in general prove their right to be crowned Best Young White Male British Blues and Soul Band (or at least to pitch for the title).

The album was in the Top 40 for twenty-five weeks and held the number three position for five.

It has to be remembered that throughout most of the second half of the 1960s, even The Beatles rarely had a stab at the number one position in the album charts, which was held relentlessly for the best part of three years by the soundtrack album *The Sound of Music*. *Sgt. Pepper* displaced it for three months or so but eventually, inevitably, the British public showed that, though 'A Day in the Life' and 'Lucy in the Sky with Diamonds' were nice for a bit of a change, in the final analysis they still preferred 'Do-Re-Mi' and 'The Lonely Goatherd'.

The single, 'Hey Girl', took three weeks to reach number ten and held the position for another week before gently dropping. It might have gone higher were it not for a little trouble with TV promotion.

There had been a resentment festering for some time about running orders. When 'Sha-La-La-La-Lee' was riding high, they'd been booked for an episode of *Thank Your Lucky Stars.*

'Although we had a single in the charts,' Steve said, 'they refused to let us do more than one number and they wanted us to open the show, which was being topped by Dee Warwick [Dionne's sister who, despite critical adulation, never had a UK hit].'

'We'd been opening everything,' Ronnie said, 'including *Five O'Clock Club* [a BBC children's show hosted by Ollie Beak, an owl, and featuring, incongruously, as its resident bandleader British blues legend Alexis Korner]. They were beginning to call us "The Small Openers". I mean, own up – we had a number in the Top Ten. So let us be second or something.'

It happened again when they were due to perform the new single on *Top of the Pops*. The producer told them they'd be opening the show. Steve told him to fuck off. Don Arden argued with the BBC. 'We always open bills – we wanted to be placed further into the programme, but they refused.' The band walked off the set.

'Hey Girl' drifted away to be followed, in August, by 'All or Nothing'.

The *NME* for one saw the new release as a sign of a band growing up: 'Gone is the incredibly happy mood of their past two great hits, the Faces are in a more soul-searching groove, reaching into themselves, sparing neither vocal chords, nor guitar and drumming ability.'

The song was featured on *Juke Box Jury*, the BBC show in which celebs aired their opinions about new releases, voting them a 'Hit' or a 'Miss'. The celebs that night – actor/singer/comic Bernard Cribbins, singer Rosemary Squires, musical theatre star Kay Medford and radio presenter Barry Alldis – decided 'All or Nothing' would be a Miss.

'We ordered champagne,' Steve said. 'That wasn't sour grapes on our part. It's just that we learned through experience not to put any faith in *Juke Box Jury* verdicts. They voted "Whatcha Gonna Do About It" a "Miss" and it was a hit and 'I've Got Mine' a "Hit" and it was a miss.'

The record had stiff competition. A Beatles double A-side, 'Eleanor Rigby' and 'Yellow Submarine', was released in the same week.

Having kissed and made up with various TV producers, they plugged the song on *Top of the Pops* and *Ready Steady Go!* and, on 11 August, 'All or Nothing' became their first and only number one. Not quite, though, according to *Top of the Pops*. The show, which compiled its chart from various sources, reckoned they shared the top spot with The Beatles, so compiled a montage of the two groups for the chart rundown, twinning the two bands – Ronnie with George, Steve with John, Kenney with Ringo, and Mac with Paul, which wouldn't have been too bad if the twinned record had been 'Lady Madonna', say, or 'Hey Jude'.

But 'All or Nothing' twinned with 'Yellow Submarine' must have stuck in the craw.

8

The Seeker

After the spats and tantrums about second-best billings, the Small Faces' reconciliation with the TV industry – indeed their triumph over television – came when, on 12 August, they took over an entire episode of *Scene at 6.30*, Granada TV's music, news and views programme, and did eight songs, finishing with 'All or Nothing'. Rod Taylor, the programme's producer, said it was, 'The most exciting spectacular we have made since the one featuring Little Richard.'

The standard career path for bands in the sixties was the one set by The Beatles. Establish yourself in the UK and Europe, then off you go to conquer the USA. Everybody did it. The *Billboard* Top 100 Bestsellers for 1966 included releases by The Mindbenders, Dusty Springfield, Donovan, The Hollies, The Rolling Stones, Petula Clarke, The Troggs, The Beatles, Crispian St Peters, Peter and Gordon, Herman's Hermits, The Association, The Yardbirds and The Kinks. In 1967, the number one bestseller of the year was 'To Sir with Love' by Lulu. But no Small Faces.

Don Arden claimed to have set up a US tour for the band during the autumn of 1966, but it never materialised. Sometimes this was blamed on a drug conviction that Mac was supposed to have had but, 'My bust wasn't the reason we never went,' Mac said. 'Don had set up a tour, but it was bogus. It was set up so we'd say no – months long, back of a bus, bottom of the bill, very little money. What are you supposed to say? No! It would have meant he lost control of us.'

Don also announced that the band had been asked to appear in Brigitte Bardot's new film *Two Weeks in September*, and that Steve had been asked to star as Oliver in the new major movie of Lionel Bart's *Oliver!*

These things didn't materialise either.

'My Mind's Eye' was recorded at IBC studios as a track for their second album. Vaguely based on the Christmas carol 'Angels from the Realms of Glory', a tape with a rough mix of the song, along with other songs, was deposited at Mr Arden's office and the band went off on a tour of Germany and Sweden.

'We were on the road in our van between gigs,' Ronnie said, 'when 'Eye' appeared on the radio. It was a rough mix, done about four in the morning and duly sent to Arden's office to ram it down his throat that we were making full use of our studio time. Consequently, a huge row with the management developed out of this.'

'We hadn't been asked about it,' Mac said. 'He took it straight from the tape of the demo, but we hadn't finished with it and even if we had, it was never intended as a single. Our reaction to him when that happened began with a C and ended with a T. That was the beginning of the end of our working relationship.'

They appeared on *Top of the Pops* on 10 November performing 'My Mind's Eye' without much enthusiasm. A week later they appeared on *Ready Steady Go!* performing '(Tell Me) Have You Ever Seen Me' and 'My Mind's Eye' – but the band were critiqued in the *Melody Maker* for 'falling about on stage'.

A few weeks later they were due to appear on *Crackerjack!*, the children's Friday at five-to-five light entertainment show, but didn't turn up. So, Leslie Crowther, the show's host, performed a piano instrumental version of 'My Mind's Eye'. As ghastly as this might sound, it was par for the course; the show often featured the cast doing rumpty-tumpty bowdlerisations of hot hits, as witnessed by a clip, available on YouTube at the time of writing, of three *Crackerjack!* stalwarts, Peter Glaze, Jan Hunt and Jack Douglas, giving it to Status Quo's 'Whatever You Want'. Enjoy.

The 'Angels from the Realms of Glory' pinch suggests that 'My Mind's Eye' could have been pitched as a Christmas number one, but, perhaps because of the band's lacklustre commitment, it rose no higher than number four, and Tom Jones' 'Green, Green Grass of Home' was the nation's choice to herald the birth of baby Jesus that year.

Elsewhere, the Small Faces, according to most sources, did find time in their busy schedules for sex. Pop stars, girls, groupies, coercion, consent and all that they entail are not easy subjects to address. The 'different times' defence will not stand. Hearts, minds and lives would have been broken.

Steve had got a 15-year-old fan pregnant. She gave birth to a daughter.

'It was all kept fairly quiet,' Kenney said. 'Ronnie got accused of the same thing, but it wasn't his child. Lots of girls were doing it. It was a thing that happened at that time.'

They were boys who – like most pop stars – were barely post-pubescent and had more hormones rattling round inside them than they had blood, bones, flesh or sense. Suddenly they had access to many things that lack of money and adult supervision had previously put far out of reach. Of course, they should have known better – just as Jimi Hendrix, Mama Cass, Janis Joplin, Jim Morrison and the rest should have known better than to take all those drugs.

It's always as well to remember, when jaunty anecdotes are swapped about backstage romps, that the men, or boys, involved were criminal bastards. And even if the girls were as predatory as the men – and often, particularly in America, they were – that doesn't detract from the men's crimes or their bastardliness.

To give them their due, though, the Small Faces were also working-class lads who knew how to do right by a girl when the right one came along.

In either Cardiff (or Blackpool, memories vary) the band had met Susan Hunt, who'd been signed up by a model agency and, under the name of Genevieve, was trying to make it as a singer. She released a couple of singles, 'Just a Whisper' and 'Summer Days', neither of which set the world on fire.

She and Ronnie hit it off.

'He was just standing there on his own, he was miles away,' Sue said, 'We connected immediately, well I did anyway, I think it took him a little longer.'

'She wasn't much of a singer,' Mac said, 'but she was good looking and a sweet girl. Ronnie really fancied her. But when her manager caught them kissing between the curtains during the show in Cardiff, he told Ronnie to leave her alone or there would be trouble. Ronnie kicked him off the stage and told him to fuck off, which he did, leaving Sue without a manager but with a new boyfriend. She eventually moved out of her flat in Sloane Square to come and live with Ronnie.'

Meanwhile, while playing *Ready Steady Go!*, Mac encountered Sandy Sergeant. She won a dance competition and went on to become the show's first cage dancer. In the mid-sixties, a young woman, inadequately protected against cold and draughts, dancing in a cage suspended in mid-air, was standard set dressing for a TV pop show – a consideration that gives one pause to wonder whether one might have been a little too adamant in one's insistence, a couple of paragraphs earlier, about the validity of the 'different times' excuse.

Anyway, in 1968, Sandy would become Mac's wife.

But otherwise . . .

'Girls, girls, girls and more girls,' Ronnie said, recalling the rare moments when they were at home in the house that Mr Arden had acquired for them in Westmoreland Terrace, Pimlico the year before. 'Oh yeah! And playing Scalextric with Georgie Fame and Zoot Money.'

Steve, Mac and Ronnie shared the house. Kenney still lived at home with his parents. Ronnie had taken the front bedroom on the ground floor. All he had brought with him was his Dansette record player and a pile of records.

The sitting room had wallpaper decorated with Greek classical statues in black on a white background and the boys (or someone in Don's office) had acquired an antique leather sofa, Mexican rugs, a £265 soundproof chair that hung from the ceiling on a long chain and . . .

' . . . one of those build-it-yourself shelves set-ups, which you add to as you go along. It seems to be growing by itself – taking over the whole place, it is.'

'We had a German housekeeper called Liesel,' Mac said. 'Without her I don't think it would have worked. She did all the cooking, all the cleaning and washed and ironed our clothes. There was another old lady called Marge living next door and it was her that coined the phrase "How's your Bert's lumbago?" Liesel would insist on cooking us all this German food, though. We'd get up around midday and she'd have mashed potatoes and meat when all we really wanted was a fried egg on toast.'

The popistocracy would call round often.

'You never knew who'd be in there,' Kenney said. 'Mick Jagger, Paul McCartney, all sorts of people. Most of us were stoned out of our heads all the time. There weren't really any hard drugs in those days – we'd smoke hash, lie back and fall asleep.'

'We got to party a lot,' said Mac. 'Of course, but if we wanted to work on a song, boom, we were there. It was like being on the road, really, except that there was always somewhere to eat, sleep, smoke a joint, have a drink and listen to music. We were having the best time.'

One day, Brian Epstein showed up with Graeme Edge, The Moody Blues' drummer. Brian had just returned from America, where he had been trying to manage the fallout following John Lennon's 'bigger than Jesus' comments. He handed round a plate of orange slices laced with LSD.

It's inevitable that people would have different memories of such an event. Some will swear that the first time they took acid they were in an attack ship on fire off the shoulder of Orion where they could watch the C-beams glitter in the dark near the Tannhäuser Gate, and who's to say they're wrong? Ronnie remembers it happening not at the Westmoreland Terrace house but at a party thrown by Brian at the Saville Theatre.

'I was naïve; I didn't know what I'd been given,' said Ronnie. 'It was horrific at first but soon turned into something beautiful.'

Mac said he and Ronnie had, 'the best fucking time. It was brilliant, unbelievable.'

Ronnie walked down to the Thames to look at the river.

Steve had a bad trip and ended up taking an early train to Manchester, where he broke up with his then girlfriend, Sue Oliver.

According to Mac, acid changed Ronnie. 'Ronnie was always a seeker, a spiritual person, but I don't remember him looking for anything but a good time before he took acid.'

Much later, Ronnie gave a strange interview to Keith Altham of *NME*, in which he described himself as going through a disturbing emotional period and feeling that his whole character was altering.

'In the last six months I've completely changed my attitude to life,' he said. 'I suddenly realised that I had achieved my ambition of playing in a big group and life must hold something more.'

'I mean we're not just this,' he indicated his skin. 'There are other things that I'm finding out about – they're as old as time. It's just that I'm beginning to see them more clearly.'

One of the things he wanted to see more clearly was where all his money had gone. Mr Arden seemed to have lots and the Small Faces not very much. He had reached Stage Three of Management Mistrust (see Chapter 5).

Ronnie, the way he told it, was fairly phlegmatic about the matter.

'We worked seven nights a week and ended up broke. There you go. Some people get bitter about that sort of thing, but I wonder what would have happened if we hadn't got through all that. I'd have probably ended up in a bloody factory.'

As always, Don saw things differently. 'As soon as the hits came pouring in,' he said, 'Ronnie, predictably, was the first one to mention money. But he was too chicken shit to talk to me about it himself. Instead, he sent his older brother round to see me. He was a big truck driver and I suppose he thought I would be frightened of him. He said, "I've come here to talk to you about royalties." The conversation didn't last long! I phoned Ronnie and he said, "Oh, I don't know anything about it, tell him to piss off!" I said, "I already have. I wasn't ringing for advice; I was ringing to ask if I should kill him because if he ever comes here again that's what I'll do." Truth is, I didn't take money from the Small Faces, I made them money. I took them from the gutter to the top of the charts and showed them a lifestyle they could only have ever dreamt of.'

The realisation was kicking in. All those shirts and shoes and limos and hotels, soundproof chairs and extendable bookshelves – they hadn't been presents. They'd been paying for all this stuff. And all the money they thought they'd been earning from the telly and the records and the endless bloody touring actually wasn't very much by the time Mr Arden had made the necessary deductions for fees, this, that and sundries.

The parents became worried. They knew their lads were working flat out. They knew they could command upwards of £1,000 per appearance. They'd had a number one record. But other than the soundproof chairs and Mexican rugs, they seemed to have very little to show for it.

They demanded a meeting with Mr Arden. They asked where the money had gone. In reply, Don said a terrible thing. He told them that their sons were all hopeless junkies and they'd spent all the money on drugs.

The band were outraged. 'We smoked grass every day,' Mac said, 'and took leapers whenever we could, but we weren't taking heroin or anything.'

'Our relationship with him kind of soured after that and it never really recovered,' Steve said.

For some time, others had been sniffing around hoping to wrest the band from Don's clutches.

Here's the story – which is probably, in essence at least, true – of what happened when Robert Stigwood tried to poach the band. Stigwood was, at the time, up and coming, but would go on to manage Cream and the Bee Gees and produce films like *Saturday Night Fever* and *Grease*.

'I had to stop these overtures – and quickly,' Don said. 'I contacted two well-muscled friends and hired two more equally huge toughs. And we went along to nail this impresario to his chair with fright. There was a large ornate ashtray on his desk. I picked it up and smashed it down with such force that the desk cracked – giving a good impression of a man wild with rage. My friends and I had carefully rehearsed our next move. I pretended to go berserk, lifted the impresario bodily from his chair, dragged him on to the balcony and held him so he was looking down to the pavement four floors below. I asked my friends if I should drop him or forgive him. In unison they shouted: 'Drop him.' He went rigid with shock, and I thought he might have a heart attack. Immediately, I dragged him back into the room and warned him never to interfere with my groups again.'

In a TV documentary made about Arden in 2013, Sharon Osbourne, his daughter and a music manager in her own right, confirmed the gist: 'My father went to his office and literally dangled him out of the window. All I know is my father came back and roared with laughter.'

It proved an effective deterrent. Simon Napier Bell, lyricist, record producer and manager (The Yardbirds, Wham! and Ultravox) said: 'Stigwood was shaken up by this – he was a friend of mine at the time. And then, two days later, who came knocking on my door but the Small Faces? Now, I didn't want to get dangled out of the window by my legs. But I do like to confront things head on, so I picked up the phone to Don and said, "The Small Faces are sitting in my office. They obviously want to leave you. I've got an idea: if they are going to leave you anyway why don't I manage them, and they stay signed to you and we split everything fifty–fifty."

"Oh Simon, what a geezer you are – that's amazing. I wish everyone was as honest as you," Don said.

"But hang on, Don, they haven't agreed to it yet – let me ask them."

'To which Don replied, "They will sign up for this or I'll go round and break their legs!"'

But nothing came of it and not even one little leg got broken.

Eventually the band hired a lawyer, Victor Gersten, to try to extricate themselves from Don Arden. Victor, according to Simon Spence in his excellent biography of Steve Marriott, *All or Nothing*, introduced the band to Tito Burns and the Grade Organisation, after which, 'The sequence of events remains slightly murky, but is said to include huge sums of cash in brown paper bags. In December the press announced that Harold Davison, who was a key part of the Grade organisation, paid Don £12,000 to take over as the band's manager and agent.'

★

By the end of 1966, there was a strange vibration all across the nation. The Byrds' 'Eight Miles High' had featured a guitar woven of the stuff from which dreams are made. The Beatles' 'Tomorrow Never Knows' invited us to let our consciousnesses slip down the river and on the same album 'Love You To' brought Indian classical music to Abbey Road and, on the same album, 'Love You To' brought Indian classical music to Abbey Road. Meanwhile, The Beach Boys' 'Good Vibrations' teased us with dense harmonies, a sci-fi theremin and more na-nas than had been heard since 'Land of a Thousand Dances', or would be heard again until 'Hey Jude'.

Then, on New Year's Eve, The Move, The Who and Pink Floyd all appeared at the Giant Freak-Out All Night Rave at the Roundhouse, with globular light show provided by Gustav Metzger, (the man who, at Ealing College, had introduced Pete Townshend to auto-destructive art and thus to the ruination of several hundred perfectly serviceable Rickenbackers, Fenders and Gibsons), and some young women who, to 'emancipate us from our national social slavery', were inspired to strip to the waist. The whole phenomenon was described as a manifestation of 'Psychodelphia' or 'Psychedelicamania'.

9

Ungrateful Bastards

The band kicked off the 1967 new year with a gig back on their old turf at ex-boxer Billy Walker's club, the Upper Cut in Forest Gate. The club was already legendary – Jimi Hendrix had allegedly written 'Purple Haze' in the dressing room when he'd played there a few weeks earlier. Tickets cost 12s 6d for gents and 10s for ladies. Pricey, but the punters thought otherwise.

Sixteen-year-old Sue Mason from Romford Road, where Ronnie's parents were still living, thought that ten bob was value for money. 'The Small Faces are worth it. The price isn't too bad because you don't have to pay fares. And I like the atmosphere of the club.'

Fourteen-year-old Jennifer Randall agreed. 'I get £1 a week pocket money and as I am at school I don't go out during the week. I don't mind spending 10 shillings for a dance over the weekend.'

There was screaming, there were tears, there were faintings. And the band, their stage closely guarded by eight bouncers, played on.

'We just keep playing,' said Ronnie. 'All we can see is girls and pretty underwear carried across in front of us.'

January and February brought the usual range of Locarnos, Corn Exchanges, Ballrooms and Winter Gardens. And Steve and Ronnie were already grumbling about the new management.

One of Harold Davison's first initiatives was to put the band in a tour with the American singer Roy Orbison (then with his career in decline, 20 years before his magnificent resurrection), cheesy boy singers Paul and Barry Ryan, Jeff Beck, and The Settlers (a soft pop-folk group). The mismatch seemed to be apparent to everyone except Davison. Jeff Beck left the tour. 'Frankly I would never tour with such artists again and play low down the bill,' he said. 'I'd rather top on a ballroom tour. It was quite a comedown.'

However, the Small Faces stuck with it.

Chris Welch of the *Melody Maker* caught them at the Astoria, Finsbury Park. 'A right phantasmagorical experience was created by the combined powers of the Small Faces and Roy Orbison,' he wrote. 'Steve Marriott, hair longer than ever, proved he is the best "mover" on the current scene and cheery waves to the audience caused mayhem. Bassist Plonk Lane, resplendent in a suit that made him look like a kindly gangster, grinned at the seething mobs, while Ian "Mac" McLagan peered over the top of his Hammond, and Kenney Jones hid inside an enormous blouse, trying to make his drums heard above the noise of the audience. Faintly their hit tunes and new material filtered through and eventually they disappeared from the sight of anybody reluctant to stand on their seat, or clamber on the back of their neighbour's.'

The band, though, didn't agree.

'The reason for our tendency towards our almost exclusive studio work later,' Ronnie said, 'was the fact that we were quite disillusioned with our live playing – we had not really worked on improving our stage act, there was no point. It was always the same with all the screaming . . . we literally couldn't even hear ourselves. We did not hear a note we were playing. It was just curtain up, wiggle your arse and a lot of screaming.'

Another reason for concentrating on studio work was that they'd signed with a brand new record company. A cool one, run by chaps not much older than they were.

Sometime in the early sixties, Lionel Bart, the writer/composer of *Oliver!*, *Fings Ain't Wot They Used T'Be*, 'Living Doll' and 'From Russia with Love', was in Cannes, France, having lunch with Pablo Picasso, the most celebrated artist of the 20th century. How the two men met is a mystery (Lionel knew everybody), but it's also irrelevant to the story.

On the way to the restaurant, they were accosted by an English teenager who recognised Lionel – 'He was a pretty astute kid. I thought he was on the game.' The boy spun a 'cock and bull story about how his parents had stranded him there.' Lionel was impressed and gave the boy £30 – in 1960, a week's wages for, say, a bank manager. As Pablo and Lionel ate, they watched the boy successfully panhandling punter after punter. Eventually Lionel went over to congratulate him, get his £30 back, and tell him, 'Gimme a call when you're back in London; you're a hustler and I think maybe you'll get on somewhere . . .'

Three years later, the boy, Andrew Loog Oldham, did get in touch with Lionel to say that he had recently become the manager of a pop group but, being under 21, needed a grown-up to sign the contracts. Lionel obliged and thus – for a short time anyway – technically became manager of The Rolling Stones.

Francis Wyndham wrote of Andrew: 'His epicene figure, pretty weasel's face and affected manner conceal a nature both calculating and tough . . . A contradictory, decadent, impatient personality, he could only flourish in the peculiar climate of English pop at that time.'

Andrew, by this time, had also made it his business to know everybody. He'd worked in the fashion business for the two grooviest designers, John Stephen and Mary Quant. Then, as a publicist, he'd worked for Brian Epstein and The Beatles, with maverick producer Joe Meek, and had promoted Bob Dylan's first UK tour.

It was he who, having taken on The Rolling Stones, decided that being bad boys loathed by mums and dads – the anti-Mop Tops – was the right PR strategy, and probably encouraged them to piss against garage walls just up the road from Ronnie's mum and dad's house. It was also he who, having discovered that it's loss-making to record songs you haven't written, locked Jagger and Richards in a cupboard, saying he wouldn't let them out until they'd written some hits.

In 1963, he set up a PR company, Image, with fellow whizz-kid hustler Tony Calder, the man who'd made sure that The Beatles' first single got the airplay it deserved, mostly to handle the Stones' publicity.

Although the band was signed to Decca, Loog Oldham, from the start, had taken a leaf out of Joe Meek's book. The usual procedure was for a band to sign to one of the majors – Decca, EMI, Pye or Philips – then to use that company's studios, producers and engineers to record their stuff. Meek was one of the first British producers to record his artistes independently – mostly using his mad professor-style jury-rigged set-up in his upstairs flat on the Holloway Road in north London. Then he'd lease his tapes to the majors, who would press and distribute the records. This enabled Meek to make a good bit more money and to retain ownership of his own master tapes. In like manner, Loog Oldham set up Impact Sound, which leased the Stones' product to Decca.

Joe Meek had also set up his own independent label – Triumph Records – which had enjoyed a couple of minor hits, most notably with the Fabulous Flee-Rekkers' version of 'Greensleeves', rechristened 'Green Jeans' and credited on the label as being by P. Flee-Rekker, which, in 1960, rose to number 23.*

Again, following in Joe's footsteps, in 1965, Loog Oldham and

---

* On 3 February 1967, Joe Meek shot and killed his landlady, Violet Shenton, who'd apparently been complaining about the noise, with a shotgun he'd taken from Tornados bass player Heinz Burt. He then turned the gun on himself, which possibly encouraged others, like Andrew Loog Oldham, to later adopt the business practice of using properly soundproofed studios.

Calder launched Immediate Records with the not very well-thought-out slogan 'A New Record Company of Tomorrow Today'. Their first release, at least numerically (Immediate 001), was the McCoys' 'Hang On Sloopy', a US record to which they had acquired the UK rights. This made number five for two weeks and stayed in the Top 50 for 14 weeks. So, good start.

It was followed up by a mixed bag, which included the Small Faces' producer Glyn Johns displaying his fine baritone on a song called 'Mary Anne' as well as tracks by Chris Farlowe, John Mayall & The Bluesbreakers and Jimmy Tarbuck, the popular comedian who'd been at school with John Lennon.

Then, in August 1966, they scored a number one with Chris Farlowe's 'Out of Time' (Immediate 035), which was written by Mick Jagger and Keith Richards, both of whom, of course, they were already managing.

The offices got plusher.

Loog Oldham and Calder were, in the words of Peter Whitehead, who made promotional films for Immediate, 'an odd couple, like Laurel and Hardy: they complemented each other well. I don't think you have got two madder people than Andrew and Tony. I think Andrew saw himself as an Arab prince surrounded by a harem or something.'

'We were all horny and greedy then,' says Loog Oldham.

In his book about Immediate Records, Simon Spence gives the Don Arden version. Don didn't much care for Loog Oldham, but reserved a particular species of contempt for Tony Calder.

It's a funny thing, how people like Tony Calder talk, 'Oh yes I bought the Small Faces from Don Arden'. Tony Calder is full of shit. First of all, if he ever bought anything, it was on behalf of Immediate. If he ever did anything it was on behalf of Oldham really. He was a bullshitter, all the time. I never liked him and I never trusted him. I sold the Small Faces recording contract to

Harold Davison then he sold it on to Immediate. Calder saying, 'Oh yeah, we bought the record contract for £25,000 from Don, delivered it to him in a brown paper bag because he needed the cash at the time'. Calder would always try to put something like that in to try to put me down. Deep down, looking back I think I always hated Calder and he hated me.'

Tony Calder's version, recalled on the *Vinyl Memories* website, goes:
'"Don Arden's here."

"Yeah, send him in."

'He said, "Tone, I know you and Steve Marriott go back to Ilford Palais (when I was doing the kids' session, Marriott pops up one afternoon and 'Allo, I'm Steve Marriott. I've been in *Oliver!* Can I play the records?' I said, 'Yeah, get on with it.') I want to sell you the contract – they'd love you to manage them."

'I said, "But they're cold Don, they've gone off the boil – you fucked them up."

'He said, "Well, this new record's not very good."

'I said, "What do Decca think of it?"

"Oh, they'll put anything out."

I said, "Give me the paperwork," and he said, "I want 30 grand."

"I'm not paying 30 grand – 20 grand."

'We settled on 25.

'I said, "I'll read the paperwork and if it's OK we'll do it tomorrow." He said, "It's got to be in a brown paper bag."

'So, Tony told Andrew and Andrew said, "Call a meeting tomorrow; I'll be there; call them in."

'They [the Small Faces] turned up, scrubbed, clean.

'Andrew said, "You're on Immediate. What do you want to do? We've rented this house down in the country; go down there and write and do an album. It's got to be an album."

"Far out man."

"And by the way, take this with you – don't open it until you get there." They were like kids with a Christmas present. It was a block of hash. And off they went.'

Kenney Jones, on the other hand, remembers that Mick Jagger played an important role in the story, 'Through Mick, we engineered a meeting with Andrew at Ronnie's flat in Earls Court. We hit it off immediately.'

And Glyn Johns is pretty sure it was him who introduced them.

There is some level of agreement that it was The Rolling Stones (still managed by Loog Oldham but never signed to Immediate) who stumped up the £25,000.

'They [the Small Faces] hadn't got a pot to piss in when they came to Immediate,' Tony Calder told *Mojo* magazine in 1994, echoing Don Arden's claim that Steve had been living in a mud hut in Finsbury Park before Don took him in hand and made him a proper gen'leman. 'So we gave 'em five grand. It was gone in a matter of days. Their drug consumption was unbelievable. It was always sniff sniff sniff with them. Ronnie in particular was very partial.'

However it came to be, on 11 February 1967, the Small Faces signed with Immediate.

'Andrew Oldham had a lot of influence over us because we were very impressionable,' Ronnie said. 'But he was a moody fucker! He'd swan around in his shades and his limousine and he was quite amusing really. He was very camp and had this camp humour.'

'We got along straight away with Andrew Oldham,' Kenney said. 'We enjoyed his company and we were able to do exactly what we wanted to do. Andrew knew. Our talent was in the studio, recording.'

The changeover was accompanied by a couple of contractual confusion singles. 'I Can't Make It', recorded at Olympic in January, before the changeover, was released in March by Decca with the credit 'Produced by Steve Marriot and Plonk Lane for Immediate Productions' on the label. The band's willingness to promote it was lacklustre, perhaps because of the contractual mess, but more likely because it wasn't very good. They did a *Beat Club* and a *Morecambe and Wise Show*, but still the song only managed to get to number 26 in the charts. Initially the BBC banned it, 'because they reckoned it had some sexual reference,' Kenney said. It doesn't, unless the BBC censors assumed that the line, 'I can't make it if you can't' was a reference to simultaneous orgasm, in which case you can't help wondering why, a couple of years later, they didn't turn a hair at The Beatles' 'Come Together'.

Paul McCartney reviewed the single in *Melody Maker*. 'Spencer Davis? Mrs Miller? I don't know. Who is it? The Small Faces. It sounds like a complete change for them. And the voice is smoother and spadier. "Spadier" is this year's trendy word for "better". Did I say "trendy"? Ouch! It's a nice record. I think the voice sounds better than on 'My Mind's Eye'. It's a tighter sound in the group. Like Spencer. Nice and it'll be a hit. Incidentally. Hi, Chrissie!'

The 'Hi, Chrissie!' was a shout-out to Steve's new girlfriend, Chrissie Shrimpton, Mick Jagger's ex and sister of the model Jean Shrimpton. She towered over him, of course, called him 'Peter', after Peter Pan, and invited him to call her 'Wendy'. In February, the drug police had raided their flat in Knightsbridge and the incident made the front page of the British newspapers.

Chrissie eventually got out of never-never land, grew up and married a man unconnected with pop. All the same, Steve never forgot. Years later, when asked what he considered his biggest achievement during his time with the Small Faces, he replied, 'Fucking Chrissie Shrimpton.'

'Patterns', on the other hand, their second contractual confusion release on the Decca label, sounds like a cheaply recorded demo by a band hoping and failing to hit the big time in about 1963. The band sensibly refused to promote it and it never came within hailing distance of the Top 50.

Loog Oldham's decision to send the band off to the country with a block of hash to write an album – not a single, an album – was a clever move. For cool bands, the album, not the single, was the cool format. Cool punters hankered for LPs with a sleeve you could stare at while, stoned, you lay on your bean bag to listen. Nineteen sixty-six was the last year in the UK and the US that singles sold more units than albums.

Walk into the room like a camel, put your eyes in your pocket and your nose on the ground and welcome to 1967.

10

We Are Stardust

'Hippie' brought together, in an indiscriminate way, various notions, most of which had been knocking about in one form or another for decades, centuries, millennia. Some of them had genuine intellectual respectability, others were delightfully gormless.

The 'hippie' belief that most if not all of the problems besetting the world were the fault of civilisation had a long heritage going back at least to the 18th century, when the French philosophers Denis Diderot and Jean Jacques Rousseau fell in love with the idea of 'the noble savage'. The islands of the South Pacific had not long been discovered. Diderot in particular put it about that the South Sea islanders lived a prelapsarian existence, untroubled by work, anxiety, morality, guilt, illness, inequality or much in the way of clothing. Instead, they sat around all day, at one with nature, eating passion fruit and having sex.

It was an ideal readily embraced by hippies, particularly the part about having sex. The more enterprising got out of the city, moved 'off-grid' into the country, where they grew their own food and their own weed, and when the rains came turning their fields to mud, had sex in it. The nature and quality of this sex was still, in 1967, entirely directed towards the man's bodily urges. The role of women was to be available and to stir the brown rice, until a year later when the Women's Liberation Movement came to the world's attention by disrupting the Miss America contest, causing many hippies, male and female, momentarily to put down their joints and say, 'Wow!'

Those who didn't have the gumption, opportunity or money to move their shit to the country did their best to create an Alternative Society in town: to drop out and squat in, perhaps, a derelict building, doing without electricity and holding Be-Ins, Love-Ins and Happenings in public spaces. This proved a workable option for much of the summer, but less so when autumn came.

Ronnie, like most working-class lads who didn't have the pretensions enjoyed by grammar schoolboys, had an instinctive mistrust of the hippie thing, but already some aspects of what can loosely be described as 'hippie music' had crept into his consciousness.

In October 1966, John Savage, writing for *Melody Maker*, provided a rough introduction to the genre. 'Psychedelic,' he wrote, 'the new in word. I know it's hard but make a note of that word because it is going to be scattered round the In Clubs like punches at an Irish wedding.

'It already rivals "Mom" as a household word in New York and Los Angeles and it even appears in the publicity for The Yardbirds' new single, 'Happenings Ten Years' Time Ago'.

"It's trying to create an LSD session without the use of drugs," says Graham Nash of The Hollies. "It's a question of trying to expand the consciousness to the limits."

'One of the British groups who are doing their own bit of psychedelic experimentation is The Fingers. "We have flickering circles flashing on the group," said singer John Bobbin. "If the audience looks for any length of time, the reaction on the retina of the eye gives them luminous rings before the eyes."

'John Bobbin used to be an electrician.'

★

The elements that came together in the Electric-Kool-Aid-Acid-Test-Underground-Freak-Out-Consciousness-Mind-Fuck-Experience had been emerging for a while.

Dylan first turned on to LSD in the spring of 1964. It confirmed his previously stated belief that 'Rimbaud's where it's at.' The 19th-century French poet was promoted from 'cool guy' to 'muse' and Arthur Rimbaud's declaration that '*Le poète se fait voyant par un long, immense et raisonné dérèglement de tous les sens*' ('The poet becomes seer by a long, immense and reasoned disruption of all the senses') became a recipe for hit singles and high old times. Disruption of all the senses was definitely the way forward.

For the next few years, Dylan's best songs were those in which his senses have been stripped, his hands can't feel to grip, his toes too numb to step, and people rode on chrome horses with diplomats dressed in leopard-skin pill-box hats that balanced on their head just like a mattress balances on a bottle of wine – and all was glorious.

He'd also kicked open the door that led to chambers of ease and certainty for fellow songwriters. For decades they'd been trying to find something new to say about love (or cars, or school, or teenage angst) and trying to torture sentiment and scansion and rhyme into some sort of sense and, even harder, produce words that would fit into a singer's mouth in a way that made nice noises. Dylan freed them. A lyric that sounded good could dispense with literal sense entirely and create a meaning of its own, the kind of brand new meaning that can only come from the *dérèglement de tous les sens* and whose purpose was guaranteed to come clear once you'd done enough acid to give you a permanent drool.

Mad about saffron, the lyricists turned cartwheels across the floor with a semolina pilchard in either hand asking is it tomorrow or just the end of time?

The need to recreate the acid experience in the recording studio also led to a general – not necessarily 'psychedelic' – exploration of new sounds, both musical and electronic. In 1965, George Harrison used a sitar on 'Norwegian Wood'. Then The Rolling Stones had one on 'Paint It Black', The Yardbirds on 'Heart Full of Soul', and The Byrds made sitar-like sounds with a 12-string guitar on 'Eight Miles High'. Indian-sounding scales and drones crept in all over the place. They called it 'raga rock'.

'Most ridiculous term I've ever heard used,' Steve Marriott said in a 1966 *Melody Maker* interview. 'We'll be able to get plastic sitars in our cornflakes soon.'

Then – again a not necessarily psychedelic but definite hippie tendency – there was the Rousseau-esque, Wordsworthian notion that children understand things that grown-ups don't but that we could regain that understanding if only we adopted a more childlike outlook on the world. This led to whimsy of the most embarrassing kind, not so bad perhaps when Pink Floyd saw Emily play, but quite creepy when Traffic – some of the most competent musicians on the scene – sang of bubblegum trees in 'Hole in My Shoe' and recruited Francine Hellman, bless her, the young stepdaughter of Chris Blackwell, boss of Island Records, to do a bit in the middle where she speaks of riding on the back of an albatross to a place where happiness reigned all year round and music played ever so loudly. Even hardened hippies were known to disgorge their lentils. And Paul McCartney wanting to take his train to bed in 'All Together Now' doesn't bear thinking about.

Meanwhile, back at Immediate, the Small Faces' time spent breathing country air liberally cut with quality hash had paid dividends. 'Plonk and Steve's songwriting output is ridiculous,' Mac said. 'They write a hell of a lot of numbers.'

Numbers enough to spare. In December 1966, Ronnie and Steve had made a demo of a track they'd written called 'My Way of Giving'. Steve approached Chris Farlowe (who had given Immediate its first number one with 'Out of Time') to see if he was interested in recording it. He was. Released in January 1967, it crept into the lowest reaches of the Top 50, stayed a week and crept out again.

Twice as Much, a duo who mostly wrote their own material (as well as songs for Chris Farlowe, P. P. Arnold and Del Shannon) did a version of Steve and Ronnie's 'Green Circles' on their second album. And a band who basked in the name The Apostolic Intervention put out a single of '(Tell Me) Have You Ever Seen Me' with another Marriott/Lane song, 'Madam Garcia', on the B-side. Nobody bought a Caribbean island off the proceeds.

'We thought it would be the English version of Stax, where everyone plays each other's stuff,' Billy Nicholls said of Immediate. 'And we all did. No one ever got credited, no one really got paid. I had my own office there and that's where everyone would hang out. We'd play all the time. It was a really, really good atmosphere.'

Ronnie, Steve and Mac had been evicted from Westmoreland Terrace by this time, but Ronnie and Steve 'still spent a lot of their free time together,' Ronnie's girlfriend Sue Hunt said. 'They were quite happy sitting up all night playing guitars and writing songs.'

'Plonk – he's a constant explosion like Stevie,' Mac said. 'They vibrate a lot. Plonk is actually a bit like me and his good points at times are like my bad points. For instance, he can get up in the mornings and I can't. He rings me up as soon as he wakes – and I can't communicate with him in the morning.

'Both Steve and Plonk are very much aware, awake – they're hard to keep up with, as it happens, both of them.'

'Steve and Ronnie,' Kenney said, 'got along really well during that time.'

But Sue could see cracks opening up. 'There was some friction. Ronnie and Steve were two very different animals. Steve was incredibly outgoing and very flamboyant whereas Ronnie was much more sensitive and very inward. He was very deep and very caring.'★

Olympic Studios, now relocated to leafy Barnes from its former home in a disused synagogue behind Selfridges on Oxford Street, had become Immediate's in-house studio. Loog Oldham had booked the place round the clock for £25 an hour and it was here the Small Faces began to stitch together their new album.

Ronnie, by this time, was taking a far more active role in the direction the band was going.

'The first Immediate album is made up of 50 per cent Steve's songs and 50 per cent of Ronnie's,' Kenney says. Although all of the songs are credited to Marriott/Lane, 'they didn't collaborate as much as people thought. When they did, they often ended up arguing and fighting.'

Ronnie and Steve had also negotiated a credit as joint producers on the album.

'That didn't reflect the true situation,' Kenney says, 'Glyn [Johns] contributed far too much to be assigned the role of mere engineer: co-producer would have been more accurate. Andrew thought of himself as a supremely creative person but in terms of his contribution to our music . . . his influence was limited. As a big Phil Spector fan, Andrew envisaged operating at that level, but he didn't possess Spector's vision. Most of our recording ideas either came from the band or the sound engineers.'

In February, they recorded 'Become Like You', 'Something I Want to Tell You' (with Ronnie on vocals), 'Feeling Lonely' and 'Eddie's

---

★ Sue was doing all right. As Susanna Hunt, she'd scored a part in the latest Bond film *Casino Royale* – the 1967 non-franchise comedy-Bond film starring David Niven, Peter Sellers and a host of other A-listers in cameo roles. Sue has a brief but important role – with dialogue – as a bikini-clad temptress testing the ability of one of the James Bonds (there are several) to resist the honey-trap.

Dreaming' – Ronnie's tribute to Eddie 'Tan Tan' Thornton, who was the trumpet player with Georgie Fame.

'He played on a couple of tracks of ours with the rest of the horn section and Speedy Acquaye, who was a conga player,' Kenney says. 'We used to score dope from Speedy. Eddie used to get a little high and he'd stutter: 'I got to . . . I got to . . . I got to tell ya . . .' He could never get the words out, and we'd laugh. Anyway, Ronnie wrote that song about him and it was a loving tribute—just a little laugh with him—and we got him and the guys to play horns on the track.'

A happy picture of the Small Faces at work in the studio on their second album was provided by Nick Jones in *Melody Maker.*

'I love this place,' sighed Steve, rushing up to the control room, saying hello to John [actually Glyn Johns] the engineer, getting some drumming from Kenney to balance up, switching the lights off, and generally grooving about.

'Marriott went into action. "A nice big jangle on Mac's piano; rock and roll bass sound; and a deep, dry crisp drum sound."

'When the bass drum "boom" was satisfactory and Plonk's bass speaker crackle was eliminated, the first backing track was laid down.

'No more neighbours. No more 'Sha-La-La-La-Lee'. No more 'My Mind's Eye'."

'The past is blocked out completely for the moment. There's only one way – forward.

'"Our outlook is one of happiness and well-being," said Stevie, "and this must come through with your music. We are living and we want our music to too" . . . Lunacy broke through again. "Orlright was it?" beamed Plonk. The boys listened to the playback. Discussed it. More ideas. Adding, subtracting, louder, softer, harder, longer. Brandy.

'Back into the studio. Shouting, joking, falling about. Red light. Another layer of bass guitar from Plonk, 12-string guitar from Steve. The sound began to grow, as the different sounds went on. Another track. Another idea.'

RIGHT: Ronnie 'Bronco' Lane,
the apple of his dad's eye in
Margate, 1951

BELOW: Ronnie, Ron Chimes
and the Outcasts in 1963

ABOVE: Don Arden 'The Jewish Teddy Bear'

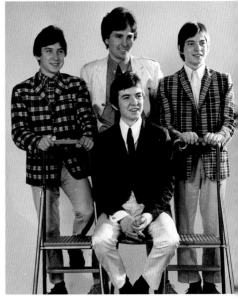

ABOVE: Even if they stood on ladders, Jimmy Winston was taller than the others

ABOVE: 'We all looked alike – Plonk and Steve might have been my brothers,' said Ian

ABOVE: 'We'd always hang out together, we were always smoking dope and taking pills, there wasn't any time we weren't stoned.'

ABOVE: 'Ronnie said in a magazine that he would like an alligator as a pet.'

ABOVE: 'Tin Soldier' is the real us and 'Itchycoo Park' was really a nice kind of send-up

ABOVE: 'We were like a bunch of old women at a jumble sale when we walked into a shop: some of the stuff we never even wore.'

ABOVE: 'The scruffiest bunch of poms that ever milked money from this country's kids.'

ABOVE: 'If you walked in and everyone was larking about, you'd say, "Well, it looks a bit happy days by town".'

OPPOSITE: Walk in like a camel, put your eyes in your pocket and your nose on the ground and welcome to 1967

RIGHT: 'The album's title just came from us thinking, if marijuana was legal what would it be called?'

ABOVE: Ronnie and his first wife Sue, 'We connected immediately.'

ABOVE: The Faces sitting on Kate and Mike's sofa, too drunk to stand up

ABOVE: The Faces on tour 'Being in The Who,' said Pete Townshend, 'was fucking grim by comparison.'

Ronnie's bass sound was idiosyncratic. Unlike, say, the thump of Paul McCartney (in his Hofner days) or the sustained, slightly over-driven sound of Jack Bruce, Ronnie's sound, at its most extreme, can be compared to the *doiinngg* of a huge elastic band.

'My guitar is a Harmony,' Ronnie told *Beat Instrumental* in July, 'a special model which I bought from St Giles Music Centre. It's the only one of its kind in the country. It was sent over for a trade fair, and I snapped it up. I used the old model for so long it was falling apart by the time I changed it. I've had the new model rewired recently to give me an even more trebly sound. I don't like a deep bass.

'The sound I want is chunky and sharp. This stems from the old days when I didn't have very good gear. The only way I could get any sound at all was by adding all the treble I could. As I bought better and better gear the volume increased, and the treble sounded so good that I stayed with it . . . As far as my style is concerned, well its simple stuff played with a thump. I always use a plectrum just to add power to my playing.'

Now and then, as the recording progressed, pop royalty paid a visit. 'There was great excitement when the Stones showed up at the studios,' George Chiantz, one of the engineers, said. 'The Small Faces were in at the same time. I think Bill sang on one of their tracks and they sang on some of The Rolling Stones' stuff. Steve said Keith wanted him to replace Brian Jones in the band. You could not get Stevie out of the studio, he just loved it in there.'

Having completed most of the work on the album, the band went off on a European tour. This was a spectacular affair.

'We would do these junkets of Immediate acts around Europe,' Tony Calder said, 'and as we were coming in to land, Oldham would stand up and say, 'We're in Italy. The only words you need to know are "fuck off" in Italian.' We would come off the plane everywhere in any country shouting, "Fuck off!"'

In Germany ('*Verpiss Dich*' is probably as close as you can get, the Germans, on the whole, using the word '*fricken*' exclusively in the sexual sense rather than the handy replacement for most other words that 'fuck' is in English) they were on the bill supporting The Beach Boys. One of the other bands was Twice as Much.

'It was just one big binge, just this sort of drug and alcohol-ridden haze of music and great times,' Dave Skinner, half of Twice as Much, said. 'I remember with Plonk of the Small Faces we went through a craze of painting our boots with eyes and cottages with smoke going up your ankle.'

They did German TV while they were over there.

'You used to do a lot of miming,' Dave said. 'You basically mimed to your single or your hit. That was it: you were on for about three minutes. As long as you could unstick your mouth it was all right. The drugs helped. Oldham was like a walking clinic and the acts on Immediate obviously dug him a lot.'

11

The Small Faces Transcend Pop

On 2 June 1967 the band's first proper Immediate single was released. 'Here Come the Nice' took its title from an adaptation of stand-up comic Lord Buckley's monologue 'The Nazz' ('Here comes The Nazz'), but where Lord Buckley was speaking of Jesus of Nazareth, Steve and Ronnie's song was about a friend of the band, Mick O'Sullivan, who sometimes used to live in the Pimlico house. O'Sullivan was the band's dealer. Uppers, downers, weed, acid – whatever they wanted, Mick could supply. He even gets a songwriting credit on 'Green Circles' (see below), although it's hard to say whether his contribution was musical, lyrical or pharmaceutical.

The first verse of 'Here Come the Nice', ('he's got what I need, he's always there if I need some speed') puts it up there with Marianne Faithfull's 'Sister Morphine' and The Velvet Underground's 'Heroin' as one of the more overt drug-related songs. It was a time when the BBC were very down on any song with pharmaceutical overtones. Upon the release of The Beatles' *Sgt. Pepper's Lonely Hearts Club Band* in 1967, memos had flown to and fro, and though, after much anxious pipe-sucking, the censors had relented on 'Lucy in the Sky with Diamonds', they had, for a short time, banned 'A Day in the Life' because of Paul's suggestion that having had a smoke on the upper deck of a bus he 'went into a dream', and they were fairly sure that Woodbines did not promote the sort of dream that involved heavily reverberated choral outpourings drifting aimlessly from left to right in the stereo picture.

'We were out of our boxes, but the fucking funniest thing was, nobody got it,' Steve said. 'How fucking obvious can you get. That was probably the best thing that came out of the Don Arden thing – he gave us this image, Sha-la-la-la-lee, butter wouldn't melt in our mouths. We could have got away with murder. We did get away with murder.'

'Don had the band down as The Partridge Family on amphetamines,' Loog Oldham said. 'Whereas to me the Small Faces transcended pop. They wrote national anthems.'

The single stayed in the Top 20 for six weeks, peaking at number 12, which is more than you can say for 'God Save the Queen' (the non-Sex Pistols version, anyway).

Then, hot on the heels of the two contractual confusion singles, came a contractual confusion LP. Don Arden and Decca pulled together a collection of discarded tracks, previous hits and other bits and bobs into a compilation they called *From the Beginning*. It included tracks written by Holland–Dozier–Holland, Kenny Lynch, Ian Samwell and Mort Schuman, and one track, 'Baby Don't You Do It', which had lead vocals by the long-gone Jimmy Winston. Despite being a bit of a rag-bag, it made the Top 20, peaking at number 17.

Three weeks later, Immediate released the proper album, called, confusingly, *Small Faces* – the same as their first album. Loog Oldham took out adverts in the music press announcing: 'Whichever way you look at it, there are only four Small Faces. But there is just one Small Faces LP. It's on Immediate.' He then sent out promotional copies with carefully curated (by no less a person than John Peel) testimonials.

The tracks, all of which were written by members of the band, were short – none of them more than three minutes and many less than two. Ronnie sang lead vocals on four of them and he and Steve shared the vocals on two. Many fans, including John Hellier and Paul Weller, reckon it's the Small Faces' finest hour (even though it runs only a smidge over 30 minutes).

It's impossible to say (even if anybody could remember) quite how the fifty–fifty split of songwriting panned out between Ronnie and Steve, but if one makes the assumption that Ronnie was more likely to sing the songs to which he made the bigger contribution, it's clear that he was moving the band in a more adventurous direction. Steve flirts with psychedelia, 12-string guitars and 3/4 time, but he still has both feet planted in what, at the time, was mainstream pop. But Ronnie draws influence from all over the place. He's injecting music hall, jazz flute, cinematic interludes, all sorts – he doesn't always quite pull it off (is the chorus of 'All Our Yesterdays' an imaginative exploration of bitonality or just a bit of a mess?), but he's clearly on a mission to craft songs rather than pitching for the next hit.

Hippie-experimental and vaguely psychedelic hints had begun to infect their songwriting and their sound back in 1966. For instance, 'Just Passing', the B-side of 'I Can't Make It', is almost something you could nod your head to slowly while grinning like a moron and enjoying a staring contest with a house plant.

The lyrical bent of 'Just Passing' ('the ceiling is light as I glide through the night') is definitely in the trippy ballpark and its spaced-out use of reverb and feedback on the final chord is whimsically punctured by the beep-beep of a bicycle tooter interrupting the main riff. Toot-toot. Blow your mind.

Some of the songs on the new album were similarly touched by the spirit of innovation. 'Show Me the Way' combines the antique whimsy of the harpsichord (a sound once described by Sir Thomas Beecham as 'two skeletons copulating') with the rumble of distant timpani, a sound not much heard in pop (except as a counterpoint to Gene Pitney's sobbing), since the days when The Brook Brothers ruled the airwaves.

But Ronnie liked to mix it up. 'When I was a kid, I never liked who you saw on TV all the time,' Ronnie once said. 'I went to see the inner circle groups like Nero and The Gladiators, The Piltdown Men,* and I used to stand with me mouth agape while Jimmy Page played guitar for The Crusaders.'

The 'Show Me the Way' lyric strays over the border into psychedelic territory, too, with Steve claiming that all the truth he had known had been scattered and blown so that he no longer knew who he was. One reviewer described the track as a 'psycho-baroque' gem, and it is, in every respect, several light years away from 'Sha-La-La-La-Lee'.

'Green Circles', the aforementioned song covered by Twice as Much, tells of a stranger whose eyes are filled with love and pain dreaming of green circles, and does strange electronic things towards the end which makes you fear for the reliability of your Dansette, either of which would qualify it with some freak-out credentials. 'Up The Wooden Hills to Bedfordshire' is decked out with Winnie-the-Poohness and goes weird at the end, so that's in the running too.

On the other hand, it has to be said that having listened appreciatively to the harpsichords, flutes and lyrical inscrutability, it is with a sense of relief that one encounters 'Talk to You', a fine exercise in white soul that gives Steve the chance to say 'gotta' and 'ha' several times. There are few sounds more exhilarating than Steve Marriott saying, 'gotta' and 'ha'.

Despite the new directions, and the fact that the band hadn't been touring as much as usual, their teenybopper fanbase (some of whom had, by now, reached the legal age of consent) were as avid as they ever had been.

---

* The Piltdown Men, an American instrumental band, were particularly fond of timpani – witness their 1960 hit 'Brontosaurus Stomp'.

Pauline Corcoran, guardian of the fandom, had moved with them to Immediate. She didn't like it. 'Life had been fun in Don's Carnaby Street office but life now in New Oxford Street was miserable.'

Two fans, Lynda and Margaret, both 15 and from Reading, spoke to *Rave* magazine about their idols.

'We waited hours to see Plonk move houses. We skipped school all day. We often ring Pauline, the fan club secretary. Once she didn't tell us, but she put Stevie on the line, and we were saying, "We love Stevie, he's so handsome", not knowing we were talking to him!'

Lynda had a holiday job, but she lost it because she stayed away too often seeing the Small Faces. 'We had a letter to go to court because we skipped school. I want to be a fan club secretary when I leave school.'

Two more fans, Hilary Tonks and Jean Miller, said they had 660 pictures of the Small Faces each and had seen the band ten times. 'I'd marry Plonk or Kenney or Mac, but not because they are famous, but for themselves,' Hilary said. They like the boys to be happy and have girlfriends and are pleased about Genevieve (Susanna Hunt's pop-singer pseudonym) and Plonk.

At the Upper Cut, Forest Gate, on 8 July, fans invaded the stage and did battle with the bouncers, during the course of which Steve's mic was broken and Ronnie's bass knocked out of tune. Nobody died, but dozens of girls were treated by the St John's Ambulance Brigade, and one taken to hospital.

'It was chaos on stage,' Ronnie told the *Stafford Express*, who interviewed him that night. 'We couldn't concentrate. We are sorry for the kids who got hurt, but it was so hot up front that they fainted and had to be dragged to the stage for their own safety.'

'Let's face it, ballrooms and clubs are a bit of a drag now,' he told the *NME*. 'We've done two-and-a-half years hard of those kinds of dates. Anyone who wanted to see us must have had the chance by now.'

In the summer of 1967, another chance came to find a new audience in the US, opening for Jimi Hendrix's first American tour. 'Fuck that,' Steve reportedly said, 'We're not opening for anybody.'

Ronnie was particularly aggrieved. Another opportunity missed.

Towards the end of July, the band went into Olympic Studios to record their next single for Immediate. 'Itchycoo Park' was, ostensibly at least, about a patch of wasteland in east London that derives its names from the prevalence of nettles.

The song, 'basically came from me,' Ronnie told *Record Hunter* magazine. 'I lifted it from a hymn, 'God Be in My Head', and I also got the theme to the words in a hotel in Bath or Bristol. There was a magazine in the room with a rambling account of some place in the country and it was about "dreaming spires" and a "bridge of sighs" – there was a write-up on this town – and I just thought they were nice lines.'

Mac found an egalitarian message in the song.

'Years after, I finally, properly, checked out the words, and realised it was about education and privilege. The "bridge of sighs" is the one in Cambridge. The "dreaming spires" are a reference to Oxford. Then '"to Itchycoo Park . . . That's where I've been", Ronnie was saying, "I didn't need privilege or education. I found beauty in a nettle patch in the East End of London." Steve contributed the middle eight, but the song was definitely Ronnie's creation.'

'Itchychoo Park' was a drug song and a total piss-take on the flower power scene, with East Ham as our San Francisco,' Kenney said.

The Bridge of Sighs in Cambridge is named after the one in Venice. Ronnie had 'no idea that in Venice you had to walk across the Bridge of Sighs before you had your head chopped off. He thought it was hilarious when he found out.'

'Phasing' (sometimes called 'flanging' – there are technical differences between the two, but they can sound very similar) is a swooshy, distant sound effect probably first heard on Toni Fisher's 1959 hit 'The Big Hurt', although Les Paul had made similar noises monkeying about with two tape recorders as early as 1952. The psychedelic crowd took to it because, just as a water-based colour and an oil one placed between two glass slides and projected on the walls could pass as a pound-shop visual recreation of an acid trip, phasing did the same for sound.

The Beatles had used it (or something very like it) all over the place, most noticeably on their trippiest tracks like 'Tomorrow Never Knows' and 'Lucy in the Sky With Diamonds'.

George Chiantz, a young engineer at Olympic, was the man who added it to the middle eight and fade-out on 'Itchycoo Park'.

'One night I get a call from the engineer at Olympic, who says, I've got this great sound called phasing and the boys have done a track, come and listen,' Tony Calder said. 'I hated studios, but I went down and, fuck me, it was a classic. I was blown away. But Steve is saying he thinks it's too pop. Fuck it! We stuck it out and it was number one in under two weeks!'

Actually, it only got to number three, but who's counting?

The BBC got the idea that the song might have something to do with drugs and were inclined to ban it. Immediate rushed out a statement: 'Itchycoo Park' is a story about a park in the East End of London. It's a slum area similar to the slums of Brooklyn. There isn't any green grass in this park. It's just a strip of wasteland with swings a sandpit and a hill. At the bottom of the hill there are loads of stinging nettles. Kids used to ride their soapboxes off the hills into the stinging nettles and get all itchy. Hence the name Itchycoo Park. There is also a little pond where the ducks land, where the kids feed the ducks.'

After which the BBC lifted the ban, thankfully not noticing that the song doesn't list swings, soapboxes or ducks among the activities enjoyed, but instead specifies getting high and touching the sky.

The song was featured on *Top of the Pops* three times over the next month, alongside other psych classics – Traffic's 'Hole in My Shoe', The Move's 'Flowers in the Rain' and The Rolling Stones' 'We Love You'.

'I don't want to sound conceited,' Mac told *NME,* 'but it was the only one of our records which I personally felt would go to number one.'

However, although the single sold 250,000 copies in the UK and 268,000 in Europe, it still only made number three. Even more galling, the stiffest competition came from Engelbert Humperdinck's 'The Last Waltz', a mum and dad song that held the number one position for five consecutive weeks. (It's also worth mentioning that, in that same chart at number 28 – its highest position – came Bobbie Gentry's 'Ode to Billie Joe', a record widely regarded by those keen on spooky lyrics with spookier string arrangements as the finest example of the genre known to humankind, proving, if proof were needed, that we live in a universe devoid of sense or justice.)

To try to make some impact on the US market – having turned down the Hendrix tour – in September, the band was sent off to Chiswick Park to make a promotional film designed to bring excitement to American high schools.

Ronnie is resplendent in orange jacket, yellow T-shirt, black Stetson, heavy gold chain about his neck and white concrete cat upon his shoulder. Steve wears a long kaftan and a straw hat. There are placards pasted to trees reading 'This Way for Your Yellow Balloon' and 'The Amazing Grotto'. An elderly woman passing by with a dog asked the cameraman if Steve 'was a girl or a fella'. Steve, overhearing this, called after her, 'Not 'alf, lady, come and 'ave a go'.

The band loon about without much in the way of a narrative dynamic. Somehow, though, it worked. The people at CBS in America, who had a deal with Immediate, got behind the record and reckoned that the band should tour the States as soon as possible. As a result,

'Itchycoo Park' climbed slowly up the *Billboard* Hot 100 until, at the end of January 1968, it peaked at number 16 and stayed there for three weeks before climbing slowly down again. Once again, though, the US tour never materialised.

Ronnie and Sue had moved into a flat in Spear Mews, Earls Court where, in October, after a vegetarian lunch with Ronnie's dad, Stanley Snr, and journalist and friend Keith Altham, Ronnie, Sue and Stanley chatted about life, love and other matters, while Keith recorded it all for *NME*.

Altham's subsequent piece appeared under the headline 'Hippy was hard for a working class lad. Too riddled with pretension for comfort.'

A week or so earlier, John Lennon and George Harrison had been interviewed by David Frost and had sung the praises of the Maharishi Mahesh Yogi and Transcendental Meditation.

Stanley couldn't see the sense in it. 'The average man in the street doesn't have the time for all this deep thinking. A lorry driver comes home, watches a bit of TV, and then goes to the local for a drink and game of cards with the lads. He doesn't want to sit there meditating on the state of the world. His immediate concerns are his family, his wage packet and his car.'

'And you know, as well as I do, that all these material things won't bring him happiness,' Ronnie replies. 'Not the car, not the TV or the money. This idea isn't deep at all. All the Maharishi and The Beatles suggest is that people would live better, more effective lives if they sat down for a few minutes each day and thought about things.

'Young people are desperately unhappy doing jobs they don't like and now they are asking, why should we? I was unhappy in the factory where I worked. During your lifetime you went through two world wars and there wasn't much time to think about things, but now there is and the chance to do something about it.'

'But you're an exception,' countered Mr Lane. 'You've worked hard, and you have talent. Most kids don't even want to entertain themselves today or anyone else.'

'You only think that because I'm your son,' said Ronnie. 'The milkman could have done what I've done if he had wanted to know and made the effort. Ultimately what will happen is that the teachings of people like Maharishi will be adopted into the normal education.'

'But you can't impress abstract and collective ideas upon individuals,' said Mr Lane. 'It's very difficult to convince a docker that he should be learning yoga when he's fighting for a wage increase to keep his wife and children.'

Stanley was indeed fighting to keep his wife. She'd had a relapse. The multiple sclerosis had her in its clutches. If they went out, Stan had to carry her.

Steve remembered meeting her at the flat when she was in a bad way and couldn't talk. 'Fucking hell, Ronnie is that your mum?' he'd said.

Ronnie was clinging hard to what the doctors had told him when his mother was first diagnosed – that the illness was not hereditary.

If only.

12

Things Fall Apart

In 1965, P. P. Arnold, from Watts, Los Angeles, became an Ikette – a
backing vocalist/dancer with the Ike & Tina Turner Revue. When
the Revue toured the UK with The Rolling Stones, P. P. palled up
with Mick Jagger, made contacts in the business, and decided to stay
on and pursue a solo career. Loog Oldham signed her to Immediate.
Her first single for the label, a cover of Cat Stevens' 'The First Cut
Is the Deepest', made number 18 in the UK and still has the power
to blow off your socks and fill your eyes with tears of joy.

In 1967 she had an affair with Steve Marriott, and he offered her
a love song, 'Tin Soldier', which she reckons wasn't about her at all.
It was about Steve's new girl, Jenny Rylance, whom he had coaxed
away from Rod Stewart and who later became his first wife. Anyway,
in the end Steve said she couldn't have the song after all because he
wanted it for the Small Faces. The band went into Olympic on 6
November and started work on the track. With remarkable generosity
of spirit, P. P. agreed to sing second vocals.

Where 'Itchycoo Park' was a nod in the direction of psychedelia,
'Tin Soldier' is a straightforward raver, something the Small Faces –
and Steve in particular – had down to a T. They know how to press
all the right buttons with precisely directed vim and vigour. And

anybody who doesn't get the hairs on the back of the neck thing when P. P.'s voice soars in the choruses barely deserves to be called human.

The single was released on 2 December. True to what had now become established form, the BBC wasn't sure about allowing it on their airwaves because the last line seems to suggest that Steve wants to sleep with the girl. Steve reassured them that the line is not, 'All I want to do is *sleep* with you', but '*sit* with you'. The BBC presumably had a few meetings to decide whether a young man and a young woman 'sitting' together might imply filth of one sort or another, decided it didn't, and concluded that the record was unlikely to deprave and corrupt.

The 4th of January 1968 was a big day. In the morning Mac married Sandy Sargeant. They did it in secret, not even telling the rest of the band, and would have got away with it if some pesky kids hadn't seen them leaving Marylebone Register Office. Then, later, the band did their new record for an episode of the kids' show *Crackerjack!*, transmitted on the 5th, then to BBC Lime Grove to do their new record on *Top of the Pops*.

'That *Top of the Pops* where we were all on stage together with Pat [P. P. Arnold] dancing behind us was the seller. They set it up well and we could all get going together,' Steve said. 'We celebrated. And I believe it was the first time we'd ever done that show without feeling very nervous.'

The record made number nine, but in the US failed to cash in on the success of 'Itchycoo Park', stalling at number 73.

Keith Altham interviewed the band for *NME* and came straight to the point.

'Your new record isn't very progressive, is it?' he said.

'We wanted to make a record that was really us,' Steve said. ''Tin Soldier' is the real us and 'Itchycoo Park' was really a nice kind of send-up. Some of the kids were saying that we were not so wild as we used to be, and we thought "yeah" and came up with 'Tin Soldier'. We can play this one live, but we could never get the same effects on 'Itchycoo . . .'.'

'Yeah,' said Ronnie. 'And we used to have a lot of trouble getting the RAF to send over jets [the sound of phasing] at the right time on 'Itchycoo Park' to coincide with the recording!'

Four days later, Mac and Sandy set off on honeymoon, but their romantic idyll was somewhat blighted when the filth busted him for 85 grams of resin. At Uxbridge Magistrates' Court on the 12th, he had to come up with £1,500 but, all the same, he was free to accompany his bandmates on a tour of Australia with The Who and Paul Jones. As things turned out, this was something they all came to regret.

It started badly and got worse.

They arrived in Sydney after a two-day flight and were – everybody was in those days – promptly sprayed with insecticide. This put them in a less than sunny mood when they encountered a gaggle of reporters. Asked about his drug bust, Mac replied 'fuck off'. Thus encouraged, Steve called them 'cunts'.

This set the tone for the band's relationship not just with the Australian press but with the entire population of the country for the rest of the tour. To be fair, the press, much of which was already owned by an ambitious young chap called Rupert Murdoch, was generally antagonistic to British and American pop groups. They even gave The Monkees a hard time about the demonstrations against the Vietnam War. (Despite claiming that they were 'just trying to be friendly', they were, by their own admission, 'the young generation and we've got something to say.')

Then there was a moment of calm before the storm.

'We had nothing much to do for a few days but get over the jetlag by lounging around the hotel swimming pool, soaking up the sun until the '''Orrible 'Oo'' arrived from the States,' Mac said. But the peace was not to last. 'The first time out of the hotel, driving to

Bondi Beach in a Jeep, we were pulled over by the Sydney Old Bill and ticketed for having "Protruding Elbows".'

The stress got to them.

Tension grew, particularly between Ronnie and Steve.

Then when The Who arrived, there were personality clashes between Steve and Pete Townshend. Mac described the two of them as being highly strung, 'like racehorses'. Pete (6ft) and Steve (5ft 4in) got into a scuffle in a hotel corridor in Melbourne that resulted in Pete putting Steve in an arm lock. Relations remained strained.

The Who had toured extensively in America the year before – bizarrely supporting The Monkees and later Herman's Hermits – and their performances reflected this. They were tight, toned and honed. By contrast, the Small Faces, having spent most of the last nine months in the studio were 'road-rusty' – under rehearsed and sloppy.

Perhaps initially brought together by their mutual antipathy to Steve, Ronnie started hanging with Pete, and the human windmill introduced Plonk to his great discovery. A year or so earlier, on a flight home from the Monterey Festival, Pete had had a bad trip and vowed never to touch psychedelics again.

Back in London, Mike McInnerney, the graphic artist whose posters embellished any psychedelic event worth its salt, who'd contributed to the magazines *IT* and *Oz* (essential reading for all hippies who could deal with yellow text on a pink background without going blind) and who later designed the sleeve for The Who's *Tommy* (1969), spoke to Pete about the teachings of Meher Baba, the Indian Perfect Spiritual Master who, many believed, was the Avatar, or God in human form. His philosophy was a 'unique amalgam of Sufi, Vedic and Yogic terminology'. Since 1944 he had been silent, communicating through an alphabet board or hand gestures to an interpreter. It would probably be a mistake to say much more than that about a deeply felt spiritual belief in a 300-page biography of a lesser-known but nonetheless vitally important pop star. It's enough to know that the teachings spoke to Ronnie and Pete, and provided Ronnie with a centre and a peace he'd maybe never otherwise have found. And, as the tour progressed, he didn't half need it.

For a start, Steve began getting very uppity indeed. At one point, he cornered Tony Calder, who'd popped out to see them, and said, 'I'm not gonna give any more of my fucking songwriting to Ronnie Lane.'

He was also very keen on getting Peter Frampton, lead singer with The Herd, to join the Small Faces. Nobody else was. Frampton's guitar playing might have been an asset, but the last thing they needed was another bloody singer. Nevertheless, Steve persisted. 'Go back to London and call him,' he told Tony Calder. 'I want him out of his contract.'

There were technical problems, too. Everywhere they went, gremlins infected the sound systems. In Sydney, the revolving stage got stuck, leaving the band with their backs to the audience. 'We couldn't turn round because of our equipment, and they never really saw us,' said Steve. 'I got 40 "geezers" to push the thing round in the second house and it wouldn't move.' Steve lost his temper. 'It was one guy in the front who was looking for trouble, calling me names and flicking things at me on stage. I just threatened to go down and sort him out.'

The next day the newspapers weighed in. The band, they said, were 'bad tempered louts'.

Elsewhere, they were described as 'weedy, bumptious, arrogant, sulking, sneering ambassadors for Britain,' and 'the scruffiest bunch of poms that ever milked money from this country's kids.'

Then they went to New Zealand. On the plane, there was an altercation about booze, which wasn't allowed on the flight. Somebody called the stewardess a cunt. The pilot landed at the nearest airport and had everyone ejected by force.

'The pilot had also read the papers about what a lot of scallywags we were,' Ronnie said, 'and made an unscheduled landing. When we landed, there were all these police and television cameras there, and we were carted off. The television camera was on the plane, so I said to everyone, 'Go out with your hands on your head, and it'll look like the plane was hijacked – it'll look really good on TV.' So we did!'

This was probably the origin of the legend that the Small Faces were led off the plane at gunpoint.

When, eventually, they did arrive in New Zealand, the press were waiting with their tongues out eager for more scandal to report. Steve didn't disappoint. In Auckland he threw a tantrum, claiming the piano was out of tune.

Then . . . 'On the last night of the tour in Wellington,' he said, 'we were so fed up with the way we had been treated that we let fly. It was my 21st birthday, and I had a party. Then we got the idea of chucking everything out of the windows. I had been presented with a beautiful record player. That went out of the window. The people were thrilled. The wicked British groups were conforming to their press image. The police were called. I lifted my head up and saw lots of uniforms. 'Who started this?' the fuzz asked. Of course, no one answered. Then suddenly this mad figure on the floor beside me started thudding his chest and screaming, 'It was me, Moon, Keith Moon, it was me, me, I'm a maniac!'

Pete Townshend was always keen to set the record straight. Contrary to popular belief, the first rock'n'roll star ever to chuck a television out of a hotel window was not Keith Moon, but Steve Marriott. Moon just claimed responsibility, and later tried to make up for the fact that he wasn't first by being the most prolific, at one point, allegedly, on the way back to an airport, getting his limo driver to turn round and go back to the hotel because he'd forgotten to eject his TV before he left.

As they left, the Australian prime minister said, 'We never wanted you to come to Australia. You have behaved atrociously while you were here, and we hope you never come back.'

The experience soured them. At one point, the tour had been mooted as a trial run for a major tour of the States, an idea that CBS, their US record company, had encouraged after the success of 'Itchycoo Park', but they'd all gone off the idea.

'He wouldn't go because he couldn't face failure,' Steve's mum said. 'If they went there and weren't accepted, it would have been dreadful for him.'

It was 'just clubs and six weeks on a coach – which we didn't fancy,' Kenney told Radio 1. 'We said no. We've done all that when we were starting up.'

And anyway, it would have been a non-starter for Mac, whose drugs bust would have made it pointless even to apply for a visa. (Although two years later, the US authorities relented and let him into the country.)

Besides, there was writing work to be done. They'd been recording tracks and demos for a new album since the previous autumn, but still needed more material. So, as a change from packing them off to the country with a lump of hash, Loog Oldham hired a couple of Thames motor cruisers so that they could mess about on the river and maybe do some songwriting.

'Steve, Ronnie, Sue, myself and our dogs were in one and Mac and Kenney in another,' Jenny Rylance, Steve's soon-to-be wife, said. 'Mac crashed his boat into somebody else's boat and down it went. Mac was the rogue of the river!'

Although Ronnie and Steve had been growing apart for some time – Steve was increasingly volatile while Ronnie was becoming more spiritually aware and laid back – they used the time productively.

'He had educated me a lot,' Ronnie said. 'We'd get the ideas individually and present them to each other. We didn't write a lot of stuff together from beginning to end, we more or less finished stuff off

107

than actually wrote it together. In many ways it was just me helping Steve write songs: a bigger percentage of ideas came from him than me. You couldn't really say he did this and I did that, it was a chemical thing. It was like alchemy . . . we'd come up with something to knock each other out with, I suppose, and once the ball got rolling it would sort of finish itself.'

'We wrote apart,' said Steve, 'just like McCartney and Lennon, Jagger and Richards: they didn't write together they just heaped it together.

'If there's someone in the room with you, it might be pouring out of Ronnie or it might be pouring out of me, but if there's someone there to egg you on, stem the flow, and give you other little tangents to go on, that's more writing together than actually sitting down and saying, "Right, now what have you got?"

'Ronnie'd say, "This is the way it goes", and we'd do that. Or I'd say, 'This is the way it goes', and we'd do that.'

The album began to take shape.

One evening lying on the riverbank, next to a fire, Ronnie (the story goes) looked up at the sky and said, 'Where's the other side of the moon?'

An idea was born. The whole of side two of the album would be the story of a man – Happiness Stan – and his search for the other half of the moon, and subsequently the meaning of life itself. The songs telling the story would be linked by a narrator.

'We thought it up on the boat,' Ronnie said. 'We just thought it would be a positive way of finishing the album: link them all up, and then, bang, you've got one side.

'The story is kind of a mystical journey. There's this kid, who kind of falls in love with the moon, and all of a sudden, he observes the moon being eaten away by time. You know the way they go; they wax and wane, don't they? And of course, when it's gone, he's all down; and then the thing is that all of a sudden – boosh! – it comes

108

back again, like life itself. And I thought that was something to pick up on really, because you can often get really brought down by something, and you're just being stupidly impatient usually.'

In early spring Olympic had had a new Ampex 8-track recorder installed. This meant that you could record vocal, guitar, bass, organ and drums all on separate tracks, monkey about with each of them without affecting the others, and still have three tracks left over to do backing vocals, daft noises – anything you liked. Or, alternatively, they could record everything on one track, leaving the other seven free for Steve to overdub his own voice and turn into a choir. The Beach Boys had used 8-track for some of their *Pet Sounds* LP, but The Beatles had had to make do with 4-track and a lot of technical wizardry when they did *Sgt. Pepper*. Within a few years, first 12, then 24 tracks would become standard-issue studio gear, but at the time an 8-track was the best toy imaginable for a band to play with.

'They were not a group of intellectuals but a bunch of East End soul boys – pint-sized herberts,' engineer Phil Browne said in his memoir *Are We Still Rolling?* 'They were all small-framed and dressed in a similar way in crushed velvet trousers or white jeans, tailored flowered shirts, chiffon scarves, felt hats, soft Italian shoes and fur coats. They had thin, drawn faces, mod haircuts and childlike smiles.

'Partly due to the zany nature of the material, the sessions . . . had a great atmosphere and were full of humour. Steve Marriott and Ronnie Lane had written the majority of the songs and were producing the album with Glyn [Johns]. They were much influenced by old music hall traditions, and this showed in the way they used rhythms, melodies and character vocals. Marriott and Lane were particularly funny and engaging and stormed through the sessions with little regard for conventional studio procedure or technicalities. Working in Studio 1, we laid down songs as a band, with drums, bass, guitar and piano or organ, set up according to Glyn's tried and tested layout.

'The members of the band were endlessly messing about, forgetting the lyrics and musical parts. The key word at times like that was "Nice". They would look at each other, smile, say "Nice", then have another go, trying not to laugh.

'The band used all the tricks of the day including heavy compression, tape-phasing, wild panning and feeding guitars and vocals through a Leslie speaker. There were harp, flute and cello arrangements as well, which were overdubbed. We used every possible space within the building to record in, including the corridors and toilets. I thoroughly enjoyed this approach. There was a strong feeling of freedom on these night sessions, with no office staff, and no 80-piece orchestra to look after. Working with just four or five band members (who did not sight-read music) was easier, much more fun and had less predictable results – I particularly enjoyed that aspect of it.

'Drugs, in the form of speed and dope, were in abundance on Small Faces sessions. In some corridor, empty office or sitting behind a studio screen, it was not unusual to find a roadie, or one of the band, with a joint in his hand or a pill in his mouth.'

At the end of March, they went off to Europe to do a handful of shows and while they were out there, they heard that Loog Oldham had released one of the tracks from their new album as their next single. It was a song partly inspired by Steve's domestic arrangements.

'Steve wrote it about his neighbours,' Ronnie said. 'He was having a lot of trouble, because he was living in this residential part along Chiswick Walk, I think, and a terrible European middle-class family lived next door, and of course there were records playing all night long and things like that, and his dogs were shitting all over the place and he didn't clear it up – there was a real running battle with them.'

Steve got it off his chest by writing 'Lazy Sunday'.

The song is an agglomeration of influences and styles. There are touches of psychedelia in the instrumental patches, lashings of *Sgt. Pepper*-style sound effects, quotes from the 'Colonel Bogey March' and hints of blues and soul, but mostly it's straightforward music hall, a style that seems to have developed organically during the recording process.

'We'd been working over and over it,' Mac said, 'and in the end we started taking the piss out of it – all that roo-dee-doo-dee-doo and stuff – and speeded it up.'

It's rumoured that at some point Steve had an argument with The Hollies, during the course of which they had taunted him for singing in an American accent (as if they never did) rather than his native cockney. He could always, at the drop of a hat, abandon his 'one of the most powerful voices on the British blues scene' persona and revert to the Artful Dodger, and on 'Lazy Sunday' he switches gleefully from one to the other. So sucks to The Hollies.

'This isn't the start of a new Small Faces sound, or anything,' Steve said. 'I doubt we'll make another record like it. It's just a progression at a different tangent. I didn't want it out at all, me. I had a right go about it. We found out about it in Italy. We got a call saying Andrew had released it, and I rang him up and went mad. I said, "No, don't do that. It's supposed to be just a little one-off thing." I didn't want that to be our theme song, which is what it became, that and 'Itchycoo Park'. To us, it was more of a giggle. We had other stuff that we were more chuffed with. But there you go.'

Despite the misgivings, back in England the band shot a promo film for the single at Kenney's parents' house in Havering Street, Stepney. It was Mr and Mrs Jones' outside lavatory that Steve went into, carrying his roll of loo paper, and their neighbour, Peggy Dawson, who knocked on the door and clobbered Steve over the head.

The neighbours that had complained so much about the noise would recognise the source of their misery in the film. It opened with Steve sitting outside his Chiswick house with his speakers: a Marshall stack, the sort of thing Hendrix used when he wanted to go *really* loud.

111

The promo film was aired on *Top of the Pops* at the beginning of April. Then on the 14th, they featured the single as part of a session recorded for John Peel's *Top Gear* show on BBC Radio 1.

By the beginning of May, 'Lazy Sunday' reached number two in the UK chart. It made number one in the Netherlands, Singapore, New Zealand and Switzerland, but in the US shifted just 35,000 units.

13

Keep Playing, We'll Try and Bring Him Back

Now and then, the band emerged from the studio to play a gig or two.

Ronnie was understandably fed up of gigs. 'You couldn't take it seriously. It was like playing in a pub and everyone's talking – only everyone was screaming. We got very half-hearted about it . . . The funny thing was we were quite a good little live act when we started out.'

One gig in February, at Silver Blades ice rink in Streatham, London, ended in even more chaos than was usual.

'A hundred and eighty-six girls fainted,' the Fan Club Letter said. 'It was all too much. The boys started on their first instrumental number, then the bouncers stepped in to help the girls who felt themselves "going". Ronnie had a go at one of the bouncers because he kept punching the girl across the head to wake her up and Ronnie nearly hit him, so the bouncer was a little more careful and Ronnie kept a watchful eye on him. There was something wrong with the mikes so Steve and Ronnie couldn't sing much, but altogether it was a marvellous show.'

Often, they cancelled at short notice.

'Dear Fans,' they announced in the *Belfast Telegraph* on 23, 24 and

25 May, 'We very much regret that due to circumstances completely outside our control we are NOT APPEARING IN IRELAND THIS WEEK-END.'

Ronnie did find time on 24 April to marry Sue at Kensington and Chelsea Register Office.

'I was there,' Kenney said. 'I was really pleased to see them get married. They suited each other well. Sue was a nice down-to-earth woman. We all got on well with her. It was just close friends and family at the wedding so not a big do.'

No photographs of the occasion seem to exist, and though the *Daily Mirror*, the *Acton Gazette* and the *Hammersmith & Shepherds Bush Gazette* all briefly reported Mac and Sandy's wedding three months earlier, no national or local paper seems to have mentioned Ronnie and Sue's – it's the price you pay for being a bass player without being Paul McCartney (or Bill Wyman).

Any time they could steal from touring or marriage was spent in the studio, mixing the new album.

The first choice to narrate the 'Happiness Stan' story on side two of the album was Spike Milligan, writer and performer of BBC's *The Goon Show*, whose name was, and still is, spoken with reverence in comedy circles. But he proved unavailable. They cast the net a little wider.

'Professor' Stanley Unwin was a former BBC engineer who, while messing about with colleagues, revealed an ability to improvise his own language – an almost understandable mangling of English later called 'Unwinese' – on the hoof. His talent was picked up by a couple of radio producers and this led to a career as an eccentric entertainer. The language was his only schtick, but it served him well from the early fifties until his death in 2002. His first LP, *Rotatey Diskers with Unwin*, which included a retelling of fairy stories ('Goldyloppers and the Three Bearloaders', 'The Pidey Pipeload of Hamling') together with talks on cultural matters ('Classicold Musicee' and the like) developed, like Lord Buckley's albums, something of a cult following among the nerdy but hip community. 'Oh, folly, folly' they would say, one to the other, and 'deep joy', and they would laugh.

The Small Faces hired him.

'Ronnie said that he'd heard me saying 'Sunnyglow the pureymost' on a TV advertisement for Gale's Honey,' Unwin said. 'He said that they had cottoned on to that. It was fairytale stuff and that's what they liked. Happy days!

'It was a good story, a little weird story, which one has to listen to again and again to get the best out of it. I still don't know whether it was worked out by any individual or whether it was all of them cooking up the story. Ronnie was the one who seemed to jump about a bit more than anyone else.'*

Gradually, an album was assembled.

'A lot of the songs came from sayings of the group. Like "happy days toy town" was something we used to say,' Ronnie said. 'If you walked in and everyone was larking about, you'd say, "Well, it looks a bit happy days toy town."'

'Mad John' was inspired by one of Don Arden's bully boys, Mad Tom, who once, when Steve said, 'Oh, hullo, Tom,' picked him up by his neck and grunted, '*Mad* Tom to you!'

'Song of a Baker', that's all Ronnie,' Steve said. 'I had nothing to do with that. I just played on it. Most of them are like that. 'The Hungry Intruder', that's Ronnie, whereas 'Mad John' is me. 'Happy Days Toy Town' was all three of us.'

'"There's wheat in the fields and there's water in the stream." It's about how hard you want to work, if you're hungry,' Ronnie said about 'Song of a Baker'. 'If you're hungry, then you learn to become

---

* The name Happiness Stan, by the way, was coined before Unwin appeared on the scene and had a more immediate connection with Ronnie's big brother Stanley.

a baker. It's a bit stupid, but I got the idea from a Sufi book, which was kind of a mystical book. Because I'm a very mystical person. I'm really deep. So that's 'Song of A Baker'.'

'The album's title just came from us thinking, if marijuana was legal what would it be called?' Mac said. 'We thought we'd be ahead of the game. We envisaged that rather than cigarette machines there'd be joint machines, with all the packaging and everything. The people at Immediate got Ogdens [who make pipe tobacco] to send over all their old designs and scrapbooks going back to the previous century, and we browsed through them. We were looking at this design on a tin which said Ogden's Nut-brown Flake, and Steve suddenly went: "Nut brown – nut gone! That's the one." We got an artist to come in and change the wording, but we kept the original design.'

They toyed with the idea of releasing the album in a tin – like an oversized Ogdens pipe tobacco tin – but that would have been too expensive. Instead, they put it in a circular sleeve. This meant the record had a tendency to roll off the shelf, ejecting the album and leaving it for the dog to use as a chew toy. Such is the battle innovation invariably faces between form and function.

The artwork was produced by Nick Tweddell and Pete Brown, art school friends of Ian McLagan, who'd also played in his old band The Muleskinners (not to be confused with The Muleskinners that Ronnie played with).

Andrew Loog Oldham took out an advert for the album in the music papers parodying 'The Lord's Prayer'.

> *Small Faces*
> *Which were in the studios*
> *Hallowed be thy name*
> *Thy music come*
> *Thy songs be sung*
> *On this album as they came from your heads*

We give you this day our daily bread
Give us thy album in a round cover as we give thee 37/9d
Lead us into the record stores
And deliver us Ogdens' Nut Gone Flake
For nice is the music
The sleeve and the story
For ever and ever, Immediate

'We didn't know a thing about the ad until we saw it in the music papers,' Steve said. 'And frankly we got the horrors at first. We realised that it could be taken as a serious knock against religion.'

The ad, the artwork, the roundness of the cover, the success of 'Lazy Sunday', or maybe diabolic intervention in thanks for the blasphemy, did the business. On the day of release, *Ogdens' Nut Gone Flake* shifted 20,000 copies. A week later it was number one in the UK album charts.

Later, *NME* voted it Album of the Year, an achievement more remarkable when one considers that other contenders included The Rolling Stones' *Beggars' Banquet*, The Beatles' 'White Album', and Hendrix's *Electric Ladyland*.

Still, it got barely a tickle from the US market, selling a measly amount and giving them the distinction of being one of the few big UK bands of the sixties the US barely noticed.

The reasons for this have already been covered. Apart from Mac's drugs bust, 'There was a lot of carve-ups,' Ronnie said. 'Steve didn't want to come, so that blew it a couple of times. And other times it just fell through. No one ever walked through the door and said, "Bang! 'Ere's a contract, you're going to America." It was always just sort of talked about.'

Like *Sgt. Pepper*, *Ogdens' Nut Gone Flake* was never supposed to be performed live. Still, they pretended to have a go at it on the BBC Two programme *Colour Me Pop*, miming, but with the mics left open for live vocals and the occasional ad lib. They did a track or two from side one, ran the promo film for 'Lazy Sunday', then did the whole of side two, with Stanley Unwin, resplendent in an ermine cloak and papier mâché crown, narrating the Happiness Stan section. It went out at 11.10 on a Friday night, just when you were getting in from the pub.

Elsewhere, Ronnie's interest in Meher Baba, first kindled by Pete Townshend in Australia, continued to grow. 'Pete started to send us things through the mail about Meher Baba,' Sue said, 'and it struck us that this seemed really true.'

Through Pete, they got in touch with the community of adherents based in London, which included Mike McInnerney and his wife Kate.

'We met at the Meher Baba centre at Wardour Street when I was 19,' Kate said. 'I was with my husband, Mike, and we met Ronnie and Susie. We got chatting and we left at the same time, so they invited us back to their place. So, they got into their Volkswagen, and we got into the Ford Popular that we had just bought from Jane Asher, and Mike accidentally reversed into Ronnie's car! So, they had to come back to our place in Richmond.'

This led to more meetings at Mike and Kate's flat, at which Pete Townshend, living not far away, was a regular.

'When you first hear about Baba, and your heart warms to him, he shows you an aspect of himself that floors you, astounds you,' Pete said.

The teaching did indeed have a profound effect on Pete.

'I've found it!,' I scream and I tear up the flying saucer magazines I've been taking to bed,' he said on a Meher Baba website. '"This is absolutely IT! Baba is *the one.*" It's like being reunited with the use of your legs after living without them for years in a wheelchair.

'What was so sneaky about the whole affair was the way Baba crept into my life. At first his words were encouraging, his state of consciousness and his claims to be the Christ exciting and daring, later they became scary.

'Baba has to be adjusted to over a few months, or maybe some older Baba lovers would say a few lives, and it is never apparent at any given moment how real or genuine your own affections are.

'Baba only asked people for their love, not their possessions or even their lives. Just their love. The thing I tell people that ask me this question is that nothing ostensibly changes when an individual hears about Baba and starts to devote time to thinking about him and his work. No all-pervading joy creeps into life, no formula for solving difficult problems. In some cases, it seems to bring problems to a head. At least they are over with that way.'

Pete Townshend's name cropped up regularly in interviews that Ronnie did around this time. In *NME*, he talked about becoming a vegetarian. 'It's like Pete Townshend says, "eat the food of Satan and your stomach will be turned into a steaming, boiling pit!"'

Thankfully, as 'Song of the Baker' says, 'there's wheat in the fields and water in the stream.'

Ronnie and Sue were, by this time, living with Steve and Jenny and Mac and Sandy in a beautiful house in Marlowe, Bucks, previously owned by Jerome K. Jerome, author of *Three Men in a Boat*. It was the middle-class English idyll – low-beamed ceilings, leaded windows, rambling roses, a sunken garden and honey still for tea.

'It's a steaming love farm down 'ere,' Ronnie told the *NME* in August.

As well as three Small Faces and their wives, the menage included, 'Smelly Arfur, a healthy black tom, who is held to be the main culprit for the subsequent litters although he is exonerated in the case of Lucy the Alsatian who is expecting pups,' two collies Rufus and Shamus, and Love, a dog of undisclosed breed.

It was in the garden that summer that Steve wrote and recorded what would be the Small Faces' final official single, 'The Universal'.

Although credited to Marriott/Lane, it was pretty much an exclusive Marriott creation. Having rowed with Mac and Ronnie, Steve recorded it alone with a 12-string acoustic guitar on a portable tape machine in his garden, accompanied only by dogs barking, birds singing and distant voices and traffic noise.

'He brought it into the studio, we overdubbed drums and stuff onto it . . . and that was basically it,' Kenney said.

The overdubs included an insistent four-to-the-bar bass drum, which was strangely reminiscent of Don Partridge – a one-man-band novelty act who had a couple of hits that year – a rooty-toot clarinet, a stick-it-up-yer-jumper trombone and an electric guitar. It was released on 28 June but barely scraped into the Top 20.

'I did take it personally,' Steve said, 'because that song was the best I'd ever written, I thought.'

'Steve was becoming more and more self-centred,' Mac said. 'He was a pain in the neck to be around.'

Part of the problem was the success of their last album.

'At the time I couldn't see how we could follow *Ogdens*,' Steve said. 'That's when I thought it's got to be over.'

Steve and Ronnie (well, mostly Steve) were also unhappy with the way Immediate was handling their finances.

After the success of *Ogdens*, Immediate wanted to re-sign them but there was some controversy about whether they should have to cover the initial outlay of £25,000 that was used to buy the band out of their previous contract. To smooth things out, Immediate offered a ten-grand advance on publishing royalties with which Steve and Ronnie bought a house called Beehive Cottage in Moreton, a village in Epping Forest, Essex.

'Ronnie got the raw end of the deal,' Kenney said, 'because in Beehive Cottage there was a garage with a flat above it and Ronnie got that, and Steve got the cottage.'

Mac and Kenney, not being the writers, weren't in on the deal.

This irked Mac in particular. He was still trying to scrape together a deposit for a house in Fyfield, just round the corner from Moreton. A share of the ten grand would have been handy, but it was not to be.

Towards the end of June, the band flew off to the Netherlands to appear at the festival The First Holiness Kitschgarden for the Liberation of Love and Peace in Colours, with Pink Floyd, Cream, The Pretty Things, The Move, The Incredible String Band, Dirty Underwear, a 'transcendental aurora lightshow', some 'chemical explosions of death and war' and a lot of other stuff you rarely got to see on *Sunday Night at the London Palladium* or at Streatham ice rink.

But Steve, like Ronnie and the rest of the band, was increasingly disenchanted with anything to do with live performance.

'We'd really got into recording and overdubbing and stuff like that,' he said. 'And doing that you get out of the habit of playing as a group.'

To freshen things up, they tried adding personnel to the line-up.

'There was a guy called Eddie Thornton [the inspiration behind 'Eddie's Dreaming'], who was with Georgie Fame at that time,' Steve said, 'and we took him on the road for a while. He had a little section. I'll never forget that we did a little tour, and to play with brass was just wonderful. I felt like I was in a *band*. I felt really professional. It was great fun.'

But taking a brass section on tour was ruinously expensive and if the fans were still screaming so hard you couldn't hear them, what was the point?

And it still wasn't safe.

On 29 June, at Castlereagh Park, Newtownards, Northern Ireland, pressure from fans trying to get to the stage caused a wall to collapse, injuring many, and a stage invasion knocked over the amps. In Bournemouth, 'a lot of equipment was damaged, and one member of the group almost lost his clothing.' On 4 September, at Chesford

Grange Hotel in Kenilworth they played behind a 7ft-high steel mesh fence, erected at their insistence to stop fans mobbing the stage. At the Colston Hall in Bristol they, together with Canned Heat, got into a fight on stage with 'hall officials' when management turned up the house lights halfway through a number. 'The management said the groups insisted on continuing after licensing time and became obscene and violent.' And later in the year, they were sued for cancelling concerts in Aberdeen, Perth, Montrose and Nairn.

On 19 October at Belle Vue in Manchester, and later in Essex, Steve got Peter Frampton – lead singer with The Herd and *Rave* magazine's 'Face of 1968' – on stage to join the band. Steve was, of course, keen on poaching Peter from The Herd and recruiting him as a Small Face, reckoning he could beef up the sound with high harmonies and good guitar.

Ronnie, Mac and Kenney were *still* not keen.

'I felt that Peter Frampton was an intrusion,' Ronnie said. 'And he was.'

Nevertheless, rumours ran riot, causing Frampton to issue a statement to *Disc* magazine: 'The Small Faces and The Herd are simply good friends. I went up to Manchester to see the group and I was persuaded to sit in with them. There is no likelihood of any link between the two groups on a business basis.'

At Olympic, they had a go at assembling an *Ogdens* follow-up, recording 12 tracks, some instrumental, none of which were ever properly signed off as finished. Some of them, like 'Red Balloon', 'Wham Bam, Thank You Mam' and 'Jenny's Song' (which became 'The Autumn Stone') would resurface after the band had split up on an Immediate records double album called *The Autumn Stone*, which also featured live recordings from a Newcastle gig.

They recorded in Paris, too. Glyn Johns asked them to go over to perform as a backing band for Johnny Hallyday – the French (actually Belgian) Elvis – on his new album.

'Glyn Johns asked us to 'come to Paris' 'cos Johnny Hallyday had always been a fan of ours and wanted the 'Smooth Faces' – as he used to call us – to come over and back him,' Steve said. 'I took Peter Frampton with me.'

'I think Glyn Johns was trying to get Steve and Pete [Frampton] together,' said Mac. 'Mick Jones [songwriter and session musician, later of Spooky Tooth and Foreigner, who wrote a lot for Hallyday] told me that Glyn Johns definitely broke up the Small Faces. I don't know why we did the album; we were short of money, I think. I can't listen to it. It wasn't a great time in my life, I was pretty pissed off.'

Nineteen sixty-eight had been a turbulent year: in Czechoslovakia, Russian tanks had brought an end to the liberalisation of the 'Prague Spring'; in the US, first Dr Martin Luther King Jr, then Robert Kennedy were assassinated; the Vietnam War got nastier; anti-war protest in the Americas and Europe got angrier and bloodier; student demonstrations, about everything from the war to capitalism in general, erupted everywhere from Mexico City to Warsaw and, in France, led to the dissolution of the National Assembly and threats to bring in the military.

And then, just when you thought the horrors of 1968 were at an end and had started hoping that 1969 would bring a better, fairer, gentler world, the Small Faces went and had a barney.

Appropriately, it happened on the stroke of midnight (give or take an hour or two) on 31 December. The occasion was the Giant New Year's Eve Gala Pop and Blues Party at Alexandra Palace, featuring Joe Cocker, John Mayall's Bluesbreakers, Amen Corner, the Bonzo Dog Doo-Dah Band and the Small Faces, £1 in advance, £1 5s on the door. Six thousand punters showed up, drink and drugs were in abundance, the sound system was dire.

Alexis Korner, British blues legend, the godfather of it all who started Blues Incorporated with Cyril Davies back in 1961 and had mentored Mick Jagger, Jack Bruce, Charlie Watts, Ginger Baker,

Long John Baldry, Graham Bond and a thousand others, was also present.

Steve, who had done a few gigs with Alexis earlier in the year, invited him to join the Small Faces on stage in a rendition not of some low-down Chicago blues, which would have been Mr Korner's comfort zone, but of 'Lazy Sunday', with its psychedelic moments and root-i-tootie excursions.

It did not go well.

At the end of the number Steve threw his guitar down on the ground and stalked off the stage, leaving the rest of the band playing on.

Alexis Korner took the opportunity to slip away too, and then Mac did the same. Ronnie, according to Kenney, whispered to him as he left the stage, 'Keep playing, we'll try and bring him back,' but after a few minutes of a brave drum solo, he put his sticks down and left the stage.

There was no booing or applause – just silence.

14

The Best Place to Be on the Planet

It wasn't, of course, the end of the Small Faces. They still had contractual obligations, gigs booked and so on, that somehow, they'd have to fulfil, with Steve on board.

But plans were being made.

When Steve got home from the Alexandra Palace gig, he phoned Peter Frampton, who was in Paris with Glyn Johns

'I've just left the Small Faces. Can I join your band?'

The following day, according to Peter, Ronnie rang him and asked whether he wanted to join the Small Faces. But Steve had got there first.

There were other considerations, too, not least the emotional fallout.

'I felt a huge personal loss,' Ronnie said, 'because we had been so very close. Just after he left, I was in a right state.'

And as if to compound that sense of loss, at the end of January, Meher Baba died. Sue, who wasn't working at the time, was able to travel to India and, along with many other pilgrims, visit his shrine.

Ronnie and Sue were still living at Beehive Cottage, the house they'd bought with Steve and Jenny, and even though they were in the barn/garage and Steve and Jenny in the big house, it was still too close for comfort, so Ronnie and Sue went back to London and got a little flat in Elsham Road, Shepherds Bush.

Ronnie's attempts to recoup the money he'd put into Beehive Cottage were met with a flat refusal, with Steve claiming that the house was bought with royalties from the hits, '*I* wrote – not *we* wrote.'

One must also never forget that Steve was blessed with a majestic ego. Most people have had the experience at work – whatever their job – of coming up with an idea that the boss immediately purloins as his or her own. It's usually not so much conscious thieving as the boss genuinely believing that the idea popped into their head, by coincidence, at the exact moment you said it. So rather than argue the toss, which would almost certainly have involved solicitors, barristers and courts, Ronnie just walked away. He was broke. His mum and dad had been living in a high-rise council flat and he'd just helped them with the deposit on a nice bungalow in Romford with a garden.

Andrew Loog Oldham and Tony Calder at Immediate provided little in the way of comfort or practical help. The break-up of the Small Faces would leave a big hole in the company's earnings. They were the biggest act they had.

Andrew put it bluntly. 'Tony said to me one day, 'Pick a straw'. Then he explained we had a choice. We could either go with the three Faces – Kenney, Ronnie and Mac – wherever they were going to go with their lives. Or we could follow Stevie. I didn't regard it as a choice. Neither did Tony. Marriott was our man.'

Steve made the announcement that 'the group is definitely breaking up', in February, and the last gig ever was the Springfield Theatre in Jersey, at the beginning of March 1969.

The day after, Mac spoke about the break-up to the *Jersey Post*. 'We can't wait for it to happen so that we can get started on our own. The Small Faces will be dead and buried forever we hope. Steve's replacement won't be a singer as such. He'll be a good guitarist who can sing.'

'We had offers from kids all over the country wanting to join,' Mac said. 'We had a letter from a young boy in Blackpool, and I could see him looking exactly like Steve, and that's just what we don't want.'

Fellow songwriter and musician Donovan was looking for a touring band and asked Mac and Ronnie and Kenney if they were interested. There is perhaps some overlap in the rumpty-tumpty rhythms of 'Sunshine Superman' and 'Lazy Sunday' but, all the same, Mac thought it was 'ridiculous'.

Ronnie was in a quandary. 'Every day, in the morning I was definitely going to keep the Small Faces. I was going to keep the boys out of the Small Faces, which is Ian McLagan and Kenney Jones. I was going to stay with them. Come the evening, I was going to go on me own, I was going to try for myself. And that was every day. Come the morning, I'd be stickin' with Ian McLagan and Kenney Jones, come the evening I'd be . . .

'It was like a love affair that was past its prime. You get into a nice, comfortable rut and while things aren't really together and you don't care too much about the girl, you hate the thought of someone else going out with her. That's how it was until suddenly I realised, well we [Ronnie, Mac and Kenney] all did, that we did want to stick together.'

In February, Pete Townshend let the three of them use his home studio in Twickenham to do some recording. 'They were making a disc,' he said, 'to see how things would work out without Steve.'

Basically, it didn't work out – not particularly well anyway – until salvation walked through the door in the shape of two renegades from the Jeff Beck group.

Ronnie Wood (who, to save confusion, will henceforth as much as possible be referred to as 'Woody') had his first brush with fame early in life when one of his drawings won a competition on the BBC kid's programme *Sketch Club* (presented by Adrian Hill, a posh man in a bow tie – and all submissions had to be on grey paper, not white because the cameras couldn't take the glare).

Woody and his two big brothers, Ted and Art, were all good at art and music. The music was in the family; their dad, in his younger days, had played with a harmonica orchestra. Woody could have gone either way – art or music – and ended up doing both. He was playing guitar in bands when he was still at school. When he left, he went to Ealing Art College (as did Pete Townshend and, a few years later, Freddie Mercury), but packed it in when the band he was playing with, The Birds (not to be confused with The Byrds) started getting more gigs and were signed by Decca.

In 1967, Jeff Beck, fresh from being fired by The Yardbirds and enjoying a solo hit with 'Hi-Ho Silver Lining', decided to form a band and recruited Woody, first as a guitar player. When Dave Ambrose, the bass player, left, Woody was persuaded to switch to bass.

Rod Stewart, born in north London to a Scottish dad and a London mum, had planned to be a professional footballer and showed great promise, but when in the end it didn't work out, he became a beatnik instead, busking with his harmonica. Then he reinvented himself as Rod the Mod, the sharpest dressed man in town. He was recruited by Long John Baldry, one of the first wave of British bluesmen, and – with solo excursions along the way – appeared with the various incarnations of Baldry's bands, culminating in Steampacket with Brian Auger and Julie Driscoll. Along with Woody, he joined the Jeff Beck Group.

Neither were happy with their berth. It is probably fair to say that, at the time, Jeff Beck was not a people person.

'Vibes were decidedly hostile,' Rod Stewart said. 'Ronnie [Wood] was well pissed off with it – you could tell he was just using the group as a filler while he looked for another band.'

Woody had seen in the papers that the Small Faces had broken up and got in touch with Ronnie Lane. 'What ya doin' man? You've got to keep the group together!'

'We were hunting around,' Ronnie Lane said, 'and Ronnie [Wood] turned up, who we didn't know. He just phoned up. I'd seen him round Steve's now and then. He always had a smile on his face. I always remember him as the smiling head.'

'Eventually the two Ronnies got together, and I would go over to Ronnie Lane's flat in Elsham Road,' Mac said. 'He had a Wurlitzer there and I'd sit in, and we'd play and work on these songs. We jammed together, and we weren't very good, but Ronnie was alright. Not brilliant, but we thought, why not? We never suspected him to turn out as brilliant as he is now. He'd just come off the bass and to be honest at first, we wondered if he was the man for the job. But we thought, 'We're none of us is brilliant, so we'll work at it together.'

At the time, Ian Stewart, former piano player/roadie with The Rolling Stones, was sharing a house in Surrey with Glyn Johns. Ian knew Ronnie and he knew Woody – he knew everybody – and arranged for them to use the Stones' rehearsal space in a Bermondsey cellar, equipped with a Hammond C3 electric organ with Lesley (a revolving speaker that makes electric organs go whoosh and wobble), guitar amps and a drum kit all set up and ready to go.

'We used to have these sessions at the Stones' Bermondsey rehearsal place,' Mac said, 'and [drummer] Mickey Waller used to turn up with other guitarists, various girlfriends and liggers and it turned into more of a social thing. But once we stopped telling everyone what nights we were gonna go down, it just left the four of us [Woody, Ronnie, Kenney and Mac] and we started working on songs.'

Then one night, Rod Stewart turned up just to watch. The next day he came back, and the next, every day for a week. He liked the vibe and the sense of humour. But he said, 'I was too embarrassed to ask Woody if I could join.'

The idea of Rod Stewart being backward in coming forward sits somewhere between 'quaint' and 'implausible', but he was right to have his doubts. The matter of his joining was far from cut and dried.

Woody was keen. His wife, Krissy, said as much. 'Ronnie [Wood] knew that he worked best when Rod was around . . . the charisma really shone when they got together both on and off the stage. Theirs was a true partnership.'

'In the back of my mind I had a vocalist for them which was Rod,' Woody said. 'But I didn't want to lay him on them straight away because they were all wary of the idea of a bossy bloke who was going to leave them in the lurch like Steve did.'

Ronnie [Lane] had more reason to be wary than the rest. He could sing. He could write songs. He could even shine, but Rod, like Steve, was much, much shinier. And Rod was 5ft 10in – 6ft if you included the spiky hair.

Mac was apprehensive, too. 'After Steve, we said, "No more lead vocalists". We thought Ronnie Lane and Ronnie Wood would sing and I kind of hoped I'd sing somewhere in there as well.'

Woody was definitely wanted in the band – if there was ever going to be a band – to the extent that Ronnie found himself fighting off the stiffest competition.

In the spring of 1969, Brian Jones was sacked by The Rolling Stones and a month later was found dead in his swimming pool. They were looking for a replacement guitar player, and Woody was a front-runner.

The story (which may or may not be true) has it that Mick Jagger phoned the Bermondsey studio and asked to speak to Ronnie. The wrong Ronnie came to the phone. When the confusion had been sorted out, Ronnie Lane told him there was no point in him speaking to Woody. 'He's perfectly happy where he is.'

Thus, Woody never heard about the offer, Mick Taylor got the gig, and seven years went by before Woody got the call again.

'I would have said, 'Is 60 seconds too late to show up?' Woody said. 'I never found out about it until years later when Brian's replacement, Mick Taylor, was about to leave.'

Anyway, back to the Bermondsey rehearsal rooms.

'One day,' Woody said, 'we invited Rod down – 'cos he used to hide upstairs and listen to us playing Booker T. and Meters instrumental stuff, the odd 'Shake, Shudder, Shiver'. When Rod came down and started singing, we did things like [Dylan's] 'Wicked Messenger'. It was really good.'

Mac agreed. 'Once he started singing, I was absolutely impressed, and I knew, we all knew, this was different. Now we could concentrate on playing our instruments instead of trying to be singers. Once Rod started singing, oh man, it was a pyramid then with the voice on the top of it.'

The certainty – and the doubts – increased when Ronnie, Mac and Kenney went to see the Jeff Beck Group's last UK gig on 25 April and saw that Rod was 'cocksure and camp' and 'a natural showman'.

'I could hardly take my eyes off him,' Mac said. 'He was so flash.'

On the one hand, then, an invaluable asset to any band. On the other, a fierce liability. Another Steve, with the front-and-centre ego problems.

A trial run for the Small Faces plus Woody and Rod line-up came from Woody's brother. Art Wood had a band called, inescapably, The Artwoods that had done well live but, signed first to Decca, then to Fontana, had never sold more than a few armfuls of records. When they eventually broke up, they still had some studio time booked courtesy of Fontana. It seemed a shame to let it go to waste, so Art invited Woody, Ronnie, Rod, Mac and Kenney and a bloke called Kim Gardener, who Art knew from college, to come and record some demos.

'I remember Ronnie Lane turning up on his bicycle and hanging his clips on the studio hatstand,' Art said. 'Rod came along with Ronnie, and we made up these songs on the spot – 'Engine 4444' and 'Diamond Joe'. More songs about trains, because everyone sang about trains, that's what you did then.

131

'It was very close to how the Faces would end up sounding – obviously because they were the same players, but they didn't know they was going to be the Faces at that time, if you see what I mean. All it did for me was show how much better a singer Rod was than me, which is not a good idea when you are doing your own demos.'

When Art did the rounds with the demos, the record executives would stroke their chins, say how good they were and then casually ask who the bloke singing was.

No recording contract materialised, but, under the name Quiet Melon, they got an agent and a few gigs, including one at the May Ball in Cambridge. Ronnie, however, absented himself from the Ball. He had other things on his mind. He had scraped together some money and, like Sue had done a few months earlier, went out to India to visit the shrine of Meher Baba.

'He's blown all his bread on the trip,' said Mac. 'He was besotted with that Indian preacher. He said it was what he'd been searching for all his life.'

He was supposed to go with fellow devotees Mike McInnerney and his wife Kate, but at the last minute Mike had to pull out because of work commitments, so in the end Ronnie and Kate went without him.

Six years later, Ronnie and Kate would marry, but we'll come to that in good time.

When Ronnie got back from India, he and Sue moved house again, first to Russell Road in West Kensington, then to a ground-floor flat in Heatherdene Mansions, in Twickenham, just round the corner from Pete and Karen Townshend.

'Ronnie Lane and I used to spend huge amounts of time together,' Pete said. 'He was my best friend. He'd moved to Twickenham two months after I'd moved there, and we used to see each other twice a week if we weren't on tour. We'd play together, record demos together. He was a really extraordinary guy. But he was a bit like Neil Young, in that he had his own space that he was going to occupy, musically, and never deviated from it.'

Immediate Records were in a pitiable state – not far from folding. Without consulting anybody in the Small Faces, they rifled the supply of outtakes and rejects and released a single 'Afterglow (of Your Love)', a perfectly credible song recorded in such a way as to make you wonder whether your radiogram was faulty. It made number 36. There was an album, too – *In Memoriam*, a compilation of outtakes and demos tracks, released in West Germany, but withdrawn when the band objected to the title. 'We're not dead!' Mac said.

And there was that similarly unauthorised double album mentioned earlier, *The Autumn Stone*, released later in the year, featuring their Immediate hits, some covers, various demos and live recordings from a 1968 concert at Newcastle City Hall. It didn't chart.

Money was a problem.

Rod was all right. He'd scored a £1,500 advance from Mercury Records, signing as a solo artiste, but spent it all on a V6 Marcos GT sports car. He was living with his parents. The others were seriously strapped.

'This morning,' Mac said in June, 'I went to the bank to cash three quid's worth of pennies and ha'pennies. I had to count them into five bobs, or they wouldn't take them.'

'I don't think any band's been treated worse than the Small Faces,' Kenney said. 'We got our very first royalty cheque from the sales of our Decca records in 1997.'

Art Wood gave up on Quiet Melon and went back to his trade as a graphic designer. Woody, without a band or a record contract was living off Krissy's wages. For Ronnie, Mac and Kenney, the pop star experiment seemed to have come to an end when Steve had run off.

'We had a terrible time trying to flog ourselves,' Ronnie said. 'As far as they were concerned, we were just a bunch of silly boys and Steve was the real face in the band.'

Looking for a deal, they approached Track and Apple. At Apple, Ringo played them some tracks by bands they'd already signed, which was nice, but not the point.

Irksomely, in September, Steve's new band Humble Pie had a Top Five hit with their first single, 'Natural Born Bugie', and were just about to start a US tour.

'Steve wanted to be in a . . . it was the time of the *supergroups*,' Ronnie said. 'He wanted to be in a supergroup and all that, and obviously the Small Faces, to him, was not a supergroup.'

And so, despite all the reservations, Kenney, Mac and Ronnie came to accept that Rod was the missing ingredient.

'It was the difference between success and failure,' Kenney said. 'Rod was just what the group needed. Ronnie didn't want anyone to run out on us and let us down like Steve did. That was his only reservation. Same with all of us but I convinced everyone that he wouldn't and he didn't.'

And Rod, despite having signed as a solo artist with Mercury – they'd cross that bridge when they came to it – was up for it. Apart from any musical considerations, Ronnie, Kenney, Mac and Woody were terrific company, something he'd missed with Jeff Beck. As Dave Thompson puts it in his book about the Jeff Beck Group, 'Jeff Beck was not a friend. Beck no more looked for comradeship among his bandmates than a bus driver expects to be friends with his passengers.'

Rod liked a drink, and so did the others, which was handy. Usually, they'd meet up in the pub at lunchtime, play through the afternoon, go to the pub, play a bit more in the evening, then make it back to the pub in good time for last orders. After a bit they noticed, however, that Rod was happy to conform to some of the most heinous of Scottish stereotypes.

'We'd go for a drink socially or we'd walk into a pub,' Mac said, 'and Rod would invariably be a gentleman and open the door for you. We soon worked out why. We'd go in and be the first to the bar and if you're first, you pay. Rod was very shrewd with his money, very tight. Sometimes we'd drive to the pub in five cars and there would be a lot of checking the car locks so as not to be first at the bar.'

Still, there were obstacles to surmount, not least of which was that the three ex-Small Faces were still under contract to Immediate.

Kenney was going out with (and would later marry) Jan Osbourne. At the Speakeasy club, Jan's brother Jimmy introduced him to an Irishman called Billy Gaff. Billy was born in the Curragh of Kildare. He did not look very rock'n'roll. Though just 27, he was short, chubby and balding. After school, he'd studied economics for a bit and briefly flirted with the idea of acting, but his nerves got the better of him, so he got a job at Robert Stigwood's agency. One of his first assignments was with Cream.

Robert said to him, 'Have you ever looked after children?'

'Yes, my sister's got three of them.'

'Good, just think of it like that and you'll be fine.'

When Cream broke up, Billy ran away to sea for a while with the merchant navy, then managed Peter Frampton's old band, The Herd, before they dispensed with his services.

He had, according to Ronnie, a permanent worried expression, or, as Mac put it in his autobiography, *All the Rage*, 'He always looked like he had just escaped from the hands of terrorists or narrowly escaped a train crash, or both. The eternal worried look on his face suggested he knew the end of the world was nigh, but he had been told to keep it to himself . . . I don't expect managing the Faces would help his state of mind.'

However, Billy was confident that he could get the three Faces out of their contract with Immediate. He wanted 5 per cent and a handshake to seal the deal.

'Nobody else really wanted to know,' Ronnie said. 'He just turned up and said to Kenney, 'I'll get you out of it.' Well, 150 others had said the same thing and not done anything about it. So, we thought, "Give him a crack of the whip, why not." Three days later he had us out and we asked Rod to join.'

Cannily, when Billy negotiated with Immediate, he didn't mention that Rod might be on the scene, so Loog Oldham, who in any case was going under fast, didn't see the three as much of a going concern.

The official announcement was made in the *NME* on 18 October: 'New singer joins the Faces'. They'd dropped the 'Small', since Woody and Rod are both about 5ft 10in.

Officially the name became 'Faces' without a 'The'. It was a time when 'The' was seen as passé. Hence Led Zeppelin, not *The* Led Zeppelin any more than *The* Pink Floyd, *The* Black Sabbath, *The* Fleetwood Mac and so on. Journalists, critics and commentators who never had a problem with Pink Floyd, always had (and still have) a tendency to stumble in the face of Faces and add and involuntary *The*. In speech it saves trouble, 'Faces were good last night' sounds daft. 'Whose faces? Which faces?' passers-by ask. Whereas 'The Faces were good last night,' merely prompts the question, 'Did they do 'Maggie May'?' Then you have to tell them that 'Maggie May' wasn't actually a Faces track. And they say, 'Yes it was, I saw them do it on *Top of the Pops* with John Peel on mandolin.' And the evening inevitably ends with the dead and wounded strewn around the floor of the scout hut.

When Don Arden learned that Rod was on board, he started sniffing around, claiming he still had some rights to a piece of the action. Billy saw him off, too, and started looking around for a record deal. They'd already been rejected by most of the likelies, but Billy learned that Ian Samwell, who had co-written 'Whatcha Gonna Do About It', was now a house producer at the Warner Bros. London office, and a loyal fan.

'He was enamoured of Rod and the Faces,' Billy said. 'I think he was hoping to produce them again.'

After a bit of argy-bargy about the name (the execs wanted to retain the 'Small', Ronnie suggested 'Slim Chance' and they compromised on 'Faces') they signed on 1 November and afterwards went out for a slap-up lunch at the Golden Egg (a chain of restaurants and one of the first to serve food on oval plates, allegedly so that the tables could be narrower). Like Rod, their first thought once they'd got their hands on the advance from Warner's was to blow the lot on flash motors. Woody got a Jaguar XK150, Kenney a white MGA, Mac a Triumph TR6 and Ronnie traded his bike and cycle clips for a Mercedes 190SL, in silver.

The new band's first gig was at an air force base near Cambridge. When they showed up at 8 p.m., they were told that they wouldn't actually be going on stage until two in the morning, by which time they were all hopelessly drunk. Nobody can remember how much this affected their performance. Or it might not have been an air force base near Cambridge. It might have been the University of Bristol. It can be hard to tell them apart when you're tired. Or perhaps they got drunk in Cambridge *and* in Bristol. Or got drunk in Cambridge but woke up, inexplicably, in Bristol. Who knows?

In December, they'd sobered up just enough to go into De Lane Lea Studios to start work on their new album, using the material they'd worked up at the Bermondsey rehearsal rooms and in Ronnie and Woody's flats.

Glyn Johns was first choice as producer. He asked for a 2 per cent royalty, which Ronnie thought was fair. 'When it came to the mix, Glyn would get it like a Cadillac – a big, warm sound.'

But the others disagreed, so in the end they produced the album themselves with Martin Birch engineering.

And that's how the Faces came to be – musically, socially and alcoholically a meeting of souls and livers that other bands could not but envy.

As Pete Townshend put it: 'When the Faces came together with Ronnie Wood and Rod Stewart, hanging out with them was the best place to be on the planet. Being in The Who was fucking grim by comparison.'

15

Raffish Incorrigibles

'We'll be playing for the kind of people who go to the Speak,' Ronnie told *Melody Maker* in February 1970. 'And the Crom, Bag, and the Rev.★ We have been playing the colleges but as nobody has heard the album yet, they are not sure of the numbers. I think they expect we'll play 'Sha-La-La-La-Lee'.'

'But don't worry. We'll get the band going all right. Me dad is going to run us down to the bookings in his van. And we're going to get some cards printed. And we are going to put an ad in the *MM* under 'An Able Band Available'. We were thinking of calling the band Slim Chance, or Blind Drunk. Super group? No! We're just a group of duds.'

'Those early gigs were poorly attended,' Mac said, 'and nobody seemed to be taking us seriously, so we'd always go to the pub first. I think we all enjoyed a drink first, playing second.'

Rod, under his solo contract with Mercury, had released his first album *An Old Raincoat Won't Ever Let You Down* (with a sleeve depicting what one desperately hopes is a benign old man – or, clutching at straws, a much-loved grandparent – playing, please God innocently, with a small child) to massive critical acclaim – but modest sales.

★ London clubs – the Speakeasy, the Cromwellian, the Bag O'Nails, and Revolution.

Ronnie and Woody had both played on it.

The Faces' first release was a single, 'Flying', written by Ronnie, Woody and Rod. It's a bewildering choice that starts off with a standard enough verse/chorus, but then moves into a choral section and an extended guitar/organ duel which possibly suggests that the band was heading towards, God forbid, prog.

'We released 'Flying' to bridge the gap until the album came out,' Mac said.

Lyrically, it's one of those songs about being far away from home and homesick that people love to sing and to hear even if they've never been further than the corner shop in their lives.

The B-side, the glorious 'Three Button Hand Me Down', is much more representative of the bands schtick. And it's about clothes, which along with modes of transport, love and one or two other things (food is debatable) is an acceptable subject for a rock song. And it features Ronnie playing bass not once but twice (and possibly in places three or four times) with overdubbed lines.

What is noticeable about both sides is that the Faces are grown-ups in a way that the Small Faces could never be. Where Steve sounds like an impersonation (albeit a brilliant and thrilling impersonation) of a blues/soul singer, Rod is impersonating nobody. Rod is Rod. Where Steve used the guitar as an effective weapon of mass hysteria, Woody plays properly, melodically, gracefully, skilfully, forcefully – whatever the music calls for. And Ronnie, Mac and Kenney up their game accordingly – Kenney in particular revealing himself as being up there with the best.

They did *Top of the Pops* with the new single, but it didn't take.

The album, *The First Step*, was released at the end of March.

'*The First Step* is *our* album,' Ronnie told *Beat Instrumental*. 'We sat down and planned it beforehand, and then produced it ourselves. A few tracks were got together in the studio, and there are no extra instruments used. It's just the band as it is.'

Later, in *Rolling Stone*, he said, 'We had nothing to do for months but rehearse and rehearse, which is one of the reasons why the first album had a sterile feel to it. I think Rod's records have been better than the band's. He works in a weird way. He does an album in a week. He just goes in and crash, bang, wallop it's finished. When we do it as a band as a whole, there are five opinions to take into account. When we play on Rod's album everyone just strolls in, doesn't give a shit and it comes out great.

'But it all seems to be going along smoothly and none of us waste too much sleep over how the band is going. It's a lot better than working in a factory.'

Rod agreed that album was overworked. 'It didn't come together the way we wanted it to; it ended up sounding like tracks that had been cut over a four-year period and put together on an album.'

All the tracks, except the one cover – Bob Dylan's 'Wicked Messenger' – are written by the band in various combinations. Ronnie has credits on half of them.

The album cover was shot at Kate and Mike McInnerney's flat (where the Meher Baba meetings took place), the ground floor of a Victorian villa, which had at one time been the love nest of Lillie Langtry and the Prince of Wales, so was packed with crumbling grandeur and saucy phantoms. Before the shoot, Kate mixed a cruel punch, which led to Ronnie allegedly swinging from a chandelier and crashing into a coffee table. They're all sitting down for the photo, presumably because standing had become inadvisable.

Early on in their career, the band had won the affection of Radio 1 DJ legend John Peel.

'I met the Faces backstage at a gig,' John said. 'I can't remember who else was on the bill – I think The Nice were, oddly enough. But anyway there was a phone booth backstage and I was sitting in that thinking beautiful thoughts. I mean, genuinely thinking beautiful thoughts, in as far as I was capable of doing that. And they came and flung the door open and said, "Hello, John, mate, how's it going, squire?" You know, "Come on, let's have a drink." And I didn't drink at the time at all. And as they went away, my first reaction was, 'Dear, oh dear, what dreadful rowdy people.' And then I saw them disappear into their dressing room that was full of scantily clad women and so forth and the sound of breaking glass and curries being flung against walls and so on, and I thought to myself, "Actually, these people are having a much better time than I am."

He booked them for the first of several John Peel sessions for his programme *Top Gear* – they did four tracks from the new album 'Wicked Messenger', 'Devotion', 'Pineapple and the Monkey' and 'Shake, Shudder, Shiver'.

Mr Peel developed a particular affinity for 'Stone', a track on which Ronnie takes the lead vocal. John described it as 'a reincarnation narrative born out of Ronnie's interest in the philosophy of the religious leader Meher Baba and which is made musically tasty by a spry Cajun swagger that's all the more delicious for a tart Limey twist' and 'a lot more fun to dance to than anything Thomas Aquinas ever wrote.'

Mac hated the track.

The 'drink first, playing second' formula seemed to be working out well. Even near-leglessness did not, it seemed, prevent Kenney and, to a lesser extent, Ronnie, keeping time and establishing a solid basis over which Rod, Mac and Woody could slip, slide and swagger. They became known, and described themselves, as purveyors of 'sloppy rock'n'roll'.

Gigs would invariably end with drunken renditions of 'We'll Meet Again' or 'When Irish Eyes Are Smiling', the five of them clustered around a single mic, giggling, then collapsing onto the floor.

'It wasn't just at gigs,' Kenney said. 'Everywhere we went we fell on the floor – airports, restaurants, hotels, bars. We were saying to people that you don't have to take rock'n'roll too seriously. Every gig was like going to a party. The Faces were undoubtedly the most fun band I was ever in.'

They knew how to have a good time and give it to the audience.

Years later, Ronnie, when asked about what happened to the change in direction for the band from the late psychedelia of the Small Faces to the bluesy raw sound of the early Faces, replied: 'We stopped taking *acid*! To be blunt about it. That's basically what it was all about. By saying that, I'm not going to encourage people to take such a thing, because it's *dangerous*. We were bloody stupid, really! All right, we was lucky! But there's a lot of people that wasn't.'

By the time *The First Step* was released in the UK, the band had left for a 28-date tour of North America, starting in Toronto on 25 March.

Ronnie was excited. It was finally happening. The possibility of a US tour had first been mooted in 1966, and several times since, but had never happened. America was the source of pretty much all the music he'd ever listened to, played, sung and revered. As Woody said, like all the British invasion bands since The Beatles in 1964, 'We were selling them their own music.'

Rod and Woody were 'all cocky about going to America because they had been there before, saying things like, 'We know this great place in New York that does boiled eggs.'

In Toronto, they played the 4,000-capacity Varsity Arena and, as Mac put it in his autobiography *All the Rage*, 'I've been told by more than a few punters who were there that night that we killed the lot of them.'

Billing was always a talking point. In Boston they were described on the poster as *Rod Stewart's Small Faces*. In other places they were the support band and Rod the headliner. It was irksome.

Detroit, as it turned out, was a turning point. They played seven dates at the Eastown Theatre, a 2,500-capacity former cinema. The Eastown was not a hippie venue. The hippies went to the Grande Ballroom. The Eastown was blue-collar and rough. According to Alice Cooper, those nights at the Eastown were 'pure rock'n'roll times'. It was, in other words, the sort of audience that would revel in five semi-drunken men serving sloppy rock'n'roll.

'It was like coming home to us in Detroit,' Woody said. 'They all worked for the Ford motor company and they'd all come in leather jackets straight from work. They were all ready to rock and it was a bit working class, the equivalent of the East End of London.'

'After the Faces first broke in Detroit,' Kenney said, 'it just spread like wildfire. By the time we got to the next city, word had already got around. The power of word of mouth was fantastic.'

'The first few gigs were naturally a bit shaky, but after that, well, they couldn't have been better,' Rod said. 'I'm sure everyone says that when they do America, but the band became tighter as we went along and American audiences really do have this power to make you or break you. I wouldn't say they made us into a great band overnight, but they certainly made us into a big one.'

At the beginning of April, the band got to New York for a couple of nights at the 250-seat club Ungano's, which Tiger Williams remembers in his blog as 'definitely the darkest, dankest, most depressing venue, probably in all of Manhattan.' It was most likely this particular atmosphere that drew in all the 'big' names who jammed there on off nights.

'George Harrison, Jimi Hendrix and the Grateful Dead all hung out there and it was a place that A&R reps and agents would go there to check out acts.'

The Faces stayed at Loews Hotel, where The Staple Singers, Tiny Tim, Black Sabbath and Muhammad Ali were also in residence at the time.

Ronnie found himself alone in the lift with Ali. He was struck dumb.

During a break in the schedule, they went to Andrew Loog Oldham's house in Wilton, Connecticut. Billy Nicholls, Ronnie's old friend from Immediate and fellow Meher Baba follower, was staying there.

He invited them, and since Ronnie and Mac felt they'd effectively paid for the house with the sweat of their brows, they felt entitled to avail themselves of any facility it had to offer.

On the way, on the radio, they heard 'Maybe I'm Amazed', from Paul McCartney's first post-Beatle album. As soon as they got to Wilton, Ronnie found the record store and bought a copy. Then they set up some gear in Andrew's house and figured out a version that became pretty much a permanent fixture of their live set. They recorded it a year later.

Ronnie and Billy came in for a lot of piss-taking for their Meher Baba affinity and general spirituality. Ronnie became convinced the house was haunted, so Woody and Mac took to dressing in white sheets and waking him up in the middle of the night.

'I still couldn't believe Ronnie believes in all that old bollocks,' Mac said.

Ronnie took solace in hours-long telephone calls home – on Andrew's tab.

The UK gigs, on their return, were dispiriting. On 5 June, they played Dudley Zoo in the West Midlands – a charity benefit for the World Wildlife Fund. Edgar Broughton, from Warwick, announced them as 'drunken East End yobbos', which was a lie. Rod was a north Londoner, Mac and Woody from the west. It was enough though. The audience booed and threw things.

Then came a string of what were essentially pub gigs – the Wake Arms, Epping (where, coincidentally Ronnie's mum and dad had met), and Cooks Ferry Inn, Edmonton. They usually sold out, but when the place only holds a couple of hundred, this was no reason to crack open the Moët & Chandon and go yacht shopping.

So, they abandoned the UK, and first went back to America, then to Europe.

On 5 September they played the Love and Peace Festival on

Fehmarn Island off the German coast. This was supposed to have been the German equivalent of Woodstock – three days and two nights of love and peace featuring some of the top names in international rock including Jimi Hendrix, Sly and the Family Stone, Ten Years After, Colosseum, Canned Heat, Ginger Baker's Airforce, Frumpy (Inga Rumpf's Bluesrockformation), and Peter Brötzmann, whose recent album *Nipples* was still taking the free-jazz community by storm.

The festival was part financed by German sex shop pioneer Beate Uhse, whose chain of quality dildo and gimp mask outlets also became ticket offices.

Well, as you can imagine, it all went terribly wrong. Two hundred Bloody Devils (a chapter of the German Hell's Angels) showed up and fights broke out between them, the assembled hippies and a largish party of Persians who, for reasons it's probably best not to go into, had been hired as security. Four of the Persians suffered stab wounds after which the Bloody Devils took over as security guards.

Then the weather closed in, with rain and high winds. Instruments and amps were dangerously drenched. Many of the bands cancelled. The Faces, however, played on through the horizontal downpour, risking, with each note, electrocution and, with each incautious word or careless glance, a bit of light stabbing.

Marvellously, Jimi showed up, too, and played a muted but nonetheless well-received set. It was his last appearance. Less than two weeks later he aspirated his own vomit and died.

The Faces went back to the US in October, playing larger venues. Rod's second solo album had been released. 'My *Gasoline Alley* album had gone up to number 23 in the charts while we were in the States,' Rod said, 'and the tour was the best I've known, including those with Jeff Beck.'

'My Way of Giving', the Small Faces track Ronnie'd written with Steve, found its way onto the album. Nevertheless, Mac, Kenney and

Ronnie were slightly less than ecstatic, not least because they reckoned that some of the tracks on Rod's solo album would have been better suited to the Faces.

The Faces' second UK single, 'Had Me a Real Good Time', an energising romp with horns, Mac playing top-notch New Orleans piano, Woody proving that he'd have been a much better replacement for Brian Jones than Mick Taylor ever was, and a false ending to keep you on your toes, found its way to the shops at the end of November, but signally failed to find its way to the charts.

On 7 December, they played the Marquee in London, home of legends.

'I think we were bloody scared to go to places like the Marquee and the Lyceum,' Rod said. 'When we did go though, we got 1,100 at the Marquee – the biggest crowd they'd had.'

The performance was filmed by German WDR-TV. Rod did 'Gasoline Alley', and they channelled Little Richard, The Rolling Stones and Tina Turner. Ronnie is sporting a rather scrubby little beard, signalling that his teeny-bopper days are behind him.

They had their rider properly organised by this time, too. The *NME* explained, 'Wine keeps Kenney Jones and Ronnie Wood's spirits up, bourbon works the same for Ian McLagan, brandy ensures Ronnie Lane a real good time and Rod himself puts his faith in two bottles per gig of Stanley Matthews, or Mateus wine as it is known in the trade.'

Mateus rosé was wine principally favoured for the shape of its bottle, which, fitted with wire, bulb and shade, made an attractive table lamp. People often wondered who actually drank the stuff. Now you know. It was Rod Stewart.

And in addition to the Mateus rosé, every hotel mini bar, every airport lounge, every backstage boozer was left drained after the Faces had left the building.

16

The Healing Power of Good Rock'n'roll

The second album had been gradually coming together. In January 1971, they went to Mick Jagger's house in Newbury to knock off the last couple of tracks.

'We didn't get to the studio generally until around two in the afternoon,' Kenney said. 'Ronnie Lane would turn up about four, Woody at six, Mac about six-thirty. By that time Rod and I had already been there for a few hours [. . .] so to kill time we'd end up going down the pub, which meant that it would always be late when we finally got around to recording.'

Some of the tracks were put together in the studio.

'We'd do a riff then see if we could make it work, rather than go in with a finished song. A few of them we'd already pre-written – like 'Sweet Lady Mary' – but mostly they were done as we started playing. Musically, I think we could have done a lot better had we been more sober.'

Called *Long Player*, the LP was released on 17 February, with a fancy retro sleeve.

'It was supposed to look like an old forties record cover with a hole in it and really dodgy printing.'

The British version is an accurate pastiche of an old, rough, cardboard

78 sleeve. The US version aims for the same retro theme but misses badly.

'I don't know who designed our American one,' Ronnie said. 'They ought to put him to sleep. They didn't even put credits on it!

'There's been a lack of information all round, as far as our albums have gone. We really ought to try and give the people a little more information about our albums. It's just that it always seems to be a rushed thing at the end . . . all of a sudden, you're told that the thing's been printed, and they can't possibly chuck it into the sewer.'

Ronnie has solo writing credits on two tracks, 'Tell Everyone' and 'Richmond'.

'Tell Everyone' owes a debt of gratitude to the Joe Cocker version of 'With a Little Help from My Friends'. The sloppy playing adds weight to Kenney's assertion that 'we could have done a lot better had we been more sober.'

'Richmond' is the plaint of a man stuck in New York City, where nobody loves him, wishing he was in Richmond, Greater London. Ronnie sings it mostly accompanied by two slide guitars. It's plaintive, simple. (They didn't often let him sing on stage – not the wistful songs anyway – fearing it would slow things down.)

Ronnie has writing credits on all the other tracks, too, apart from the three covers – William Blake and Hubert Parry's 'Jerusalem' (credited as 'Traditional' and played by Woody as a slide guitar solo), Paul McCartney's 'Maybe I'm Amazed' and Big Bill Broonzy's 'I Feel So Good', recorded live at Fillmore East in New York.

'I Feel So Good' gives some indication of what they were capable of as a live band (and runs for nearly nine minutes), but the live recording of 'Maybe I'm Amazed' doesn't capture the glorious majesty of the vocals – you had to be there.

The opening track, 'Bad 'N' Ruin', is some riffs and some lyrics that at first storm away in a generally uplifting fashion, but after a minute or so invite the question, 'would it kill you to change chord now and then?'

In general, it's a 'not quite there, yet' album, with the already-released single 'Had Me a Real Good Time' and possibly 'Richmond' as the only stand-out tracks. It made number 31 in the UK album charts, and 29 in the US.

Woody held Morgan Sound, the London studio where much of the album was recorded, at least partly to blame for the imperfections.

'We just had so many troubles with the board there,' he said. 'The headsets kept going wrong and it just got on top of us. Apart from that, the bar there was open 24 hours a day so anytime anything went wrong it was, 'Let's go down and have a drink while they're mending it,' and that went on for months.'

Ronnie thought otherwise. 'The main problem was that we could never get that sound and feeling in the studio that we got on stage. We had a very haphazard idea about recording. *Long Player* took so long I almost completely lost interest in it.'

Later, he said, 'It was almost instantly apparent that this was not a band built for dreary rehearsal rooms and tiresome studios. This band was meant for the stage. We weren't by any means a musically accomplished outfit. We were sloppy and loose, which took the band naturally in the direction of good time rock'n'roll.'

The next US tour proved Ronnie's point. The band was meant for the stage. Without a proper hit to their name, they were selling out bigger and bigger venues – 12,000 capacity at the Detroit Cobo Hall, 11,000 at the Denver Coliseum, 8,000 in San Diego and 17,500 at the LA Forum.

Back in the UK, they got stuck into some TV and radio. On 19 April they were at BBC TV Centre to record a late-night show called *Disco2*.

Music Echo's Caroline Boucher joined them for rehearsals.

'The Faces wander up in that particular fashion they have – all scuffling and jostling one another like a pack of small boys going down the street.

'There is a plan in minute detail as to where they should all stand. It is a feat of mathematical skill that they can get in there at all . . . but immediately they decide they would like to sit down! Stools are sent for from the basement as Granville [Jenkins, the director] growls that perhaps it would be better to glue them to their seats too.

'There's one testy engineer who suggests that the Faces should treat the microphones with a little more care; but on the whole the staff eye the group with slightly indulgent amazement.

'Filming starts. Ron Lane has dragged a canvas chair onstage because, he says he feels too weak to stand.

'By the end of the third number everyone is beginning to wilt, except the Faces who have procured some wine from somewhere and keep saying it's only tea.

'By the end everyone is exhausted, except for the Faces. They perk up as they rush to the nearest bar.'

The next day they do four tracks for Bob Harris' BBC Radio 1 show *Sounds of the Seventies* and the following week they're on *Top of the Pops* doing 'Richmond' and 'Bad 'N' Ruin' from the album.

Somewhere in the middle of that they played, according to *Melody Maker*, 'probably their best British concert yet' at the Roundhouse as part of the Camden Festival.

'The Faces are becoming the most popular live band in the country,' wrote Phil Symes in *Disc and Music Echo*, 'and it's not surprising – they have one of the most entertaining and exhilarating acts about. But perhaps "act" is the wrong word. They don't go out of their way to amuse and musically satisfy an audience. They just have a ball among themselves, and the good vibrations spread.

'By the time they're ready to leave the stage the whole mass of grinning faces refuses to let them.'

Mac reckons they had a 'unique chemistry'. Rod had become a

'vamp . . . he was camp and he was comfortable with it. Woody was the guy's guy, with a cigarette stuck in his mouth or between the fingers of his right fist, eyes blinking continually with concentration as he worried the guitar and sang and camped it up with Rod.

'Ronnie puffing like a blowfish, ambled backwards and forwards across the stage in his characteristic "Ronnie Lane Shuffle", laying down the solid and melodic bass lines that were the foundation to all of our songs, and singing so sweetly. Kenney kept us all together, whacking his kit mercilessly with a fixed stare.'

'The Faces weren't like The Stones, or The Who,' Adam Blake wrote. 'Like them, they were a London band – the quintessential London band of their time – but they weren't about ruthlessness, brutishness, power, psychotic rage. They were about fun, and cama-raderie, and the joys of being a bit young and foolish, a bit reckless. They were about friendship and the healing power of good rock'n'roll.'

At the Bilzen Jazz Festival in Belgium the band played their set and were poured into two cabs to get back to the airport to fly home.

Ronnie, his bladder filled with Mateus rosé, asked the driver to stop so he could have a piss. When it was safe to do so, the driver pulled over. Ronnie got out of the car, fell into a ditch and pissed himself, then, covered in mud and stinking of urine, got back in the car. The driver was disgruntled so by way of appeasement . . .

'After a few minutes Ronnie stuck his tongue in the cab driver's ear,' Mac said. At which, 'the unfortunate fucker screamed and nearly crashed the car . . . we were both in fits, we laughed, we hiccupped and then we knew what was coming next . . . he threw up!'

And thus, the driver, too, came to understand the friendship and healing power of good rock'n'roll.

Two days later, at the Weeley Festival, just outside Clacton in Essex, they were booked to go on immediately before T. Rex, whose single 'Get It On' was riding high in the charts.

Marc Bolan had a notoriously reedy voice, which, double-tracked on record was compelling, but as a live phenomenon could be unconvincing.

'From what I can remember,' John Watson, a punter in the audience, said, 'the Faces went on first, got the crowd buzzing, they came on and did a few encores. When T. Rex came on, the crowd still wanted the Faces and booed Bolan who then started shouting abuse to the crowd – which resulted in a load of bottles and cans being hurled on to the stage. He ended up leaving the stage in tears.'

'We wiped the floor with him,' Rod said, 'and he was brave enough to come in and say, "Guys, I can't follow you. You were that good." I was very impressed with that.'

The difficulties of being upstaged by your support act were perhaps best dealt with by Les Prior of the comedy/rock band Alberto Y Los Trios Paranoias, who toured for a while with The Police as their support band. On the first night of the tour, the Albertos, with growing dismay, witnessed Sting, Stewart Copeland and Andy Summers whipping the audience to the heights of ecstasy.

As they came off, Les pulled Sting to one side and said, 'So, that's your game, is it? Being really good.'

In July, they were back in the US.

We have already learned that Steve Marriott was, at least according to Pete Townshend, the first rock star ever to chuck a TV out of a hotel window, but Woody reckoned they'd all mellowed since then, and hotels were, on the whole, let off lightly. 'We've only wrecked about four on this tour.'

The mellowing can largely be attributed to police and security guards, who, alerted by the band's reputation, had a tendency, at the first sign of mayhem, to weigh in with fists and clubs flying.

The hotel wrecking was not always the band's fault. Sometimes it was an inevitable consequence of the after-show parties, which had a tendency to get out of hand. As time went on, though, and the police got rougher, they learned as far as possible to rein things in. So, at the Howard Johnson Hotel in Toledo . . .

'There were about 400 people there,' Ronnie said, 'and they were all quiet. As soon as anyone made any noise, everyone would go, 'Shh, you want to get your head beaten in?'

Nevertheless, the filth showed up.

'They were for real those police; they nearly dragged me off. I was trying to explain to them that it was all going to be all right and they grabbed me and said, 'Oh, he'll do.'

'In Houston, some little guy came on to pat Rod on the back, and Rod was sort of, 'Yeah, great.' The guy turned around, and the police got hold of him and smashed him off the stage,' Woody said. 'Rod turned round and oooh . . . he's had a go at the police about five times this tour.'

'He'll come unstuck one night,' Ronnie said.'

Kenney is cagey about the shenanigans that went on when questioned now. 'What went on on those tours, that's private and privileged information. Let's just say we had a great time. You should've been there! We were drunk most of the time!'

Gradually, the 'Lead Vocalist Syndrome' – the reason Ronnie, Mac and Kenney had been iffy about Rod joining the band – began to make its presence felt.

'My dislike of Rod's high camp antics on stage was becoming more and more apparent to the fans,' Ronnie said. 'News of the disagreements between the two of us was reaching the press. Me and Rod were poles apart in our outlook and there was an underlying stand-offishness between the two of us right from day one.'

Billing continued to be a sticking point, too.

'What niggled Mac and Ronnie most of all,' Rod said, 'was if there was any chance that they could be construed as my backing band. Ronnie was so furious [about being billed someplace as 'Rod Stewart and the Faces'] that he clunked Billy Gaff around the head with a bottle. Invariably, any venue that offended in this way would have the dressing room trashed royally on the way out as an act of vengeance.'

Then, to fan the flames further, Rod's next solo album, *Every Picture Tells a Story*, was released – and generally regarded as a masterpiece. By October it was number one on both sides of the Atlantic and 'Maggie May', a single from the album, released in September, was number one in the singles chart. *Rolling Stone* dubbed it album of the year.

The Faces personnel all played on the album but due to contractual restrictions, the sleeve notes keep it vague, with name checks for Mac and Woody but none for Kenney or Ronnie.

On 18 September at the Oval Cricket Ground in Kennington, south London, the Faces appeared at a benefit concert for Bangladesh, organised by The Who.★ On a day of glorious sunshine, 35,000 people (including Caroline Stafford, co-author of this book) paid their two quid at the gate and were treated to a top-notch afternoon's entertainment from the likes of Mott the Hoople and Quintessence. Faces came on at around seven. Rod wore a leopard-skin ensemble from cult fashion boutique Granny Takes a Trip (which he later auctioned for the Bangladesh charity and raised £500), Woody a tiger-print jacket, Mac a red suit and Ronnie went for white flares and a purple satin jacket. No one could see what Kenney was wearing.

Their stage wear, it seemed, grew fancier by the hour.

'We all wore crepes and satins, bright colours, exotic prints, scarves, sashes,' Rod said. 'I look back now at photos of the Faces onstage and for some shows we seemed to be answering a challenge to wear as much as it was humanly possible to wear at one time.

'Carrying 200lbs of velvet and satin around the stage for 90 minutes – that's man's work, let me tell you.'

★ Two months earlier, George Harrison had held a similar event at Madison Square Garden, featuring Bob Dylan, Eric Clapton and others.

As so often was the case at gigs back then, the PA was a heap of shit. The headline act, The Who, had had the good sense to bring their own PA, and Rod listened to their opening number, apparently, with a face of stone, bridling at the difference.

The Faces played a nine-song set and were the only act to do an encore ('Had Me a Real Good Time' segueing into 'Every Picture Tells a Story'). The highlight was when the opening bars of 'Maggie May', storming up the charts at the time, brought a great roar from the crowd. When hasn't it?

The general consensus was that they wiped the floor with The Who.

Rod was voted Top British Male Singer of 1971 in *Melody Maker*'s annual poll and the Faces made the cover of the *NME* in September.

On a personal note, the same Caroline Stafford, at around this time, was at Fiorucci in Knightsbridge, trying on some loon-style velvet trousers. It was the fashion for such garments to be cut tight around the arse and thighs and the struggle to get into them often involved contortions of one sort or another. Caroline, trying to force one leg in while balancing on the other, fell backwards out of the changing room and found herself looking up at no less a person than Mr Rod Stewart who, shopping with an entourage, paused momentarily to admire her knickers. Blushing, she hopped back into the changing room. When, she re-emerged, with her clothing and composure intact, and went to the counter to pay for the loons, she was told by the assistant that Mr Stewart had already taken care of the bill. Never known to buy his round in the pub, then, but always ready to put his hand in his pocket to buy glad rags for ladies who fell at his feet.

On 30 September, despite it not being a Faces track at all, the band turned out to mime 'Maggie May' on *Top of the Pops*. It is one of the most memorable of all their *TOTP* performances. John Peel, their unwitting friend and adorer, appeared with them, miming the mandolin part as unconvincingly as can be imagined.

The Musicians' Union had tried to stop it. Mr Peel was not a paid-up member. John had to reassure them that he was not being paid for the performance. All the same, the studio director and cameramen were instructed as far as possible to keep the non-union bloke out of shot. Accordingly, Rod took every opportunity to stand next to or directly behind him in such a way as almost to make John the star of the show. After a while, the band seemed to get bored (the song is over five minutes long and the pubs were open). In the full-length version (there are shorter versions on YouTube) Woody wanders off stage and comes back with a football. All pretence at mime is abandoned. End-to-end play ensues.

And you really do still come across blokes in pubs, now in their dotage, who will fight you if you challenge their certainty that John Peel played mandolin on 'Maggie May' (or, come to that, that Bob Holness (late-lamented host of ITV's hit quiz show *Blockbusters*) played saxophone on Gerry Rafferty's 'Baker Street' (although it is true that Bob Holness once played James Bond, but only on South African radio).)

Rod had bought a half-timbered executive home in Winchmore Hill, far north London – an area favoured by retired footballers and successful used car salesman. The accountants had suggested that Woody might like to do something similar with his pesky excess wealth.

Woody thus acquired Wick House, an exquisite Grade I listed Georgian house, previously the property of Sir John Mills, actor and film star, on the corner of Nightingale Lane and Richmond Hill, overlooking the Thames. It had 20 rooms and was four storeys high. For the next God knows how many years it became party central, where at any time of day or night one might run into a Hollywood A-lister watching *The Goodies* or a Rolling Stone looking for the toilet.

Woody didn't have quite enough to buy the whole package but

persuaded Ronnie to buy the cottage, which stood in the grounds of the main house. He and Sue moved in.

It was cosy and meant that Woody, Ronnie, Mac (near Richmond Park), Kenney (in Kingston-upon-Thames), Mike and Kate McInnerney, and Pete Townshend were all practically in dog-walking distance of each other – or at most a short drive in the Merc.

On the next US tour, Billy Gaff paid $12,000 to have the performance transmitted on giant screens either side of the stage (commonplace now but a novelty back then). Each performance was announced by four trumpeters who stepped up on stage and played a fanfare, while two dancing bears (Mickey Mouse and Donald Duck) ran their routine. Then a man in a turban would announce, 'Here, at last . . .'

At some of the earlier performances, Rod brought on cases of wine and tried to hand bottles out to the audience, but the police soon put a stop to that, presumably, because then as now, you could buy field artillery and machine pistols if you looked vaguely post-pubescent but needed (need) over-21 ID to buy liquor (to be consumed in a *private space*). They were, however, allowed to kick the great stock of footballs into the audience, which must have created something of a stir in that then almost soccer-free country by being round.

In Beverley Hills, John Ingham interviewed Ronnie and Woody for *Phonograph Records* magazine. He asked Ronnie if most of his songs were based on personal experiences.

'Yeah. Rod's much better at writing about imaginative and fictitious things than I am. I can't do that sort of thing at all. What usually happens is that me and Ron [Woody] will find a melody, or he'll find one piece and I'll have another bit and we'll stick it together. That's how 'Had Me a Real Good Time' and 'Flying' come together. And then we'll sort of look at each other, and can't think of anything to write about, so we'll give it to Rod.'

'And he's always bound to come with a lyric,' Woody said. 'He regards every track that you give him as a challenge, 'All right, I'll put some words to this.'

'They're very entertaining, his lyrics,' Ronnie said. Ingham failed to mention how tightly Ronnie's teeth were gritted when he said this, or when he added, 'I wouldn't mind [singing on stage more], but I think it's a bit stupid while Rod's around. I should think people would far rather listen to him.'

The approach to the third Faces album was a bit more workmanlike. For a start, they booked Olympic Studios, where some of the Small Faces' finest tracks had been recorded. And second, they brought in Glyn Johns – fresh from The Beatles' *Let It Be* album and the soaring, majestic perfection of The Who's *Who's Next* – to co-produce.

Nevertheless, 'There was a pub just up the road from Olympic,' Kenney said. 'Any excuse, y'know? I think it helped to get us in that relaxed-drunken-stupor mood that we always preferred to be in.'

There was trouble finding material because, 'Basically, at the time, Rod was doing his solo albums, so a lot of the good stuff went on those, and we were left with the songs we were knocking up at the time, y'know? But we made them sound great, so there you go.'

They worked on and off between tours, recording the final tracks and mixing in September.

The album, *A Nod Is as Good as a Wink . . . to a Blind Horse*, was released on 17 November. The cover photo had been taken at their 28 July gig at the Houston Coliseum by Tom Wright – or rather Tom Wright, having decided that the only place to get the angle he wanted was from high in the lighting rig and being leery of heights, enlisted roadie Chuch Magee to climb up there with the camera and press the shutter.

Tom Wright, by the way, had objections to the band being called 'sloppy'.

'The Faces drank, no doubt about it, but not to the point of sloppiness,' he said. 'I've seen a hundred shows, soundchecks, late-night jams and "sloppy" is a word that doesn't fit anywhere. It would be like calling the kid who can ride his bike with no hands, shoot the finger and yell something all at the same time a sloppy driver. The Faces were so good they made it look easy.'

The original issue of the album came with a 3ft x 4ft poster containing 349 snaps of the band and their lives. The collage included pictures of pills and pharmaceuticals, naked groupies, crew members and photos from family albums, artfully arranged by Ronnie's friend, Mike McInnerney. After a few weeks Warner Bros. got cold feet and withdrew the poster, making it an instant collector's item.

On the back of the album cover was a tableau of marionettes of the band – dressed outrageously with a pantomime horse behind them. For some reason, Ronnie hated those marionettes and smashed his with a hammer as soon as he got his hands on it.

The opening track, 'Miss Judy's Farm' like 'Bad 'N' Ruin', is a one-chord riff song, but whereas on 'Bad 'N' Ruin' you beg for variation, on 'Miss Judy's Farm' it's the last thing you want and need. Woody reveals that not only would he have been a better replacement for Brian than Mick Taylor, if anything should, God forbid, happen to Keith, he could have fitted right in. There is a middle section in which Woody and Ronnie weave elegant patterns around each other, then a speeded-up ending. Unlike 'Bad 'N' Ruin', it's also recorded properly and doesn't sound like something run up on cassette tape in your auntie's front room.

Ronnie takes the lead vocal on two tracks on side one: 'You're So Rude', a song about the joy of bringing your girlfriend home when you're a sweet teenager and the family's out visiting Auntie Rene, and 'Last Orders Please', a 'fancy running into you after our acrimonious break-up' song. Both are as fine examples of English honky-tonk as you're likely to encounter.

Side one ends with the Faces' finest hour. The sublime, pure rock'n'roll certainty of 'Stay with Me' makes hearts leap, lumps come to throats and tears to eyes. Yes, okay, it's possibly one of the most misogynistic lyrics ever conceived, but it's worth convincing yourself – however implausible it may seem – that it's meant *ironically* in order to access the greater glory of the music. It invites questions. Does Woody do better open-tuning riffs than Keith? Does the fluidity of Ronnie's bass line put him up there with Jaco Pastorius and Stanley Clarke? Did the inventors of the electric – and indeed the acoustic – piano do so only because they knew, by means of some unholy precognition, that one day Mac would come along and play it *properly*? Does Kenney's sense of time mark him as a contender for Messiah status? Is Rod half-man, half-gravel? The answer to all these questions except one is, of course, 'No', but all the same they have to be asked, because rock'n'roll is nothing without hyperbole. The real teaser though is how drunk can you be and still negotiate those switches to half-tempo with such uncanny accuracy?

The other sublime track among an album filled with contenders is 'Debris', Ronnie's love song to his father and to the market they used to go to on Saturdays. 'Oh, you was my hero.'

'Before he wrote it,' Billy Graff said, 'he did a driving tour of his school-day haunts, he wanted to see them all again before they disappeared forever.'

'It wasn't until I got to New York City that I realised I missed it. I was feeling homesick at the time.'

'Stay with Me' was released as a single in time for the Christmas market. Though it had barely made the Top 50 by Christmas Day, it eventually rose to number six. The Christmas honours that year went, understandably, to Benny Hill's 'Ernie (The Fastest Milkman in the West)'.

17

What the Fuck's Happened to Ronnie Lane?

By the beginning of January 1972, *A Nod Is as Good as a Wink* was at number five in the album charts, just behind Rod's *Every Picture Tells a Story*, which had slipped from the number one spot. By the end of the month, the single from the album, 'Stay with Me', was at number six.

Ronnie had money to chuck away – literally.

'Once we were driving down the M1 in an open-top Mercedes,' Billy Nicholls, Ronnie's friend from Immediate and fellow Meher Baba devotee, said. 'He opened his wallet, and all this paper money flew out. Hundreds and hundreds of pounds. He'd just come off tour. There was absolutely no question of him stopping, going to get it. He just carried on driving as if nothing had happened.'

Later, Ronnie gave the Merc to his brother Stan, because he said he liked it.

On paper at least, he was leading the life of Riley. He was living in a beautiful house in a top location, he rode around in a fancy Merc, his wardrobe was mostly by Granny Takes a Trip and his wife was a beautiful actress, model and singer.

But everybody was starting to get the sense that he wasn't happy. 'He'd become withdrawn,' Kenney said. 'He had been agitating for a more prominent role in the band, singing and songwriting, but it wasn't happening.'

In February, they played a three-night residency at the Rainbow, in Finsbury Park.

Mike McInnerney had designed a life-size yellow vintage Rolls-Royce in which the band would make their entrance. It was supposed to 'symbolise our rises in fortune.'

At the start of the show, the roadies, carrying it onto the stage, lost their grip and the thing went flying, spilling the band out.

At the end, as usual, they unleashed a torrent of footballs into the audience.

Something of the magic was captured when the ever-faithful John Peel featured them in a Sunday concert at the Paris Studio – a former cinema that for years did faithful service as a venue for BBC radio audience shows. Some of the tracks were later released as part of *Five Guys Walked into a Bar*, the four-disc compilation released in 2004.

In Germany, they kept the audience waiting for two hours. 'Sorry we're late,' Ronnie said, when they eventually showed up, 'Rod's hairdryer broke.'

In Puerto Rico they discovered that past misdemeanours had led to a ban from the Holiday Inn chain of hotels. This was particularly galling because Ronnie, in breach of the customary 'no wives or girlfriends on tour' rule, had brought Sue along.

The tour manager pleaded with the reception staff, to no avail. An emergency band meeting was held. 'What about we book in as Fleetwood Mac?' somebody said.

Quite how this worked in practice ('Yes, I know it says Ronnie Lane on my passport, but my stage name is Christine McVie.') is hard to say, but legend has it that it worked, and that the same ploy was subsequently used several times.

Towards the end of April, they flew into Memphis to start their Rock'n'roll Circus tour for eight days, taking in parts of the south that they hadn't reached before. This was, the MC announced, 'A new concept in American entertainment. Introducing for the first time in the history of showbiz – circus acts with rock and roll.'

There can be few people who wouldn't get goosebumps of excitement at the thought of seeing a sword-swallower or trapeze artist who might possibly have had backstage access to an interesting stash.

According to a review in *Disc*, the evening, at the 12,000-seat Mid-South Coliseum began with Blinko the clown and his novelty balloonerama.

'Are you ready for some fun?' asked Blinko. His act pivoted on the concept that the more noise the audience made, the more balloons Blinko would blow up.

'How about that,' said the MC 'Didn't they do a great job? And now the group will be ready for you in just a few minutes.'

The support act, Free, whose album *Heartbreaker* went Top 10 in the UK and Top 50 in the US, did their set. Then Carlo, who balanced on a rubber ball and twirled hoops, was followed by Miss Doris who also balanced on a ball, rolled it up a ramp and then did a handstand on it. After that, somebody came on and did cartwheels and somersaults, 'without', the MC was keen to emphasise, 'the aid of a springboard or trampoline'. The highlight of the evening for fans of suspended-by-the-hair strippers was Miss Wung, who worked 50ft above the ground, stripping while suspended by her hair.

The idea of following a suspended-by-the-hair stripper must have been daunting, but nonetheless the Faces rose to the challenge, despite being a bit out of practice, having not played much since the Puerto Rico gig six weeks earlier.

'They stumbled around a bit early in the evening, missing each other's cues,' the *Disc* review said, 'but they settle down eventually. 'Maybe I'm Amazed' is especially beautiful. And the crowd love them. They've probably never seen anything so gigantically zany.'

The gig at Clemson, South Carolina, was covered by Dave Marsh of *Creem*. He asked Pat Costello, the band's publicist, about the wreckage the band allegedly wrought wherever they went, referring particularly to 'broken lamps, banana-fucked groupies' and the time 'two members wanted adjoining rooms so knocked a hole in the wall which resulted in hotel bills for damages alone of $250 a day.'

'It's the old biker idea,' Pat Costello replied. 'It's *class*. Like, it's class to be totally outrageous. Piss in your best friend's living room. It's just . . . *it's total gross-out.*'

At Louisville, Kentucky, according to Dave Marsh, they nailed it.

'Stewart bounds across the stage with his Groucho walk, leaning into the mike and crooning like some obscene parody of Bing Crosby; Wood has all the perfectly timed and intuitively choreographed moves of the best British guitarists; Lane tromps about like a drunken sailor. McLagan and Jones don't do much, but they provide the backbeat that's a necessity as backdrop for the theatre.

'The show is so finely tuned that it even works where once it was weakest: when Stewart hands the vocal mike to Ron Lane.

'Lane is a good singer, but he's not Rod and always before it has seemed like he was merely giving Rod a break. No more. His songs are good, and his ideas about how to present them are fine. He mocks himself so well you're never sure how serious he is.'

The photographer Tom Wright was aware that Rod's standing in the band was becoming an increasing problem. 'The Faces always maintained the "we're all in it together – we're a band – it's not Rod Stewart and the Faces – it's the Faces" line. The reality was something different. The band may have started as a unit . . . the Small Faces had plenty of hit records before they met Rod Stewart. They didn't see themselves as back-up guys, but rather as English royalty who'd allowed Rod to join in on the good life. But by the end, Rod was the focal point.

'The band gave Rod his edge. Night after night, the Faces would nail your ass in your tracks: the Faces got ripped all the time and made it look like a blast. Fans would throw joints up onstage and Ronnie would catch 'em and smoke 'em.'

'Big old human pile-ups were a regular feature of the act,' Rod said in his autobiography, 'Woody falling on top of Ronnie, me lying on top of Woody, Mac coming off the piano to jump on top of all of us – we used to feel that it hadn't been a particularly good show if we didn't end up lying in a mound in the middle of the stage at the end of it.'

In Tampa at the end of the tour, members of Free joined them on stage.

'Touring with the Faces was wonderful,' Simon Kirke, the drummer, said. 'They always had such fun on stage. There were drinks in abundance, and Woody was there with the ever-present ciggie hanging out of his mouth or tucked in the end of his guitar. Ian would be grinning from ear to ear. And they dressed so flamboyantly, too, all silks and satins and flares. I loved 'em. They just had a great time, whereas Free were slightly serious.'

Free bassist Andy Fraser remembered the Faces as 'big, big drinkers. We'd be at the same hotel, and Rod especially would be like: 'Come on, fellas, let's have a couple of drinks.' Which essentially meant getting totally plastered. Watching the Faces perform was a bit like a pub singalong on an arena scale.'

Back in England during May, Ronnie and Woody spent a productive few weeks in Olympic Studios with Glyn Johns recording a soundtrack for the film *Mahoney's Last Stand*, produced by and starring Ronnie's friend Alexis Kanner, who was part of the Richmond Meher Baba set and had shot the promo film for the Small Faces' final single 'The Universal'.

The plot concerns a young, urban, half-crazy drunk who rents a derelict farm in rural Canada, is joined by a couple of crazy old friends and hooks up with his landlord's daughter – played by Maud

Adams. Pete Townshend gets his own credit on the film for 'Special Electronic Effects', which are mostly comic boings and squelchy noises. The music covers a range of styles, from hard electric blues, to Cajun-tinged acoustic two-steps and waltzes with fiddles and mouth-harps, to a folk/gospel close harmony a capella.

The budget was practically non-existent, but the vibe was good, so Ronnie was able to put together an assembly of top talent, including, along with Mac and Kenney, Ian Stewart, Bobby Keyes, Jim Horn, Mickey Waller and Pete Townshend. In fact, anybody passing would be invited in for a drink, a sax solo or cowbell obligato.

The film and soundtrack album might have been more successful were it not for distribution problems. When the film did eventually emerge – in 1976 – it was sometimes under the original title, sometimes as *Mahoney's Farm*, and sometimes *Downtown Farmer*. Similarly, the album's release was delayed until 1976, by which time Ronnie had moved on to other projects and Woody was a Rolling Stone. Some people wondered whether it was a reunion, but they were few in number because there was virtually no publicity, so you had to be paying close attention to know the album was there at all.

The whole *Mahoney's Last Stand* project – from the idea of taking over a rundown farm, to making acoustic good-time music with ragged assemblies of pals – could be taken as a blueprint for Ronnie's future. Self-sufficiency, no pressure, no managers, no lead vocalist being diva-ish.

Ronnie had acquired a four-year-old and very beautiful 26ft Airstream Caravan – with the rounded ends in polished aluminium – and had it shipped back to England. It would become, he decided, a mobile recording studio.

This turned out to be one of Ronnie's shrewder investments – perhaps the only one of his many projects that actually turned a profit. Ron Nevison, a friend of Pete Townshend's who worked at Island Records, supervised fitting it out with £45,000 (Ronnie's take from three US tours) worth of gear: Helios desk, Tannoy monitoring, Studer and Revox tape machines and all the fixings.

It was called LMS – Lane's Mobile Studio.

In July they went back to America, leaving the usual trail of destruction across several north-western states.

'Billy Gaff would go to check out,' Rod said, 'and it wouldn't be, "Anything from the mini-bar last night sir?" it would be, "Here's your bill for the future cost of redecorating the ninth floor." In Cleveland one time, Billy found his path to the exit blocked by an irate manager and the local police sheriff. It cost him $5,000 in cash to get away.'

They played the Mount Pocono Festival at Long Pond, Pennsylvania, in rain, mud and sometimes dense fog to a crowd of 200,000. The Faces were top of the bill, with each band member's name printed underneath – none of the other bands got that. Even more gratifying, the names were in alphabetical order, so Jones got first place, and Stewart fourth, just above Wood.

More gratifying still, also on the bill, lower down, among Three Dog Night, Black Sabbath and Emerson, Lake & Palmer, without so much as a namecheck for the lead singer, was Humble Pie, the band Steve Marriott had formed with Peter Frampton.

Sadly, there is no record of any meeting that may have taken place.

Tickets were $11 and doctors, nurses and a team of 65 from the County Drug Council were recruited to handle the acid casualties. The traffic was hell. Halfway through The Groundhogs' set, the combination of damp and vacuum tubes caused their amps to go up in flames.

'The peanut butter and mescaline sandwiches were a big hit,' said one witness. 'By the time the Faces started playing at dusk the fog was so thick you could not see the stage.'

'The mosquitoes were as big as hummingbirds,' said another. 'They almost carried me off.'

'I was fading by the time Rod Stewart and the Faces came on,' said a third. 'Their helicopter landing through the fog was something, and I remember them starting the set with 'Long Distance Operator'.'

And then it all became a blur.

Back in England, the band went into Olympic Studios with Glyn Johns to work on their fourth album. Ronnie, Woody, Mac and Kenney did, anyway: Rod was otherwise engaged for the first two weeks. By the time he showed up, most of the backing tracks had already been recorded.

'And when he came down, he'd say, "I don't like that" and he'd be a real downer,' Mac said. 'It was like being up in front of a teacher – it was very disheartening. All right, some of the tunes were in the wrong key, but how were we supposed to know what key to put them in. 'Oh La La', for instance, we recorded about four times [. . .] Rod was supposed to sing it but didn't like the key or the way we'd done it, so we did it again and he didn't like the words. Then Ronnie tried to sing it, but it wasn't his key and didn't suit his voice at the time. Eventually Woody sang it.

'The album was hard work and it dragged on and on and on.'

In August, they took a break to go back to the US. On the 25th they played the Hollywood bowl, where, according to *Phonograph Record*, they gave a 'definitely sub-par performance . . . the band played well but without a lot of real spark and carried on in the fashion, but without the substance we have come to expect – Rod careening and sliding like a besotted ice skater, Ronnie Lane chugging about like a cigarette smoke-puffing locomotive, Ron Wood running in huge circles while shooting an arc of sparkling wine from his mouth, like a crazy caricature of a fountain's spouting figurine.'

The sub-par performance may have had to do with some adjustments to their customary medication.

'At the gig at the Hollywood Bowl,' Mac said, 'I had this white carnation in the lapel of my tuxedo, and I'd filled it with the cocaine.

Ronnie Lane came over to have a sniff. I said, 'What the fuck? Get your own!'

The band would often go into a huddle on stage and pretend to be going over a setlist while they took turns snorting coke off the top of the amplifier. Rod, by this time, was well established as the leader, the diva in satin.

'Sometimes Warner would book the band regular hotel rooms and Mercury [the record company who dealt with Rod's solo career] would book me a suite. Of course, I could have refused the key and insisted on downgrading. But then . . . I wouldn't have a suite, would I?'

The day after the Hollywood Bowl gig, they all went to Vegas to relieve themselves of some of the cash they'd been earning.

'Mac and Ronnie went to see the fat Elvis dinner show at the Hilton. They loved him, perhaps a little too much, and almost got thrown out for expressing their appreciation too enthusiastically.'

Both Mac and Ronnie were having marital problems.

Mac's wife, Sandy, had left, taking their son. She'd had enough of his infidelities, and he was, by his own account, 'playing badly, drinking far too much and doing too much blow [via his white boutonnière] in an effort to forget my troubles.'

Ronnie's Meher Baba mates, Kate and Mike McInnerney, had moved down to Wales with their baby daughter, Alana.

According to Russ Schlagbaum, roadie and friend of Ronnie's, 'There was a birthday party held at Mike and Katie's house in Wales. Ronnie and Susan came up and suddenly Susan's walking around saying, "Has anybody seen Ronnie?" And McInnerney and everybody's going, "Have you seen Kate?" That was when they jumped in Ronnie's Land Rover and took off.'

But Kate maintains that the trip came about because Ronnie, exhausted by his last tour of the States, badly needed a break. Sue couldn't go with them as she had auditions to attend and Mike, Kate's husband, was on a strict deadline to finish a book cover. At this point Kate is adamant that there was nothing but friendship between the two of them.

They drove to Fishguard and took a boat to Ireland.

'Ronnie and Kate were planning a holiday trip to Ireland and asked me to go along,' Billy Nicholls said. 'I don't know what their other halves, Sue and Mike, were thinking when all this was going on, but off we went in Ronnie's Land Rover, which he called Rosie, along with Kate's ten-month-old daughter, Alana, and Ronnie's dog, Mollie, which was a wedding present from Steve Marriott and Jenny.'

'In Ireland we were on cloud nine,' Kate said. 'Ronnie would say, "Where shall we go next?" and I'd say, "Follow the sun!" We went off a cliff once and rolled the Land Rover over. When the Garda turned up, they took Alana and Billy Nicholls off to the hospital to check them out and Ronnie and I went off to stay with the head of the police in Tipperary for a few days. Lovely bloke.

'I used to make stews of Guinness and anything else I could find on the side of the road. We used to like sleeping in the Land Rover. The Land Rover was called Rosie. Ronnie wrote this tune he used to play in Ireland and called it 'Rosie'.'

They drove around southern Ireland and went to stay at Mick Jagger's mansion, Castlemartin, in for a couple of days. It was here that Sue caught up with them. She didn't stay long. It was obvious that the marriage was over.

They stayed a while in Ireland. Ronnie and Billy played a few pub gigs – calling themselves 'Foot and Mouth' and doing Everly Brothers and Bob Dylan numbers. Ronnie's absence meant missing a *Top of the Pops* with the other Faces miming the backing to Rod's new single 'Angel'. He sent a cardboard cut-out of himself as a stand-in.

'When we came back from Ireland the shit really hit the fan,' Kate said. 'We had always been mates, but this was different. It was pretty awful as we'd always been friends, always been a foursome. But Susie was pragmatic. And in the end, we remained friends. She wanted to break through into films and pursue her acting.'

Ronnie's dad, Stan, knew that there was something special going on between Ronnie and Kate and he told his son that he thought they would be great together.

Sue moved in with Woody and his wife until Ronnie arranged for a flat for her on Wandsworth Bridge Road. Mac and Sue had a very brief affair – finding consolation in each other after they had both been dumped.

Mike McInnerney was also distraught – he had always thought of Ronnie as a good friend and felt betrayed. 'Mike told everyone I was dead!' Kate said.

But as Meher Baba put it: 'Why should you not be happy? What need is binding you to unhappiness? Binding is self-created. It can be overcome if you really want to be free. You are your own obstacle to freedom and merely wishing for freedom is not enough.'

Kate's influence on Ronnie was both profound and instantaneous. Gone were the flamboyant Granny Takes a Trip outfits that he favoured. Instead, he dressed like an Irish poacher from the thirties – tweed jackets, Romany kerchief and little gold earrings.

This did not please the rest of the group. 'His attire was an embarrassment,' Mac said.

He stopped travelling with the group, too, preferring to take the Land Rover with Kate at his side.

'Ronnie always used to dress so impeccably with his three-piece suits – "three-piece", that was his nickname,' Russ Schlagbaum said. 'We knew he had run off and left Sue, so all of us were, like, "What the fuck is Ronnie thinking?" In he walks with Kate in tow and baby Alana in a wicker basket. His ears were pierced, he's got all these bangles, he's turned into a gypsy. And he's walking around, miles away from everybody. He's not joining in the frolics like they would do, falling over each other and all that shit. He was completely aloof, and everybody was wondering, 'What the fuck's happened to Ronnie Lane?'

It was around this time that writer and journalist John Pidgeon, researching an article about life on the road, embedded himself with the band by becoming a Faces roadie, alongside Russ Schlagbaum and Chuch Magee, on their December UK tour.

Ronnie explained to him, 'If you're going to be on the road and if you want to live at home, you may as well just live at home, because unless you totally accept that you're on the road and that's it, that's your lot, private jets back to London for a few hours a day isn't going to make it home. You're living a split and you ain't going to get any benefit out of it at all. What's wrong with living on the road? . . . You can say, "I won't take the motorway here, I'll take the B road because it goes through this county and that village, and I'd like to see this, and I'd like to see that." You might as well enjoy it. I can't understand all this rushing there and running back business. I ain't going to rush anywhere, not unless I absolutely have to.'

After the Sheffield gig, Woody and Mac wrecked their hotel room. The night manager called the police. But Ronnie wasn't there. He'd gone back to London, perhaps via Grindleford and Hassop so as to take in the Sheepwash Bridge at Ashford in the Water.

18

I'm Leaving the Group

'You can't be the Faces onstage and harbour a great rift down the middle; it wouldn't work,' Kenney told *Disc* magazine in January 1973. 'We couldn't split up, we're all very indebted to each other. We have arguments and say "right, that's it. I'm leaving the group" but it's only a threat and we never mean it. We're such good mates you see . . .'

The band had no gigs that January. Ronnie made his first recording in the Mobile Studio – Eric Clapton's Rainbow Concert on 13 January, which was released later that year.

'It's turned out incredibly well, but that was luck. I'd spent about sixty grand,' Ronnie said, 'and all of a sudden in the last month before it was completed, it hit me like an anvil that I'd bought this bloody caravan because I loved the look of it, and it was nothing to do with the acoustics. It all came together so beautifully it was like the gods were on my side.'

On 7 February, the Faces appeared on *Top of the Pops* to perform their first single since 1971, 'Cindy Incidentally', written by Rod, Woody and Mac.

The next day, they went to the Paris Studio in Lower Regent Street to record another session for John Peel's Radio 1 show.

Mr Peel introduced them: 'The BBC has asked me to come along this evening and introduce five lovable young men whose music is currently taking the country by storm – Brian Poole and The Trem . . . no, okay, the Faces.'

The session was never aired and much later cropped up on bootlegs under the title, *Too Drunk for the BBC*.

There is the odd glitch. Woody might have been a bit more punctilious about tuning his guitars – the intro to 'Twisting the Night Away' reaches heights of microtonality that Derek Bailey might have envied. Rod often seems to be off mic, or on the wrong mic, and Ronnie's vocal at the beginning of 'Maybe I'm Amazed' is a bit karaoke-Kevin at a stag party, but there are moments, like the end of 'Memphis Tennessee', when the band could even be described as disciplined and together, and when, on 'Three Button Hand Me Down', they lean back on a rock'n'roll lope, what they lack in precision they more than make up for in feel and energy.

'The Faces, there,' Mr Peel says at the end, 'still the best rock'n'roll band in the world for those of us who really care.'

The problem was possibly not that the band was too drunk to play but that the audience, and the BBC high-ups who reached the decision not to broadcast, were too sober. It might even have been, dare one say it, that the BBC technicians weren't up to the mark when it came to capturing all that joy and anarchy on tape. Anyway, sometimes the bootleg is available, and sometimes the session finds its way to YouTube, so you can decide for yourself. Have a couple of light ales before listening.

Whatever, the BBC didn't seem to hold a grudge and invited them back to the Paris on 1 April (Ronnie's birthday) for a return match. 'We had already been to the Captain's Cabin,'* Mac said 'and we wanted to go back. So, the show was a little bit in the way. It must

---

* The Captain's Cabin was a pub a minute's walk from the Paris where BBC producers often popped for a swift half after a recording only to wake up three days later in Swansea, married to a Norwegian stoker called Bergthor.

have been 20 to 11, because the pubs close at 11 and they wouldn't serve us after that. England's so miserable.'

Nevertheless, the BBC deemed this one fit to be aired. Among a smattering of favourites and hits (including a fine version of 'Stay with Me') they played five tracks from the new album, only one of which was co-written by Ronnie – even though he'd contributed to six out of the ten tracks, two of which were solo compositions. There may or may not have been some significance in this.

The album, *Ooh La La*, had been released a week or so earlier with a launch party at the Warner Bros. office, which then moved on to Tramp, the nightclub in Jermyn Street. Can-can girls were in attendance. Ronnie, abandoning his poacher's garb for the night, wore a bronze lurex suit and striped shirt, Rod seemed bare chested under his brocade jacket and Mac went for fuchsia tartan. Rock journalist Chris Charlesworth, who was at the party, thought Ronnie looked more drunk than the others, but the distinction was fine.

Most of the reviews agreed that *Ooh La La* was their best album yet, and – irksomely perhaps – the only one that could match the quality of Rod's solo offerings.

Rolling Stone, having complained about the amount of filler on previous albums reckoned, 'Only three of the ten tracks are candidates for the poop chute and the rest alternately rock real hard or are fine vehicles for Rod's mellower and subtler vocal talents.'

Even more irksome was the criticism of Ron and Woody's vocals. *NME* reckoned they sounded 'pallid when set beside Rod's,' and said of the title track, 'Ooh La La', sung by Woody, 'I wish Rod had sung it.'

Nevertheless, *Creem* said, 'When all the tumult and shouting have died, I think it'll go down in rock history as a goodie.'

Everybody liked the tricksy sleeve, though. It was a picture of Gastone – a character played by the Italian comedian Ettore Petrolini, very big in the 1920s. When you press the top of the sleeve, Gastone's eyes move from side to side and the jaw opens and closes, so you can make him say, or sing, 'Ooh la la'. The inner sleeve shows the lads leering appreciatively at a can-can dancer.

On 21 April, *Melody Maker* published an interview with Rod, conducted by Roy Hollingworth, under the headline, 'Rod Stewart: Our New Album is a Disgrace'.

'It's a bloody mess,' Rod said. 'But I shouldn't say that, should I? It was a disgrace. Well, I should say it in a few weeks' time. Not now. I mean, the public ain't gonna like me saying it's a bloody mess. It was a disgrace. Maybe I'm too critical. But look, I don't like it. One of the best tracks is one I don't sing on, and that's 'Ooh La La'. All that fucking about taking nine months to do an album like *Ooh La La* doesn't prove anything. But I'm not going to say anything more about it. All right? That's it.'

'It was very mean spirited of Rod to slam *Ooh La La* in the press immediately after it came out,' Mac said. 'He was making his own albums, fair enough, but he didn't have to slag ours off and he had no right to because it wasn't a bad album . . . The irony is he could have contributed more to it, but he didn't so he had even less of a reason to criticise.'

Either in spite of or because of Rod's comments, or maybe because of the fancy sleeve, the album was a hit, reaching number one in the UK album charts on 28 April.

They'd been promoting it with a UK mini-tour and played Sunderland the night they beat Arsenal in the semi-final of the FA Cup (and went on to win it, a second division team beating the mighty Leeds United). John Peel, who was there, judged it to be, 'The best-ever gig.'

'I'm supposed to have danced in the wings with a bottle of Blue Nun in my arm,' Peel said (Blue Nun was a very popular brand of German wine). 'And I'm a person who never dances. Never, never, never.'

The UK tour was followed by a 12-city US tour, which began, on a sour note, just two days after the publication of the *Melody Maker* article.

Before the Columbus, Ohio gig on 28 April, a heavily pregnant Kate flew out with Alana to be with Ronnie. 'Ronnie bought me and Alana a ticket to Chicago and we were supposed to meet him there,' Kate said. But she missed the plane and ended up meeting Ronnie in New York. Although even that didn't go smoothly, as she was arrested for jaywalking. She managed to turn it round though: the policeman who arrested her ended up joining the Faces road crew as a personal security guard for Ronnie and Kate for the rest of the tour.

With Kate was her friend Barbara Morice, Russ Schlagbaum's girlfriend and Ronnie's PA, which put Russ' nose out of joint. 'In Columbus, Ohio there were a load of girls that I knew from college around. I was working for one of the world's biggest rock'n'roll bands and I'm all set up. I walk into the lobby of the Holiday Inn and there stands my English girlfriend who I thought I'd left behind in Richmond. It was like "Holy fuck, what do I do now?"'

'For the three weeks left of the tour we decided to drive and not fly in the private jets,' Kate said. 'We picked up all these different cars in different states – great big American cars – gas guzzlers.'

'I have to give Laney credit,' Russ said, 'because he busted his ass to drive those distances from gig to gig with these women and a kid until the end of the tour in Indianapolis.'

'On that tour they used to do things like rearrange all the hotel rooms and put all the furniture in the lobbies and unscrew appliances and even the legs of the beds,' Kate said. 'But they weren't that bad. Not throwing tellies out the windows bad anyway.'

Rolling Stone caught up with them at the Spectrum in Philadelphia.

'Philly loved the Faces. They loved Rod's wrist-length white gloves, loved his red ostrich feather sash, loved his gold satin trousers

– especially when they ripped. ("Uh oh, me trousers is falling. I told you we wanted to give you something special tonight, Philly, but I didn't mean it this way. Don't worry, though, I take full responsibility for everything that happens up here. Just stay with us.")'

The show ended with them all around the mic stand that Rod had mangled, singing 'We'll Meet Again'.

'The brief finale,' said *Rolling Stone*, 'was the only time all evening that Rod had embraced Ronnie Lane, who since the band's earliest touring days often seemed bound to Stewart's waist. Lane played aggressive bass lines all evening, crisscrossing the stage with an uncharacteristic soberness and none of his usual pratfall antics.'

After the gig, Rod – in gloves and satin trousers – rounded on Ronnie, who was in what had become his customary rag'n'bone attire – and asked, 'What are you trying to be – a spiv or a Ted?' and Ronnie came back with, 'Well I'd rather look like a fucking Teddy boy than an old tart who's going through the change.'

On stage at the Nassau Coliseum, Ronnie threw a glass of wine over Mac. Mac threw a tambourine at Ronnie and afterwards they locked themselves in their dressing rooms.

By the time they got to Roanoke, Virginia, 'nobody was speaking to Ronnie except Woody, who was his usual bubbly self,' Russ Schlagbaum said, 'you know, "Let's put all the bad stuff behind us and have some fun." Laney always used to wander round in circles onstage so that his guitar cord would end up in a huge knot, which was always a problem for me, but that night he just stood still back by his amps and played bass.'

That was the night the onstage fights escalated.

'In the middle of a number he came up to me, doing the Ronnie Lane glide,' Mac said, 'and he looked at me and said, "Fuck off". I got up from the piano and kicked him so fucking hard he didn't know what had hit him.

'Ronnie wanted to get Rod out of the group. He saw there was a power struggle and he thought if he said he was leaving that we would agree to kick Rod out and make him leader of the group. But he was wrong.'

'Ronnie was pretty jaded,' Kate said. 'He was moving away from all that stuff.'

'It was like a bad joke gone wrong,' Woody said, 'because we all used to mess about and say: 'I'm leaving the group!' It was like a stock saying whenever anything went slightly wrong. Then one day Ronnie actually did come in and say he was leaving. I went: "Yeah right, pull the other one." But he said: "No, I really am."

'Ronnie ran off with Kate and left Sue Lane, who we all used to love. We'd all said: "What are you doing? How can you do this?" And he said he was going off to live in a caravan, become a traveller and form his own band. There was nothing more we could do.'

A fortune teller had once told Ronnie that a woman would arrive to put right both his troubled career and his never-ending personal problems. Maybe Kate was that woman.

Ronnie's brother Stan was aghast. 'I used to say to Ronnie, "You only jump off the boat if it's sinking." And for the first time in his life, he was making plenty of money. But I think that Kate was a bad influence at that time because she wanted to be a hippie and live on a farm and all that shit. I think she was the force that dragged Ronnie away from the Faces plus he was pissed off with Rod, so I think between the two of them it turned him.'

Years later, in his autobiography, Rod wrote: 'As for Ronnie Lane, I adore him, odd fellow though he could be from time to time. He was a very creative guy, tender and poetic in many ways, but he was absolutely straight up as well. If he didn't like something I was doing he would tell me and not beat around the bush. When he eventually left the band, Ronnie Wood and I talked about it and agreed that was probably the engine gone.'

Billy Gaff told *Rolling Stone*, 'I'm sure it's in the cards, and they're all aware of it, that somebody might want to go their own way. They're very practical. They've established themselves financially, and really don't have to worry, and I'm sure that eventually they'll want to go on to separate things. For each of them it's been eight years. Rod and Woody have been together for eight years as have Ronnie, Mac and Kenney. And after eight years . . .'

Back in England, the band was booked to play 1, 3 and 4 June at the Sundown in Edmonton. A week before this, the front-page head-line of *Sounds* was 'Plonk Quits Faces'.

'Following speculation about the future of the Faces, Ronnie Lane announced this week his decision to leave. Prior to leaving for a holiday in France, he said 'It's time for me to move on. I feel the need for a change.'

When it became known that the Edmonton gigs would be the last three Faces gigs with Ronnie Lane (and maybe the last three Faces gigs ever) there was a stampede for tickets. Some fans queued for seven hours.

The stage was decked out with bar, palm trees and a candelabra on top of Mac's Steinway. The last night was filmed by Mike Mansfield's TV company. It kicked off with a line of can-can dancers, who were followed by Rod in a sparkling vest and trailing tartan scarf. Dotted in the audience were banners saying 'Farewell Ronnie', but nothing was said on stage about it. The fight seemed to have gone out of them, though.

Towards the end, Rod snuck up to Ronnie, called him 'Old Pal' and asked, 'Shall we do 'Twistin' the Night Away' before they close?' to which Ronnie replied, 'Too late, they are closed.' Ronnie joined the rest of the band to take his final bow after the encore and sang the usual verses of 'We'll Meet Again'.

Ronnie left the gig with his brother Stan and went to the night-club Tramp. According to Stan they met Marc Bolan there and Ronnie asked, 'You haven't got a job for an out of work bass player, have ya?'

For Ronnie it was: 'I've played it, I've done it, but I don't want to do it again. The bubble's burst, it's not there anymore.'

'I think Ronnie's direction in music was changed,' Kenney said. 'He was branching off to do his own thing. He was a bit more gypsy and a bit more country and that's why he formed Slim Chance.'

The times had indeed changed. The gloss was going out of glam and being replaced with earth tones. In July 1973, Ziggy Stardust played his last gig. His estranged cousin, Alvin, kept going for a little longer, but eventually even he realised there was a limit to the number of coos you can coo ca choo.

You can, it's said, go blind if you spend too long looking at shiny satin on stage. Chiffon scarves are a tripping hazard. Feather boas cause allergies. Fairport Convention never went near anything shiny. They wore ordinary clothes and possibly got their trousers out of a Littlewood's catalogue. Pentangle looked like people you sometimes saw in Basildon on Sunday afternoons, cleaning cars and mowing lawns. The Band, in America, when they dressed up at all, dressed up as 19th-century dirt farmers who had more dirt than they knew what to do with. They also proved that there is a world of difference between having a beard and just not bothering to shave ever.

And different sorts of music came from these people, folksier, rootsier, smellier tunes that, rather than the '59 Les Paul and Marshall stack and the 58-piece drum kit with Rank Organisation gong behind it, favoured things that went wheeze, whee, zooch, plink and, perhaps most significantly, plonk.

There were questions of scale to be considered, too. 'Pub rock' bands like Brinsley Schwarz, Kilburn and the High Roads, and Eggs Over Easy, had proved you could make wonderful music in ordinary trousers, build fantastic relationships with audiences, shift a few records and perhaps even survive financially playing modest venues about the place without hype, pizazz, pantechnicons full of gear, or private jets with built-in water beds.

Ronnie craved that ordinary trousers music.

Kate moved into Wick cottage, the place in the grounds of Woody's house, with Ronnie. In August, she gave birth to their son, Luke Kito Lane.

The next day, still drunk from the celebrations (he had crashed his car on the way back from the hospital), Ronnie went into Olympic Studios where his old friend Glyn Johns was working with Benny Gallagher and Graham Lyle, two Scottish musicians who had been founding members of McGuinness Flint.

At Glyn's request, Ronnie played a few of the things he'd been working on, including a folksy/English honky-tonk number called 'How Come?' that he'd written with Kevin Westlake, an Irish born drummer/guitarist/songwriter who'd been knocking about the music scene for years.

Glyn liked it, as did Gallagher and Lyle. They set about gathering a band of musicians to record it.

Steve Simpson, a fiddle/mandolin/guitar player who'd worked with various outfits including Joe Brown's short-lived Brown's Home Brew, was playing at the Barmy Arms in Twickenham, 'when a little guy in a green velvet drape jacket stepped up for a chat. He said he was making a record and asked whether I'd like to play on it. This guy turned out to be Ronnie Lane, who then loaded up his pockets with several bottles of barley wine and led me off to Wick Cottage, where he played me a rough of 'How Come?' and introduced me to Kate and one-week-old Luke.'

Other recruits included Billy Livsey, a keyboard player from St. Louis, Missouri; drummer Bruce Rowland, from Joe Cocker's Grease Band and Fairport Convention; the aforementioned Kevin Westlake; Benny Gallagher on piano accordion; Graham Lyle on mandolin; and Chris Stewart, another Irishman, formerly with Eire Apparent, on bass. Ronnie didn't want to play bass anymore. He'd recast himself as rhythm guitarist.

When the track was done, he took it to Billy Gaff, who, with Brian Hutch, had started a record label – GM Records. Mr Gaff said, 'Yes, please.'

★ ★ ★

Ronnie, always the mystic, felt he was being influenced by the spirit world. The pocket watch that his father had given him kept stopping. He would look at it and see it was wrong, so put it away, but then the next time he looked at it, it would show the right time, as if somebody had put it right. When he mentioned it to one of his and Kate's old Meher Baba gang, they sent him to a psychic called Dodo.

Russ Schlagbaum remembers that Ronnie went to see 'this tiny little creature who lived in East Twickenham in a huge old Victorian house that was as cold as a refrigerator. Dodo told Ronnie, 'There's someone from your past who's trying to get your attention, and he's using this watch as a means of doing so. He was a travelling showman; and I'm not quite sure what it was he wanted to tell.'

Oo-er. The fact that this 'someone from your past' was a showman and had been a traveller in Europe, convinced Ronnie (and Kate) that what had, up until now, been a vague notion, was, in fact, his true destiny.

When Ronnie told Brian Hutch at GM Records that he wanted to travel the country as a musical circus under a tent, Mr Hutch confirmed that it was all meant to be because Mr Hutch was Circus Boy, brought up under the big top with the smell of sawdust and elephant shit in his nostrils. His parents were still circus people, working in France. So, he could introduce Ronnie to all the right people, some of whom could ride two horses at once, standing up. Others had very large shoes.

ABOVE: 'Carrying 200lbs of velvet and satin around the stage for ninety minutes – that's man's work, let me tell you.'

ABOVE: Night after night, the Faces would nail your ass in your tracks

ABOVE: *Ooh La La* – every hotel mini bar, every airport lounge, every backstage boozer was left drained after the Faces left the building

RIGHT: Kate, Alana and Ronnie in the fortune tellers caravan, 've got a family now.'

ABOVE: One of Ronnie's shrewder investments, LMS – Lane's Mobile Studio. (Courtesy of Keith Smart)

ABOVE: The fire eaters, 'EL Zippos', were a couple called Johnny and Jackie. 'They had a volatile relationship.' (Courtesy of Drew McCulloch)

ABOVE: 'The idea of a tent was such a romantic thing. It's there one day and gone the next.'

ABOVE: Slim Chance in the garden at Fishpool – Charlie Hart, Colin Davey, Brian Belshaw, Steve Simpson and Ronnie

ABOVE: 'Me and Pete, we love each other a lot, but we rub each other up the wrong way, as well.'

ABOVE: 'My best mate was Eric: I can't remember how that all came about, but we were quite inseparabl[e]
for a while.'

ABOVE: Back stage at the ARMS Concert 1983 with Paul Rodgers, Eric Clapton, Glyn Johns, Andy
Fairweather Low, Jimmy Page, Bill Wyman, Kenney Jones, Jeff Beck, Charlie Watts and other luminaries

BOVE: Quizzing Andrew Loog Oldham about where all the money went

BOVE: Back with the old gang in 1993, 'It was an awkward situation.'

ABOVE: Ronnie and his third wife, Susan. 'I've seen more in my life than many people see in three of theirs.

And so, it came to pass. On 5 November 1973 – Guy Fawkes Night – Ronnie and his band appeared as part of the Penny for the Guy Festival in a Chipperfield's Circus tent on Clapham Common to debut their new act.

'Ronnie was amazing,' Graham Lyle said. 'He would come onstage and do that little step dance of his and everyone just loved him. He had something magic about him. He really did.'

'The press turned out in force,' drummer Bruce Rowland said. 'The circus people rose to the occasion, with clowns, jugglers, tiger cubs and lion cubs. The atmosphere was sensational, and the music swung unbelievably.'

When *Melody Maker* asked Ronnie how it had gone, he replied, 'Oh, a shambles. But if it had been more professional, it wouldn't have been as good. The idea for the show has been in my mind for ages, but now it has come together just at the right time.

'All the problems I thought would have been around, people have come along and said, "Oh, I can take care of that." It's really weird the way it's coming together.

'I could have got a band together and gone out doing the same sort of circuits as the Faces, and that would be very depressing. It had to be a complete change.

'It's horrible going over the same ground. And there seemed no end to it. I woke up one morning and thought: "When's it all going to end?' I'd been at it for eight years, and I still hadn't got around to singing any of me songs."

The single 'How Come?' by Ronnie Lane accompanied by the band Slim Chance was released on 16 November. On the 11th, they'd done a Peel session at Maida Vale Studios. Later in the month, Slim Chance appeared on TV for the first time on *The Russell Harty Show*.

The Mobile Studio was turning out to be a lovely little earner, too. The Who used it for some of the recording on *Quadrophenia*.

In December, Ronnie sold Wick Cottage to Woody for £40,000.

185

He and Kate moved into a caravan at the bottom of Pete Townshend's garden. Then Kate found a prospect in *Exchange and Mart* – a farm called Fishpool, near Hyssington, on the border of Shropshire and Montgomeryshire.

And thus, the East End tearaway became the Shropshire lad.

19

Wanting Leads Inevitably to Suffering

The Whole Earth Catalog was a publication that ran through various editions and provided a general guide to the counterculture – or the alternative society as it came to be known. Stuff you needed to buy or steal if you wanted to build a geodesic dome, a school or a lavatory, get on with nomadic Arabian tribes, survive an attack by an enraged bull, make a TV programme or hypnotise yourself. More specific instructions, in the UK, came from John Seymour's *The Complete Book of Self-sufficiency*, which provided invaluable information about crop rotation, beer and cheese making, basket weaving, rabbit skinning, tree pruning, electricity generation and respect for the land. In squats with bookshelves made from salvaged planks supported by house bricks wrapped in silver foil, copies of both books were as essential as an Indian musical instrument that nobody knew how to play and the smell of pachouli. They were the manuals of self-empowerment and though they didn't have much to say about how to run a band and set up tours without getting too involved with management, promoters, stars and breadheads, the spirit of the thing was all there.

Ronnie and Kate bought their farm in Wales, allegedly with a carrier bag full of cash, and it is generally agreed that they got royally ripped off and paid way over the odds for it. The farmhouse was practically derelict – they reckoned that it hadn't been touched for 50 years. The water came from a well at the top of the hill, the fences were all flattened to the ground and windowpanes were smashed.

But it was their dream.

'Yeah, it was ideal,' Ronnie said. 'We had to have it!'

The English border was a couple of fields away and the whole area was steeped in the sort of history that inspires mystics and mages. The quarries at nearby Corndon Hill provided the stone for ancient battle axes and stone circles. You could hardly walk more than a couple of miles in any direction without stumbling on a burial mound, a hill fort or a motte-and-bailey castle or tripping (in all senses of that word) over a ley line or two.

They renovated the three-bedroomed farmhouse to minimum living standards and brought the Mobile Studio down. There was a paddock, gardens with an orchard, stables and a rickety old barn, perfect for a rehearsal space. Visitors knew they'd come to the right place because Ronnie had nailed one of his old gold discs to the front door.

'The goal of each and every one is to attain the "no desire state",' Meher Baba said. 'This is the goal. Wanting leads inevitably to suffering. So, try your best to want less and less.'

On Valentine's Day, Ronnie was invited to join Jimmy Page, Keith Moon, John Bonham, Roy Harper and others – performing under the name of the Intergalactic Elephant Band – on the stage at the Rainbow in London's Finsbury Park, to celebrate the release of Harper's new album (and his 'resurrection' from an illness that had almost seen him off). This was who Ronnie was these days, then. A superstar among superstars.*

---

* Two tracks recorded that night turned up on Roy Harper's *Flashes from the Archives of Oblivion*, released later that year. The album caused a strike among female workers at the EMI factory in Hayes because the sleeve featured a picture of Roy naked except for a pair of Manchester City football socks.

At the beginning of 1974, Slim Chance appeared on *Top of the Pops* three times,* and 'How Come?' reached number 11 on the charts. The Faces' latest (and penultimate) single, 'Pool Hall Richard', out and about at around the same time, had peaked a few weeks earlier at number eight. The picture sleeve still showed Ronnie as a member of the band even though the track had been recorded at least a month after he left, with his replacement Tetsu Yamauchi on bass.

On 23 April Ronnie and Slim Chance got a BBC *In Concert* special, recorded at Golders Green Hippodrome. The band wheezed through old Faces numbers, like 'Flags and Banners', 'Ooh La La' and 'Last Orders Please', and newer Lane compositions, like 'Tell Everyone' and 'I've Done This Before'. Kate turned up to dance the can-can for the last number.

Back in Wales, work began on Slim Chance's first album. Chris Stewart, the bass player, had secured a gig with Joe Cocker and was replaced by Steve Bingham, who'd been with The Foundations.

'One day in the early part of 1974 I received a call from my good friend, the late great drummer Bruce Rowland,' Steve Bingham said. 'He had joined Ronnie Lane after Ronnie's departure from the Faces and his bass player Chrissy Stewart had recently joined up with Joe Cocker to tour America, leaving the band Slim Chance without a bass player. Ronnie himself was an excellent bass player both with the Small Faces and the Faces but he preferred to play rhythm guitar while singing lead vocals, hence the call from Bruce, who was someone I'd done many recording sessions within the past. I had recently recorded the album *Ennismore* and toured the country with Colin

---

* Alana Lane was told years later that, at that time, the barman's mum in the More Arms at Shelve wouldn't believe that Ronnie was actually a famous musician who was going to be on the telly (not just another bloke in the bar talking himself up). She challenged him to wear her brooch on his jacket next time he was performing. He did. If you squint at the YouTube footage of Ronnie singing 'How Come?' on *Top of the Pops* you can just about see it on his lapel.

Blunstone so it seemed like an ideal opportunity to join Slim Chance as I'd always been a fan of Ronnie's.

'I subsequently travelled with Bruce to Ronnie's Fishpool Farm on the borders of Shropshire and Montgomeryshire and met Ronnie and Kate at their small cottage in the middle of nowhere! The afternoon progressed with a visit to the local pub and then back to Ronnie's farm, where he showed me to my overnight accommodation, which was an old caravan with a leaking roof and no toilet in the farmyard!

'The following day I met up with the other guys who had joined Ronnie and they included Benny Gallagher and Graham Lyle, Billy Livsey, Jimmy Jewell and Kevin Westlake, and it proved to be the start of some great friendships as I actually ended up recording with all of those artistes as well as Ronnie.'

Bruce Rowland gave Steve a word of advice when he arrived.

'If you get offered any stew, just say you've eaten and then we'll go to the pub later to eat,' he said. 'Kate uses the same pot to boil his baby's nappies in as she uses to cook the stew.' This is strenuously denied by Kate – and to be fair it does sound like an urban myth. Alana remembers there being a pony in the kitchen – although this might not have been a permanent fixture.

'Kate was the consummate hippie chick,' Billy Livsey said, 'with potions to heal and strange meals.'

The accommodation that Kate and Ronnie offered to visiting musicians was rustic – usually in one of the old caravans dotted around – but the recording process was the perfect combination of hi-tech and down-home camaraderie.

'The bed was damp, and I had slept with most of my clothes on,' Steve Bingham said, 'but I was introduced to a way of recording that I'd never experienced before and indeed have never experienced since! There was an old barn with assorted instruments and amplifiers and a beautiful bullet-shaped mobile recording studio parked outside, which was ready and waiting to record anything we played, and I can remember standing around in a circle playing Ronnie's wonderful songs, and most of them were recorded on the first take as Ronnie was only interested in capturing the right vibe and feeling. The album was to become his first solo album entitled *Anymore for Anymore* and it's widely regarded as his finest work as a solo performer.'

Anybody passing might be roped in to help out on a cowbell or tambourine. The Tanner Brothers, builders working on the outbuildings, were pressed into service as backing singers.

Benny Gallagher ('Bring the family, and your mandolin') was lairy because he had two sets of twins and staying in a leaky caravan with four kids can provide the sort of material Dante used to write about. 'But it was great to wake up and go to the barn for recording.'

'It was a real commune attitude,' Graham Lyle said. 'Kate would be washing the clothes in a tub and putting them through a mangle. An enormous cauldron of soup sat on the fire from day to day.'

And, if Bruce Rowland was to be believed, the difference between tub and cauldron was largely academic.

'We recorded the album in a barn, surrounded by hay bales,' Billy Livsey said. 'The piano was out of tune half the time. We'd have a few pints in the pub, then wander back and start playing. Ronnie normally completed songs before we started recording so it was just a matter of getting the feel. Not sure if he aimed to be protective of his songs but he had a vision and we followed.

'All I remember was the boozy nights by the campfires outside. One night I thought I would shock everyone by climbing up the hill overlooking the farm and do a streak across the landscape with the road crew shining their torches at me. It made an underwhelming impression as they were all so pissed they didn't even notice. I sat down very disappointed until I realised I had sat in a pile of stinging nettles. Other nights were spent going down to the pub and then coming back to record in the barn. I never knew a more relaxing time recording.'

Stan, Ronnie's beloved dad, came to stay for a bit too, while mum went for a seaside holiday sponsored by the Multiple Sclerosis Society.

And in this relaxing, family-friendly, home-made, organic fashion, the album, *Anymore for Anymore*, came together.

The title track, a song co-written with Kate, had originally been composed, the music anyway, for the Faces back in 1972. Rod's comment on it at the time was, 'Who wrote this tripe?'

Seven of the eleven tracks were written either by Ronnie, or by Ronnie with Kevin Westlake or Kate. In addition, there were covers: of the old blues standard 'Careless Love'; of the music hall pub-singalong tear-jerker 'Just a Bird in a Gilded Cage'; Dave McEnery's 1939 song about the then recently lost aviatrix, 'Amelia Earhart's Last Flight'; and a heavily reconstructed version of banjo player Derroll Adams' 'Roll in Babe', in which Ronnie could pass for the *Nashville Skyline* Dylan.

Nearly all the album was made on the Lane Mobile, except for 'The Poacher' – an orchestral number recorded at Olympic. But something rather more ambitious than a home recorded album was coming together.

For a good while people had felt that the words 'rock'n'roll' and 'circus' should somehow go together. Maybe it all goes back to John Lennon finding a 19th-century poster advertising Pablo Fanque's Circus Royal, appearing in Rochdale, in a junk shop and turning it into the *Sgt. Pepper* track 'Being For The Benefit Of Mr. Kite!'

In 1968, *The Rolling Stones Rock and Roll Circus*, a TV special, never fully aired, featured strongmen and fire-eaters along with The Who, John Lennon, Eric Clapton, Jethro Tull and other notables playing in a fake big top set up on a soundstage. And, of course, in 1972, the Faces had toured the southern US with Free and a real-live circus.

'We had a couple of clowns, two girls on a motorbike; one driving it and one balancing this bloke who's really high up on this little pole,' Kenney said 'This motorbike kept going faster and faster in this small circle and doing all kinds of things.

'And there was this Chinese [woman] who was hoisted up to the ceiling by the roots of her hair. It was no messing around, it was her real hair. She went up there and started taking these half-dozen kimonos off.'

As well as sawdust and elephant shit, there is the smell of pagan/hippie/mysticism about circus. The ritual of sitting in a circle, witnessing acts so impossible as to be akin to magick – fire-eating, sword swallowing, tumbling, lions lying down with lambs – is as old at least as ancient Greece and could very spuriously be argued as having its roots in some ancient rite. 'Was Stonehenge originally covered in canvas?' Discuss.

It was there. In the zeitgeist. And its appeal to Ronnie was irresistible. He would take his music to the people, with an ever-changing group of musicians (the ever-changing nature was usually the result of their not being paid) and wear a spotty kerchief around his neck whenever possible. And the enterprise would be called the Passing Show, a name borrowed from Meher Baba, 'Except God, all things are a *passing show*. God is never changing; all else is ever changing.'

'Once the album was completed,' said Steve Bingham, 'Ronnie asked me if I'd like to join the band Slim Chance for a tour of the country in a circus tent, which became Ronnie Lane's Passing Show. It was the most amazing project and looking back on it I can only marvel at the courage Ronnie must have had to risk everything on backing such a huge undertaking, and it was both a privilege and an unforgettable experience which has now gone down in music business folklore and indeed it's never been attempted again to my knowledge.'

Kate had it all figured out.

'I had the idea of the Passing Show when I was about 15,' she said, 'because I'd read a book about a Victorian travelling show, and it had been whirring around in my head ever since. The original idea was that it all would be horse-driven and go round the country slowly. When I got together with Ronnie, I shared this idea with him, and he really liked it . . . So, I thought, well, what can we do, where can we take it? But he wasn't so keen on the horses.'

Kate's brother Paul Lambert was now working as Ronnie's press officer in two of Ronnie's companies – the one that managed the Lane Mobile, and Ronnie Lane Enterprises, which was tasked with organising the Passing Show.

'We're now in the process of buying a load of old single-decker London Transport buses, 'cos they're in good nick. We'll put bunks in and turn them into box offices,' Ronnie told *Melody Maker*. 'I've got a family now. I was given a family overnight. And I don't want to keep putting them second to the band. This way, at least we can all go together. The old lady will be dancing and working in the canteen. The kids will be working an' all.'

'Ronnie liked the old-fashioned vehicles,' Kate said, ''cos they've got noses! They really had character. Nothing could dent our spirits now. This was the beginning of our travelling circus.'

Larks ensued.

'It looked perfect on paper,' drummer Bruce Rowland said, ruefully.

'We got pawned off to the wrong people,' Russ Schlagbaum said. 'Ronnie first went to Chipperfield's, but they couldn't take it on. Then he asked Gerry Cottle who said, "I can't do it, but I know a fellow who has all this gear in storage. He's been off the road for a while." What he didn't say is that he'd been off the road for 20 fuckin' years!'

The man that Gerry Cottle passed Ronnie on to was Wally Lucken. In the fifties and sixties, Wally, with his brothers Arthur and Maurice, had run a travelling circus featuring the Amazing Arco ('see him lift 12 men!') Peppi and the International Clowns, the 'neat and tricky' Jan Francissca and 'Your Favourite Cowboy' Chick Rogers. There were also dogs dressed as French maids and the 'Royal Performing

Geese'. Whether Her Majesty the Queen had actually endorsed the geese is hard to establish.

Wally, like many who rubbed their hands at the sight of well-heeled hippies, charmed Ronnie and Kate with his tales from the sawdust ring and quickly grasped that neither had been taught to distinguish between shit and shoe polish. They paid £6,000 up front for a fleet of vehicles to transport the show around the country. The vans, Russ said, belonged in a museum. 'These vehicles – some dating back to the forties – had been stored in a barn for years. They pulled them out, shovelled 8in of dried chicken shit off them, slapped on some gaudy paint and that's what we were presented with.'

The Passing Show was to be staged in a 120ft x 80 ft elliptical tent, with everyone, the artists and technical staff (Andy Knight, sound engineer, Michael Hirst in charge of lighting and David Smith, maintenance engineer) living in ten caravans on site. The band would travel in private cars, and the gear in a box van driven by Russ.

Benny Gallagher and Graham Lyle had by this time pulled out of Slim Chance, and the hunt was on for replacements. At the Marquee Club, Billy Gaff came upon Robin Lucas and Drew McCulloch. They had not long moved to London from Ayrshire, had signed to British Lion Music, and had toured with the likes of John Martyn and The Pretty Things.

'At the time Robin played guitar, and I played guitar and keyboards,' Drew said. 'We were invited round to Billy's house, and he played us a few Slim Chance tracks. There was one problem in our mind. Benny and Graham played an assortment of instruments, mandolin, banjo and accordion all now an integral part of the sound, and we had never played them in our lives! So, we did what had to be done; we lied and said we could play all these things! We then went round to a studio next to Wardour Street (I think), where Ronnie was putting the finishing touches to 'The Poacher'. A few beers later, the deal was done, Ronnie introduced us to Kenny Slaven, the eccentric Scottish fiddle player he had found playing in a restaurant somewhere. Kenny was brilliant; he had really set the scene for 'The Poacher' with some stunning multi-tracked fiddle parts. We got on like a house on fire.

'OK,' said Ronnie, 'you're in.'

'Fine, when are the rehearsals?'

'Rehearsals! We don't bother with rehearsals. The first gig is in Marlow – we'll see you there!'

'Marlow was about three weeks ahead. We immediately went out and bought a mandolin, a banjo and an accordion, and spent the next three weeks learning how to play them. I played keyboards anyway, but the accordion was like playing a piano on its side, which took some getting used to.'

Their introduction to life with the Passing Show seems to have been par for the course.

'I can't remember the names of the circus people who met us,' Drew McCulloch said, 'but they took us into their caravan, gave us tea in the dirtiest cups I had ever seen, and made us very welcome.'

The 'circus people' were the owners of the tent, all of whom were also clowns, fire-eaters and possibly lion tamers.

Elsewhere, Ronnie and Kate had an old palm-reader's gypsy caravan that he'd acquired somewhere. Chris Welch of *Melody Maker* was treated to a guided tour. 'Inside the caravan, actually planted on a modern transporter to save its tired old wheels, was a bizarre world of tiny knick-knacks, drapes, mementos, a large bed for Master Lane and his good lady. It looked like the 19th century in miniature.'

And so, at the start of what was to be the wettest summer for 30 years, the whole ensemble limped along to Marlow in Buckinghamshire and set up the tent on the local football team's training pitch.

'There was a tinker some way back in my family's history,' Ronnie said. 'And the Lanes used to travel some distance as haulage, y'know, heavy duty? And me dad was a long-distance lorry driver.

'I always seemed to like travelling around, that's for sure. I get itchy

196

feet pretty quick. That's why I never built the studio in any one place. I thought, soon as you build it, you'll want to move.'

Keith Altham, Ronnie's friend and former PR man, remembered, 'Ronnie Lane fell in love with the Romany way of life from the days when he used to bunk off school to work for the travelling fairs that graced our English village greens.' Which is a romantic way of describing Ronnie's brief experience at Battersea fun fair, but then Keith, like all good PR people, was skilled in embroidery. 'He would ride the bumper cars, collecting the fares. He loved that whole concept of travelling and moving on that went with the gypsy way of life.'

'We were on the Chicken Shit Express, all very nostalgic,' Kate said. 'I organised the can-can girls – me, Russ Schlagbaum's girlfriend Barbara and Josie Livsey, the wife of our American keyboard player Billy. I got us costumes from Sotheby's, so we looked like a cross between those girls in Degas and Toulouse-Lautrec paintings. The audiences loved us, and the level went up once we arrived for 'Ooh La La' and 'Ain't No Lady'.'

Ronnie had hired a Scottish comedian called Bill Barclay (Kate: 'He was a bit like Billy Conolly.') to open the show.

'Bill was a great character, and we decided that the Scottish contingent should share a caravan. By the end of the tour the caravan was a wreck!' Drew said. 'Bill had thrown Robin out of a window for a joke. A fire extinguisher had been thrown in through another window for another joke.'

In a moment of either folly or inspiration Ronnie asked Vivian Stanshall, lately of the Bonzo Dog Doo-Dah Band, to act as ringmaster and general master of ceremonies. Celebrated for his erratic behaviour and for rarely drawing a sober breath, Viv didn't last long.

'One episode I remember was when Viv came into our caravan for a "wee drinkie",' Drew said. 'He had already had several wee drinkies. Kenny Slaven had bought two Fender Twin reverb amplifiers, with an Echoplex machine. He was trying out some weird fiddle effects in the caravan when Viv came in, drink in hand, and sat on an amp, spilling drink over it.

'Do you mind not sitting on my new amp?' said Kenny.

'Terribly sorry, old bean!' says Viv, who then staggers to his feet, and falls on top of Kenny's fiddle – breaking it into the bargain.

'It took us about two hours to convince Viv that he should visit Kevin Westlake's caravan, where the drink was much better.'

This seemed to work. But the next morning an irate Kevin confronted Kenny and Drew. Soon after arriving at Kevin's caravan, Viv had crashed out. Kevin left him to sleep it off and eventually went to bed himself.

In the middle of the night, he was awakened by strange unearthly scrabblings and trumpetings. Viv no longer lay where he had been left.

'Kevin traced the noise to a walk-in cupboard,' Drew said. 'When he opened the door there was Viv, trousers at his ankles, saying, "You don't have any toilet paper do you, old bean?"'

Viv disappeared from the tour shortly after.

Finally, they opened. There were problems, the most pressing of which was the PA system, which had just arrived from America and had been delivered with the wrong leads.

When Ronnie took to the stage, all the microphones went dead, one by one. But Ronnie could handle adversity.

Billy Livsey, the keyboard player said of Ronnie, 'Never known a performer like him. He would go onstage absolutely tanked on barley wine, and he'd stare into the crowd with a smile on his face and the gig would become an instant party.'

Music was made. Songs sung. People had a good time. The show went on for over three hours – so it was well worth the admission price of just over a pound and only ended, according to Ronnie, when a man from the council turned up to say there'd been complaints from the neighbours about the noise and the disruption.

The show followed the circus tradition of opening on a Monday night and playing all week before the top was dismantled and the whole shebang travelled to the next venue on the Sunday. Accordingly, on the Sunday, everything went on the road to Bath.

In no time at all, the decrepit trucks began to die.

Russ Schlagbaum was driving a 1947 Bedford flatbed, towing his caravan. 'I never even got down the motorway. I pulled in to the first service area and went into the garage and told the mechanic, 'I don't know what's wrong but start by changing the points and plugs.' The guy pulled out a spark plug and said, 'I've been a mechanic for 25 years and I've never seen one like this.' I finally managed to coax the fucker to the Bath site. I was fuming because I'd spent all fuckin' night just to travel 100 miles . . .'

Miraculously, they all arrived in Bath. But immediately they were beset by yet more problems.

'The fire service was the hardest thing to contend with,' Ronnie said. 'When we got to Bath the guy wasn't going to let us go on because we only had four fire buckets. And the extinguisher wasn't good enough.

'So just before they were going to close the show, Bath Arts Council turned up and lent us a fire engine. Should have seen it. Next time the fire inspector turned up we said: 'We've got our own fire engine, it's round the back.'

'So, we took him round and there were a couple of geezers with long hair, standing there in old jeans with fire helmets on, looking all pale and wan, by this bleeding old fire engine. So, we snapped our fingers – show 'em boys! And this miserable squirt of water came out the hose. The inspector walked off shaking his head – he'd had enough. He let the show go on.

'So, we thought – what a great ruse and talked 'em into coming round the country with us on their fire engine. As it turned out, the fire engine was the biggest fire risk on the show. It kept blowing up.'

Wally Lucken, who'd supplied the main body of sick and lame vehicles, had also hired a beefy, bearded circus old hand by the name of Captain Peter Hill, former professional wrestler and lion tamer, as a mechanic for the dilapidated fleet of trucks and 'tent master'.

Fiddle player Kenny Slaven admired Captain Peter's style. 'Peter broke a tow bar going up the M6 and stopped near an exit to cut down a "give way" sign and weld it into shape as a tow bar. The police pulled up and asked him what the hell he was up to. "Well," (in his Hampshire accent) "as you can see, I'm cutting up this 'give way' sign to make it into a tow bar". Just as they were taking out their notebooks to take notes, he told me he took out his show-man's licence and flashed it at them. They crossed themselves and cleared off.'

Kate remembers the Captain saying to the policemen, after they challenged him, 'Well it's no use to you now, is it? So, if I were you, I would just turn a blind eye and walk away.'

'We had a lorry towing a lorry, towing a caravan; a Range Rover towing a bus, towing a caravan,' Ronnie said. 'And the law used to come along, and they couldn't believe this . . . THING coming along. So, we had a ruse. We had a tent-man called Captain Hill, a total pirate, big geezer with a red beard. And whenever we got pulled up by the law, we'd snake up, all over the road, jamming the road both ways, and this geezer would get out and start arguing. The law would see this jam building up and shout: "Get going, get going!" And we got away with it.'

The Captain knew how to erect the tent, stack the seating and how to work the generators. He knew that the contents of the cara-vans had to be offloaded into a septic tank every day or the whole site would stink like a cesspit.

'He knew everything about the circus,' bass player Steve Bingham said, 'so he was in charge of the clowns – whom the band hated because they were so useless – the fire-eaters and the dancing girls.'

'The fire-eaters, "EL Zippos", were a couple called Johnny and Jackie,' Kate said. 'They had a volatile relationship.'

The clowns – who according to Kenny Slaven were 'so hopelessly inadequate that they were caricatures of themselves' and, according to Kate, 'so unfunny they reached a point of brilliance' – were sent ahead to the next town to put up posters and hand out flyers to drum up interest. But they didn't seem to have bothered, because when the circus reached the next venue, people seemed very surprised to see them and nobody had bought tickets.

Audiences dwindled as the procession moved further north.

It's hard to pinpoint the exact course of the Passing Show's itinerary all these years later but they seemed to have played at Shrewsbury, Chester Racecourse (where according to Russ there were only 15 in the audience), Sheffield, Carlisle, Falkirk and, lastly, Newcastle Town Moor.

Singer-songwriter Norman Lamont (no relation to the politician) was one of the happy few who showed up when the circus limped into Scotland. He wrote about it in his blog.

'Ronnie Lane's Passing Show, his rock'n'roll circus, gave me one of the most magical nights I've ever had at a gig. It fetched up in Falkirk, on a green in the town centre, one evening in 1974. I had seen one of the few adverts and was among the small audience who turned up under the big top for a range of acoustic support acts, ringmaster, dancing girls and clowns, followed by Ronnie's band. I've been to many gigs where the love generated from audience to performer was almost tangible, but this was one where audience and performer were joined in joy at the sheer delight and craziness of being together under canvas, smelling the grass (not that kind of grass this time), and knowing that tomorrow, just about no one else will believe this.

'Little Ronnie, a huge acoustic strapped round him, glittered in the lights and his unstoppable grin filled the tent. I had to leave before the end for the last train to Glasgow and as I dragged myself to the tent door, I looked back at him and knew that I was a Ronnie Lane fan forever.'

Life on the road in leaky caravans playing to audiences that barely made double figures eventually takes its toll.

'We got pissed a lot,' Jimmy Jewell, the sax player, said. 'He'd buy us bottles of Blue Nun – horrible stuff – where it was Guinness, barley wine and a bottle of Courvoisier for Ronnie. I got fed up because I was dragging my wife and child in a broken-down caravan and getting paid 30 quid a week. It was this thing about, "Let's all be gypsies, but you lot can be gypsies on no money." It was very romantic for him, but not so romantic for the rest of us.

'I had asked for a pay rise. He said no. So, I said, "Enough."'

Jimmy's wife used to sell the tickets in the box office and when they got to Scotland Jimmy and his family left after the evening's performance – with the week's takings, leaving a note. 'Goodbye cruel circus,' it said, 'I'm off to join the world.'

Shep, Ronnie's dog, was a constant source of mayhem. He liked rounding things up. It was in his nature. Every time he saw more than two of anything he felt obliged to herd them. Not such a problem when the objects in question were dustbins say, or trees, but in Falkirk they encountered a police horse training unit. The horses did not take kindly to being rounded up and neither did their riders.

After Scotland – about halfway through the planned itinerary – they moved south to Newcastle. By then they'd done seven weeks and 23 shows. On the way, the engine of the 1947 GUY GS bus blew up. Undeterred, they set up the tent on Newcastle Town Moor and played three shows to an average audience of ten people a night. A decision was made.

'I didn't have any more money, it's as simple as that,' Ronnie said later. 'We were flogging everything in the end just to buy enough diesel to move the show, and I always seemed to be arguing with local fire officers and local authorities over regulations they claimed I was infringing.

'We broke every regulation at one point or another. If a guy came around and said we'd broken a law I'd call over someone and say, '"You're fired", and then they'd be happy. We fired the same guy about 20 times.'

Everybody, not just Ronnie, lost money.

Bruce Rowland, his friend and drummer said: 'I lost about four-and-a-half grand, a lot of money in those days. Everything was broken and we had to bring it home. I took a 40ft caravan down the M1 with a Land Rover, then went back to Newcastle on the train and drove the pantechnicon down. It had two gears, no reverse, back brakes only, and no starter. I drove between 5mph and 10mph most of the way. It took me three days.'

'The only thing that stopped it being a financial success was lack of publicity,' Steve Bingham said. 'But to those fans who actually attended the gigs it was something they would never forget, and indeed I still get people asking me to sign ticket stubs from the 1974 tour just because I was actually there! We played as far south as Bath in Somerset and as far north as Falkirk in Scotland, with the tour eventually grinding to a halt on Town Moor Newcastle. Many of the vehicles had mechanical problems and they eventually limped home to Shropshire, and that was the end of the Passing Show. Sadly there is no video footage of any of the performances but in a funny sort of way that makes it even more mystical.'

Kate, looking back on it, said: 'Of course it went tits up, but I was glad it did. Added to the fun. It lost a lot of money though, which scarred Ronnie 'cos this was his dream.'

And so it was.

'At the time,' he said, 'I had quite a bit of money that [the Faces] made over in America. I thought I'd try something out with it. I put on a show in a tent . . . in a big top, you know? . . . and I took it around this country and lost all my money!

'The idea of a tent was such a romantic thing. It's there one day and gone the next. You can chuck up such an illusion in that time and space. I wanted to do that. I want people to remember it. Even when it's just a stained patch on the grass.'

Some of the stained patches on the grass are probably still there after all these years. But that's Viv Stanshall for you.

20

Melodious Winos

Meanwhile, back in the real world, GM Records had released Slim Chance's second single, 'The Poacher'.

'The idea for 'The Poacher' came to me when I was living in a fortune teller's caravan by the side of the River Thames in Pete Townshend's back garden,' Ronnie said.

It is a fine example of gentle British pastoralism, a rejection of materialism and glitz a million miles away from 'Stay with Me', and, with its orchestral arrangement, not particularly close to 'How Come?' either, or the fun-with-a-home-made-circus. 'The Poacher' was a prayer to a salmon 'bigger than a newborn child'. Like Mac said of his old bandmate, 'Ronnie was prone to gazing off into the middle distance sometimes.'

'Ronnie created something unique in British music – a genuine form of native country music,' John Pidgeon, music writer and fan, wrote, ' – no capital letters, no inverted commas, just music that came out of this country and couldn't conceivably be created anywhere else.'

'It would have been a hit had it not been for the BBC technicians' strike at the time,' Kevin Westlake said. 'We turned up to do *Top of the Pops* only to be told there wouldn't be any show for a few weeks by which time the record was dead.'

Without the television exposure it needed (Ronnie sang it only once on TV, on London Weekend Television's *Supersonic* in January 1976) the song stalled at number 36 before disappearing.

Ronnie put on a brave face. 'It's only a game. I find the singles market totally like . . . stupid. It's a bit of muscle to your arm, that's all. I think albums matter a little more.'

The album *Anymore for Anymore* was released on 26 July, ten days after the Passing Show had limped back to Fishpool.

'I don't really know what to say about the new album. I think it has its moments,' Ronnie told *Melody Maker*. 'I wouldn't say it's the greatest album I'll ever make, I know all its mistakes. I know all the bad points.'

It was well reviewed but sneaked into the Top 50 for one week only. It was, it has to be said, up against some tough competition. Paul McCartney's *Band on the Run* was at number one, and Mike Oldfield's then ubiquitous *Tubular Bells* at number two, with Elton John, Stevie Wonder, Pink Floyd and Gary Glitter also riding high.

Part of the problem was that Billy Gaff, still Ronnie's manager, was engaged in complex transatlantic contractual negotiations for Rod. 'He was like doing a Dr. Kissinger, backwards and forwards to America all the time.'

He didn't put any resources into promoting Ronnie's album. Billy found Ronnie's attitude problematic – Ronnie always hated his managers – although his feelings didn't go as deep as they had for Andrew Loog Oldham and Don Arden.

GM Records would fold shortly, anyway.

The band that Ronnie had taken on tour fell away, too.

'I was ready for a change,' Billy Livsey said, 'and moved on to recording and being a member of Gallagher and Lyle's band. Looking back, it was fun; I wouldn't change it for the world and loved my time with Ronnie. He was the ultimate showman but sadly the outside world didn't recognise him at the time.'

'I'm just going to try to get a totally different band together now,' Ronnie said. 'I don't think it'll ever pay the dividends of running round huge halls playing to thousands of people for a load of bread but that's not what I'm after anyway. I'd far rather enjoy myself and enjoy my life than run after that sort of thing. It depends on what you want. I'm not disillusioned.'

Thankfully the Lane Mobile was still making money. Bad Company, Rick Wakeman and Rory Gallagher were among the many artistes to use it that year.

It wasn't long before Ronnie started putting his new band together.

Brian Belshaw, formerly a bandmate of Kevin Westlake's in Blossom Toes, was recruited to play bass. A friend, Ruan O'Lochlainn, keyboard and saxophone player originally with Bees Make Honey, had recently formed a band called St James Gate with Charlie Hart (keyboards and fiddle) and Steve Simpson (guitar, mandolin, fiddle). The second incarnation of Slim Chance was taken largely from St James Gate.

'Ruan went to talk to Ronnie to see if maybe we could join forces,' Charlie Hart said, 'and Ronnie looked interested by the proposal. We met up and played some songs with him, but the problem was he had his own bass player. Ruan was very good so he managed to "sell me" to Ronnie: "You know, Charlie can play a lot of instruments, keyboards, fiddle." My test came when accordion was needed and Ronnie just threw one at me, I realised it was my test. I'd never played accordion in my life, and I played well enough to stay in the band. I enjoy playing different instruments and Ronnie didn't want any virtuoso players, everything with him was about the intent.'

Around this time Ronnie switched management too. After a couple of false starts, he landed with EG Management, a company set up by David Enthoven and John Gaydon, two proper chaps whom Bryan Ferry described as 'gentlemen at play. They had their Harley-Davidsons, and they were like public schoolboy Hells Angels with their leather jackets and cowboy boots.'

David Enthoven brokered a deal with fellow Harrovian and boss of Island Records Chris Blackwell.

Blackwell, a scion of the Crosse & Blackwell empire (manufacturers of fine soups and tangy mayonnaise), had been brought up in Jamaica, where he had fallen in love with and began to record the music – ska and later rocksteady and reggae. He set up Island Records in 1959. Eventually the label came to sign Bob Marley, Roxy Music, John Martyn, U2, Alexei Sayle and a clutch of other superstars. In 1988, the label was sold to Polygram for $300 million.

Moving to Island, however, was not so great for Ronnie. He liked Chris Blackwell very much but didn't rate the rest of the staff. 'The others I knew from when I was in the Small Faces. They were tea boys then and by 1976 they were heads of the company. They couldn't run a piss-up in a brewery.'

Nevertheless, with Slim Chance Mk II, he started work on his new album, parking the Lane Mobile in the grounds of Stargroves, the stately home that Mick Jagger claims he bought when he was on an acid trip in 1970 for £55,000. To save a few bob, Ronnie recorded over the master tapes of *Anymore for Anymore* and had the whole thing done and dusted in two weeks.

In November, Island released their first Ronnie Lane single, a touching 'sorry' song, 'What Went Down (That Night with You)', with Ronnie singing at his plaintive best. He and the band did a telly (albeit Thursday teatime) and a Peel session, but the single didn't get much airplay and never charted.

Ronnie ended the year playing for the Island Christmas party – a poorer man but wiser.

The new album, called either *Ronnie Lane* or *Ronnie Lane's Slim Chance*, depending on which bit of the sleeve/label you're looking at, was released in February 1975. It presented a wonderfully eclectic selection of songs. Countryish originals written either by Ronnie or in collaboration with members of the band made up the backbone, along with jaunty rock'n'roll classics like 'Blue Monday', 'You Never Can Tell', a pub piano version of 'I'm Gonna Sit Right Down and Write Myself a Letter' and a sentimental/drunk take on the classic (probably best known from the Harry Belafonte version) 'I'm Just a Country Boy'.

Two of the songs were co-written with Kate – 'Tin and Tambourine', a song that, after spending a short time channelling the Sons of the Pioneers, tips a proud hat to Dylan's *Nashville Skyline* with an arrangement so replete with mandolins, accordions and mouth-harps that it sounds as though the entire contents of the Hobgoblin music store has been thrown at it, and 'Ain't No Lady', a sweet number with a 12-bar blues chorus that features some wonderful, not to say surprising, soprano sax solos, about losing your heart to a woman who's been, 'looking like a cowboy and there ain't no horse 'round'.

Though it didn't quite set the world on fire at the time, the album has, down the years, acquired some discerning admirers. Many (including the writers of this book) consider it his best album.

And in 2017, Billy Bragg wrote in the *New Statesman*, 'The photo within the gatefold sleeve shows Ronnie standing with the band against what looks like an old barn wall. Lane's long sideburns, drape coat and scarf give him the look of the dodgy outsider in a Hardy novel who ultimately wins the day by pulling the squire from the mill pond. With mandolin, violin, accordion and Dobro guitar to the fore, this band, under Lane's direction, created something seldom heard in British pop.'

The poor sales understandably irked Ronnie. At gigs, fans told him they weren't able to get hold of a copy. When Ronnie reported this back to the record company, their answer was that unless the album was in the charts, they couldn't persuade the record shops to order any copies.

It didn't get much airplay, either. They did a couple of tracks – 'Anniversary' and 'You Never Can Tell' – for BBC Two's *Old Grey Whistle Test*, but not much else.

Ronnie's thoughts strayed to the Passing Show. In retrospect, he reckoned the biggest problem wasn't the transport blowing up, the poor sound system or the lack of publicity, but the timing – 'If I had taken the Passing Show across London in a series of four or five dates it would have been really successful. With hindsight I should have done a regular tour last year, and done the Passing Show this year.'

Instead, they did the Passing Show last year and something vaguely approaching a 'regular' tour at the start of 1975 in low-key venues – colleges, civic halls, ballrooms. This dismayed him, too.

'Most of the halls we've been playing on this tour have been appalling. It's either bad acoustics, or the stage is too small, and you're separated from the audience by an orchestra pit, or there's been a fight there the night before and the atmosphere's lousy.

'There are so many obstacles to overcome that the band is only working to half its true capacity all the time. It's not fair on the audience, it's not fair on us, and quite honestly I'm tired of it all. I'll do it, but only with a view to getting the Passing Show together again. But just to get caught in it, doing tour after tour, without it going anywhere or turning into anything – that's when it pisses me off . . .'

'Ronnie's approach was very much: don't get too hung up on the musical niceties,' Charlie Hart said, 'you are there to entertain . . . He was actually a precursor of a lot of bands like The Levellers and The Pogues.'

Kate often went along to the gigs, if only so she could get some wear out of the can-can costume she'd bought for the Passing Show.

There was a bit of a turn-up at the University of Exeter. When Ronnie and Slim Chance returned to the stage for their encore, they were followed by none other than Steve Marriott, who picked up a nearby guitar and pounded out the intro to 'All or Nothing'.

Steve Clarke of *NME* was there.

'So what if things aren't quite in tune?' he wrote. 'It's great to hear Marriott singing that song on a stage, Ronnie Lane standing right next to him. It's all over and the two break FA rules by hugging and kissing [there had been attempts at the time to stop players "kissing, hair-ruffling, hugging and body-hoisting" after goals]. They leave the stage for three more numbers, 'Whatcha Gonna Do About It', 'Honky Tonk Women' and 'Going Down'. The band are surprisingly tight, rocking like bitches for the last song. Marriott swears at the audience – after all this is the first time the two of them have been on stage for years and they want some response. They get it, and finish with the curiously apt '30s song 'Side by Side'.'

Despite the kissing and camaraderie, the incident, like most other things, irked Ronnie. He was embarrassed when Steve hijacked the set.

'I like showing off, doing a song and shaking a leg on stage, but I don't want to play all those silly games that go on anymore. Stardom – it's not even real. All right, let the little girls' magazines say it's glamorous and all that, but Christ, we're grown men, aren't we? We should know better.'

There was a subsequent attempt at a reconciliation when Steve came to stay at Ronnie's farm for three days' straight drinking, one night to the point where Steve passed out having locked himself in the bathroom, and Kate had to climb through a window to check if he was still alive.

Charlie Hart (keyboards and fiddle) moved into Fishpool for 18 months, during which time he grew very close to Ronnie, despite their different backgrounds. Charlie was from Oxford. His dad was a professor of philosophy. Perhaps the friendship was not so surprising when one takes into account Ronnie's insatiable curiosity – especially for all things philosophical.

'He wanted to do something different,' Charlie said, 'go into new territory, and have someone in the band who was philosophically minded. Ronnie was that way as well; he was interested in what words mean, the afterlife, spirituality, philosophical questions.'

Steve Simpson, guitar, mandolin, harmonica, lived for an entire summer in a tent pitched in Ronnie's top field. He described Fishpools as 'a parallel universe . . . a different kind of world'.

The new Slim Chance had already run through a couple of drummers (Jim Franks and Glen Le Fleur). 'As I told John Peel, we seem to go through drummers like a dose of liver salts.'

Finally, in March, they found Colin Davey. Colin had been doing mainly session work for a while and was keen to be touring again. He spent some time at Fishpools, too: 'It was like being in a wonderland. I slept in an old bus. We had no water to wash.'

The fact that he noticed should be ample evidence that some drummers, despite what you hear, are not strangers to soap and water.

At the end of March, Island released another single, a knockout version of 'Brother, Can You Spare a Dime?' replete with wailing fiddles, guitars and saxes. The song had been written during the Great Depression and has been recorded by everybody from Bing Crosby to George Michael and Tom Waits. Ronnie's version was used on the soundtrack of a two-hour BBC Two documentary about the Depression, directed by Philippe Mora and produced by Sandy Lieberson and David Puttnam and aired at the end of March.

'I really feel for that song,' Ronnie said. 'Some of the words are quite embarrassing, especially the middle eight – that "once in khaki suits, boy, we looked swell" business – but I love the sentiment of the song. Songwriting to me is sentiments; you try and encapsulate a sentiment in something.'

And, in *Sounds* magazine: 'Why didn't I think of putting out 'Brother, Can You Spare A Dime?' a long time ago? I've always loved the song and wanted to record it. But if I'd put it out without it being the soundtrack of a film people would have thought "Come on . . ." But because it's a soundtrack it makes it acceptable. That's a silly game. All these rules and restrictions . . .'

Again, the single didn't make the Top 50.

That summer Ronnie bought a cottage next to Fishpool, which

brought Ronnie's estate up to 100 acres. Stan, Ronnie's brother, had broken up with his wife Sandra, so Sandra moved into the cottage with her and Stan's daughter, Lisa, and worked for Ronnie, doing his bookkeeping and accounts. Lisa, who was six at the time, loved it. She had playmates in Alana and Luke. The school bus used to pick them up every morning and take them to the little village school at Church Stoke.

And they always got on with the neighbours.

'We used to hang out at the Miners Arms,' Charlie Hart said, 'just a mile or so from the farm the other side of the hill. All the locals drank in there. There were some amazing, hilarious characters and Ronnie knew them already. Because it's Shropshire border country they're not prejudiced or insular. They were used to working with newcomers and just took Ronnie and us lot on board. We used to entertain them too; the after-hours lock-ins were notorious and often involved a song or three. It was very idyllic, like Ronnie had found his place in this beautiful part of the world.'

But it must be borne in mind that, as Alana said: 'Shropshire folk only respect you if you respect them.'

'Ronnie threw himself into farming 100 per cent,' Kate said. 'Just like he did with everything. Every day was market day somewhere in the vicinity and market day meant the pubs were open all day. He figured out that in order to get in with all the farming gentry he should attend all the farm sales – especially the livestock ones. He decided he needed animals. One of the first sorties he made was in Welshpool [in Powys]. I was with him on that occasion. It was very nice. We started at the Oak and struggled on to the auction and he put his hand up here and there and it was all very good and then we went back to the Oak and then we went on to the Compass, as it was on the way home. And I think the Miners got a look-in before we landed up back at home.

'Ronnie had bought a flock of sheep. This was going to be day one of farming. The next morning started early – there was a terrible cacophony outside the bedroom window. Our fabulous neighbours were standing there with at least 100 ewes. They were milling around the garden – or what was supposed to be our garden. So, we said, "Come on, Farmer Lane, get up and sort it out!" He didn't have a clue. But we did have a sheepdog, Shep [who'd won some experience, as has been mentioned, rounding up police horses]. He was a bloody good sheep dog.'

One of the neighbours, Clive Powsenby, used to see Ronnie in the Three Tuns in Bishop's Castle, 'either playing darts in the public bar or deep in conversation with people looking suspiciously like poachers and horse traders. He seemed at ease and in his element.'

In the summer, there was usually a fire in the yard. People would gather with bottles and instruments. If something musically promising happened to develop, they'd fire up the Lane Mobile Studio and get it down. And it was always best if Ronnie's loyal engineer Ron Fawcus, 'meticulous and long-suffering', was on hand to lace the tape up properly and remember which buttons you had to press.

'Lots of bands recorded in it,' Kate said, 'The Stray Cats, The Pretenders . . . it was great because they would all be sitting around and when they got inspired they could capture the moment by going into the LMS [Lane Mobile Studio] and record it. Ron Fawcus was always in there. Everyone was relaxed and there was no pressure.'

On 13 September Ronnie and Kate got married.

Both the bride and groom wore white, Ronnie in a white suit with brown and white co-respondent shoes, Kate in a floor-length tiered creation with arms full of bangles and her waist-length hair loose and flowing. The reception was at the Miners Arms and the whole thing was filmed by Keith Benjamin, who went on to produce a retrospective of Ronnie's career for local TV. Les Caulfield, who owned nearby Woodgate Farm and was an honorary uncle to Luke when he was little, was Ronnie's best man.

Ronnie wrote a special song – 'Steppin' and Reelin' (The Wedding)' – which would later appear on the album *One for the Road*.

'Kate supplied a lot of the imagery and ideology for Ronnie's work,' Charlie Hart said. 'It wasn't successful commercially so it's easy to say he was led astray. But it was very successful from a cultural point of view. Lots of people followed, so it was seminal.'

Yet, despite the rural idyll he was living, Ronnie was still haunted by the idea of the Passing Show.

'I'm a traveller,' he told *Sounds* journalist Mick Brown. 'I don't like the word 'gypsy' – it's over-used. But I'm far happier when I'm on the road than when I'm at home getting cluttered up with things. I prefer to be a stranger travelling through a situation than to have neighbours and be gossiped about. I couldn't cope with living in a suburb. I get claustrophobic driving through a suburb. I get a terrible feeling that my car's going to break down and I'm going to get stuck there.'

He tried to persuade the posh boys at his management company, EG, to stump up some money to get the Passing Show back on the road, 'But they laughed!'

They did, however, put some money into a new album, *One for the Road*, all recorded on the Lane Mobile, impeccably produced by Chris Thomas and engineered by Ron Fawcus and George Chkiantz.

This time, all the tracks were written by Ronnie, except the instrumental 'Harvest Home', which he wrote with Charlie Hart. 'And we celebrated by sowing a whole field of barley,' Charlie said, 'Ronnie on the tractor, me riding on the sowing machine behind.'

'Harvest Home' was a number that I wrote for a lady who died,' Ronnie said. 'Her name was Mrs Caulfield. She lived down the road from my farm, and she died, and it was really weird. It was very hot that summer, extremely hot. It was night time, and it got dark. Of course, in the summer it gets dark very late. I went to a pub, and someone told me she'd died. I couldn't believe it . . . well, I could believe it, but it knocked me about a bit. I came out of the pub, and it was dark, and all of the tractors were coming up from the fields with their lights on, and their carts all filled with hay, bringing the harvest home. I was just very choked, and I went home, and I wrote 'Harvest Home'. Yup.'

One for the Road is, again, best described as 'eclectic' – mostly countryish, shades of Dylan are there, along with Emmylou Harris, Daniel Lanois, Commander Cody and His Lost Planet Airmen, and (if it can be believed, on the title track) Bruce Springsteen.

Released at the end of January 1976, the cover shot shows them all arranged among Ronnie's motley collection of vehicles, including the GUY bus and 'Queenie', the palm-reader's caravan.

Like the others before it, the album was critically well received with phrases like 'rootsy rowdiness' and 'twangy country weepers' being bandied around, but with very little airplay or publicity, it didn't sell as well as the previous two albums, and their sales had been average to diabolical.

Ronnie told *Melody Maker*: 'In a way the album has been a documentary on the last eight months.

'This is just an album. It's no big deal – just a bunch of songs. But these days you're supposed to make a big deal out of it. But I've got no big speech to make. I live the way I do, and if I can't make this business into my life, then I'll leave it. I really will. I'm giving it another six months.'

'Much as musicians hate to be categorised,' Charlie Hart said, 'somehow it has to happen or the powers that be don't know which category to sell you in. The same goes for investment. That is what Ronnie needed. He needed managerial guidance and he needed investment to explore what he was doing. Even so, in that short period of time he came up with some amazing stuff, stuff that is now classic, it really is. Proper craftsman.

'It used to frustrate me because I realised that with a bit more of a push, we could have had hit singles – we weren't far off it, but you had to really play the game.

'And Ronnie didn't help. A journalist would show up and he would get him sloshed and then take the mickey out of him all night. Well, yes, get him sloshed but don't take the mickey. I would think, "Come on Ronnie, we are trying to get a hit single off the ground here." And in the end, it didn't work because the money did not come in.

'In some respects, Ronnie was maybe just a bit ahead of his time.'

That November, another band notorious for their unwillingness to 'really play the game', as well as their contempt for journalists, played their first ever gig at St Martin's Art College. They only lasted ten minutes on stage but that was enough to allow the Sex Pistols to mark their territory.

The Mobile Studio worked hard that year and turned out at least parts of *The Who by Numbers*, Rick Wakeman's *Lisztomania*, Bad Finger's *Straight Shooter*, Led Zeppelin's *Physical Graffiti* and Mott the Hoople's *Drive On*. Nevertheless, Ronnie was barely holding his financial head above water.

And on 17 October, while they were recording the *One for the Road* album, Stan, his dad, died at the house Ronnie had bought for his parents in Romford. Ronnie buried his pain deep inside and went back to work.

Mum, Elsie, went into a care home in Hornchurch.

21

Well, Hello

It's hard to say whether the core of Ronnie's problems in the mid-seventies were down to drink, money or illness. Nothing seemed to satisfy. Everything irked.

In one of those complex deals beloved by music entrepreneurs, Tony Calder – Andrew Loog Oldham's old partner at Immediate – bought the name NEMS, Brian Epstein's old company, from Robert Stigwood, who happened to own it at the time. Then Tony, through NEMS, bought Immediate Records Ltd., his own old company, from the liquidator.

By some sleight of hand, though the deal included all the company's assets, it did not include any of its debts or obligations. It is hard to believe that such a thing is legal or possible but apparently it is – or can be if you're canny.

Anyway, one of the first singles issued by NEMS/Immediate was a rerelease of 'Itchycoo Park' in December 1975, with plans afoot to follow it up with 'Lazy Sunday'.

To promote the single, Calder thought it would be a fine idea to re-form the Small Faces. The timing was perfect: Mac and Kenney were free – the Faces had played their last gig in the November when Rod went off finally to pursue his solo career – and Steve and Ronnie,

by all accounts, appeared to have made some sort of tenuous reconciliation.

As a starter, he offered the band £1,000 each (which probably
never actually materialised) to do some promotional work.

They made a couple of videos at the Island Studios in Hammersmith.

'We recorded the video plus a second for the soon-to-be released
'Lazy Sunday' in one afternoon,' Kenney said. 'We had a laugh. Yes,
awkward tension at first but that quickly faded. If not exactly like
old times, there was still a spark . . .'

The single got airplay, most notably when, on 8 January 1976, Pan's
People, the *Top of the Pops* dance troupe, did a routine to the song
wearing crocheted shawls and often sitting on an oversized papier
mâché toadstool (or was it magic mushrooms?) amid a great deal of
dry ice. They essentially gurn into the camera while playing a coy
game of ring-a-ring-a-roses. It's well worth looking up on YouTube
and provides a vivid illustration of how delightfully bizarre British
pop at its best can be.

So perhaps thanks to Pan's People, the reissue rose to nine and
spent a lucrative-for-some 11 weeks in the chart. 'Lazy Sunday',
released in February 1976, didn't do quite so well and only made
number 39, but then that one didn't have the boost provided by
crocheted shawls.

The Small Faces reunion began to be a more attractive proposition
as Slim Chance's fortunes continue to spiral down. Their final single
for Island, 'Don't Try to Change My Mind', vanished without trace.

Ronnie gave an interview to *NME*'s Chris Salewicz at the office
of his management company EG. It was a cosy affair. Ronnie and
Kate parked the kids in front of the television in the office (apparently
the Lanes didn't have a TV down in Fishpool) and went to have a
chat in the Phoenix pub round the corner. Ronnie talked about the
problems that he had faced over the last couple of years

'In a way I just ended up trusting a lot of people to do things which they said they could do which they couldn't, you know? It sort of backfired on me more than anyone else, really. Bit of an amateur night out. I mean I was pretty amateur too. I just used to take pot luck, but I can't really do that anymore. Because I can't afford to.'

He was about to embark on a tour, starting in Edinburgh.

'I'll enjoy it when I do it. When I left the Faces, I couldn't really face the prospect of going back on the road to do a tour like what I'm about to embark on now.

'Don't get me wrong. I really enjoyed looning about in the limousines. It was a good game. But it never became any more than a game. We was just playing pop stars. That's all. It's like Cowboys and Indians. You had to grow up some time. This is a different sort of band.

'I mean, what I'm doing now . . . The band's basically a vehicle for the stuff I write. I mean, it is a band and the way it's been got together it's good for the stuff I write, whereas the Faces – and even the Small Faces – weren't particularly good for the stuff that I personally conceived.'

Chris asked about the possibility of a Small Faces reunion.

'They're re-forming tonight,' Ronnie answered.

Chris was understandably excited and pressed him for details – was it going to be a one-off?

'Depends how tonight goes,' Kate answered for Ronnie.

And it wasn't a gig they were talking about anyway. Just an initial meeting at Kenney Jones' house in Hampstead.

They had more meetings down at Fishpool.

Kenney tells the story. 'After a few beers with Ronnie, listening to him procrastinate – "Oh I don't know if I want to. But I love you guys. I just don't . . .." – we found ourselves in the kitchen with Katie cooking something in a big cauldron. Someone's head by the look of it . . .'

According to Mac, at one point Ronnie had suggested that he and

Kenney join him in Ronnie Lane's Slim Chance, 'Like we'd be his band.'

Everything was left up in the air.

There was talk, as there had been so many times before, of some variation of Slim Chance taking America by storm. Russ got Ronnie a meeting with an American manager, Irving Hazell, who was interested in taking them on and everybody got excited. But the will wasn't there.

Ronnie later regretted not going: 'I should have taken Slim Chance to America. We'd have gone there as small time again and that would have suited me fine. I'd have liked to have gone there and toured in humane conditions and to have turned it into a life instead of tearing about all of the time, then sitting at home for a month with nothing to do.'

There was, Ronnie knew, money knocking about here and there, but it was hard to put your hands on. Some of it might have been in Jersey. Royalties dribbled in, but you need specialist accountants to figure out from the statements whether you're being paid what you're owed and Ronnie never had a high opinion of accountants.

What was obvious, though, was that he could no longer afford to keep Slim Chance together.

According to his drummer Colin Davey, Ronnie didn't have the courage to tell them face to face: 'I was with Steve [Simpson] at a recording studio and greeted him as usual with, "Hi Steve, how are you?" To which he replied, "Not too bad for somebody that's just been fired. Have you had the letter?" I immediately got on the phone and rang my wife, Alison, at home and said, "Is there a letter?" "Yeah," she said and she opened it. She said, "It's not very nice."

The letters were from EG management. The band was finished.

The Small Faces reunion idea was still vaguely on the cards. Somebody even managed to get the re-formed band a record deal with Atlantic. Contracts were signed.

So, in early summer, Ronnie, Steve, Mac and Kenney assembled at Joe Brown's recording studio in Chigwell.

Joe was a good pal of Steve Marriott's and had said they could use the studio for free and just pay him back if their endeavours later made some money.

After a bad start, however, things got progressively worse.

Ronnie was on the offensive. The fact that Steve had written a couple of songs with Mac 'put Ronnie's nose out of joint', Mac said. 'The Marriott/Lane glory days were over, nothing creative was going to happen between them.'

Then Ronnie said that Steve hadn't written a decent song since he left the Small Faces.

Then Ronnie (accounts vary) fell over a guitar and nearly broke it.

Then Steve and Ronnie had a flaming row.

They did, however, get one track recorded before knocking off to go to the pub with Joe.

And there they were, drinking and joking, when, 'all of a sudden Ronnie got pissed off,' Mac said, 'and started talking about going home. He got nastily drunk . . . he said it was all a load of bollocks in the studio, then became abusive.'

Kenney Jones remembers Steve acting 'like an ass, constantly taking the piss, overly confident and arrogant.'

Steve was also 'going through a spitting stage. I think he was a bit insecure at the time, don't know why; maybe it was because his hair was falling out, yeah let's put it down to that.'

And Ronnie did always have a very fine head of hair.

'It was really that Steve had changed so much,' Kenney said. 'I regret continuing with it. I should have walked out at the same time.'

In the end, Steve and Mac laid into Ronnie before chasing him out of the room and down the driveway. Ronnie phoned Russ to come and collect him and drive him back to the farm.

A year later Steve Marriott, in an interview in *Sounds* magazine, admitted, 'Yes, I suppose there'll always be bad feeling. Because we love each other in a way, me an' Ronnie. We were brought up together, man. That always creates bad feelings. I did hear he wanted to call this band Slim Chance and give me the elbow. A close friend told me. I couldn't believe that. Devious Ronnie . . . Ronnie was drunk when we had that row. And I had been up for three days. It was good that it went down, 'cos it would only have gone down later on, you know.'

'It's all right to visit your old school,' said Ronnie later, 'but you don't want to attend classes.

'I dunno. I find Steve Marriott kind of hard to take in my old age . . . I really wouldn't go out of my way to talk to him. I don't know what's going on in his mind . . . I really don't.'

Steve dismissively told an interviewer, 'We sent him out for a packet of Rothmans . . . and he never came back.'

And that, this time, was definitely the end of the Small Faces with Ronnie Lane on bass. The other three carried on recording – bringing in Rick Wills to replace Ronnie, and even, eventually, released an album on Atlantic under the title *Playmates*, copies of which are usually available on discogs.com for between £2 and £10.

Ronnie returned to the farm and the 1976 drought and heatwave. There were forest fires just over the border in England.

Nothing good was happening anywhere. The soundtrack album from *Mahoney's Last Stand* was finally released. Most people thought it was a Ronnie/Woody reunion rather than a side hustle they had going when they were both in the Faces. But despite the fact that Pete Townshend, Kenney and Mac all had credits on the album and that Woody was now a fully fledged Rolling Stone, they could have been selling blue asbestos to schoolkids.

Then Atlantic told Ronnie he owed them an album. That contract he'd signed when the Small Faces reunion was imminent was binding.

As Meher Baba put it, 'He whom I love most will always be a wreck financially, as thereby he automatically gets clean. He gets so clean that, with my *nazar* [glance], his ego goes, and Baba comes!'

Ronnie drove to Twickenham to have Sunday lunch with his old pal, Pete Townshend. He had to make this new album. Would Pete produce it, please? Pete had a better idea. Why didn't they make an album together and get Glyn Johns to produce it?

EG, who'd been pressuring him to think again about the Small Faces, were well up for it and could already hear the ching of the cash registers as punters queued up at HMV and Our Price for the new Lane/Townshend/Johns product. In the end, glory be, they got Eric Clapton, John Entwistle, Charlie Watts, Gallagher and Lyle, and Ian Stewart thrown into the mix, too.

Sessions started in September at Olympic Studios. Ronnie wrote four tracks, one in collaboration with Kate and one with Kate and Eric Clapton, Pete wrote five tracks, they wrote a single track together and there was a cover of Don Williams' 'Till The Rivers All Run Dry', dedicated to 'the Old Man'.

Ronnie would have liked a closer collaboration on the writing.

'I couldn't make out why we couldn't spend an hour or two in the evening to write songs together. I'd got a few ideas. Pete had a few ideas. My ideas weren't finished. So, I said "Why don't we get together and write some things?" He turned round and said, "What? And split the publishing?" I was floored.'

'It was recorded at the fabulous Olympic studio in its heyday, when it had that fantastic big room,' Charlie Hart remembers. 'Eric's on it, Benny Gallagher, Dave Markee on bass, myself and obviously Ronnie. We all sat around in a circle with virtually no screens or baffles, so there was maximum eye contact between us. The whole thing was live and probably all done in one take. Then we went into the control room and listened to it. Glyn had a bit of a soft spot for Ronnie, but there were two sides of him. He could be very severe and quite tough on people, but he was very tuned in on other levels. He went, 'Oh yeah, I think this is it,' and more or less mixed it in front of us. Then he stood back from the faders, without touching anything. It was one of those idyllic recordings.'

From the start there was friction between Ronnie and Pete. 'I'd known both of them for a long while and had a friendship as well as a working relationship with them,' Glyn Johns said. 'They fought like cats and dogs on a couple of occasions so there was some stress while it was being made.'

'The sessions were quite funny,' Ronnie told Dave Marsh in his book *Before I Get Old: the Story of the Who.* 'A lot of rowing. Me and Pete, we love each other a lot, but we rub each other up the wrong way, as well. He's a much bigger fellow than me, he's got a longer reach than I have.'

In February, Eric Clapton came to Olympic to visit Pete. Pete had organised a comeback concert in 1973 for Eric at the Rainbow Theatre in London after his heroin addiction had kept him from performing on stage for nearly two years. This concert was one of the first to be recorded by Ronnie's Mobile Studio and Glyn Johns had produced it.

The two musicians had met a few times over the years – Eric remembered meeting Ronnie in Denmark Street in the sixties – and Eric was attracted to Ronnie and his alternative lifestyle.

'I kept going along to the studio hoping I'd get to play,' Eric said. 'But a lot of the time I was just sitting around keeping the peace between the other two. They kept having heated arguments about philosophy and politics and so on – all totally irrelevant to the work in hand. I felt more like a referee than a guest artist on that album.'

Or as Pete put it: 'Ronnie and I would talk about life. That would mean Ronnie insulting me and me hitting him. Sometimes Eric Clapton would come and play. That would mean him insulting him,

Eric hitting him and Ronnie falling over. Glyn and Ronnie often discussed Ronnie's songs. This consisted of Ronnie trying to keep Glyn in the studio until three or four in the morning while he insulted him.'

It's there in the sleeve notes: 'Ron and Pete play various acoustic and electric guitars, mandolins and bass guitars, banjos, ukuleles and very involved mind games.'

All the same, Glyn maintains, '*Rough Mix* was an enjoyable album to make. I had been really good friends and worked with Ronnie and Pete for years, so to do it when asked was a no-brainer. It turned out to be an all-time favourite album of mine and one track that stands out for me is Ronnie's 'April Fool'. Ronnie did a wonderful vocal and I got Dave Markee to come in and put a bowed double bass on it. Eric [Clapton] added a solo with a Dobro, which complimented what we already had. There are moments in my recording career that I treasure, and this is one of them. I played Ronnie the track and I noticed that his foot was tapping as he ran through the song. I quickly put a microphone on his foot, and we recorded the next run-through. It was note perfect and quite beautiful. Ronnie's performance was perfection.'

'April Fool' is indeed a beautiful and plaintive song, which seems to foreshadow how Ronnie's life was changing. He was finding it difficult to tour around and perform, and his relationship with Kate, which was always challenging, was starting to deteriorate. It is of course always presumptuous to read meanings into artists' words but it's hard not to feel the truth behind Ronnie singing in his world-weary voice.

'As far as Ronnie's stuff was concerned, I really enjoyed working on them,' Pete told Chris Welch in a joint interview in *Melody Maker*, 'but Ronnie's contribution to my stuff was much, much deeper. It's hard to explain. For a start, I don't think I would have done the album or the kind of material I did, if it were not for Ronnie's encouragement. And that hasn't just started with this album. It has been constant. Ronnie's been one of the few people that I've played demos to, and he has always encouraged me to do stuff away from the mainstream of Who clichés.'

'We knocked about together over the years,' added Ronnie. 'But basically, the thing that kept us together was Meher Baba, which meant there was a mutual understanding about it. I'm not wishing to preach about it, I'm just saying that. But it's basically kept us together.'

Another time, Pete summed it up in elegiac tones. 'What Ronnie brought to the table was gentle Gaelic influences of acoustic mandolins, violins and accordions whose sound still echo in the pastoral folds of the English countryside.'

'Annie', Ronnie's delicate little ballad (co-written with Kate and Eric Clapton) about the old lady who used to come in to look after the Lane's children when they were away or busy, is in some ways the spiritual centre of the album. Lisa Lane, Ronnie's niece, who was living on the farm by then, remembers Annie sitting by the open fire with Ronnie's Alsatian at her feet, and every night, whether they needed her to babysit or not, she was there.

Kate loved her medical tips and hints like, 'If you put ivy leaves in your shoes that would stop your feet aching.'

Try it.

22

We Used to Roam So Freely

'By now, my best mate was Eric,' said Ronnie. 'I can't remember how that all came about, but we were quite inseparable for a while, we even cut ourselves and became blood brothers. We did low-key gigs together in my local pubs and his.'

'I loved hanging out with Ronnie,' Eric said, 'because we were both drinkers and as we spent more time together Ronnie's musicality also began to rub off on me.'

He became a regular down at Fishpool and was generous with his presents.

'Eric came to one of the livestock shows in Bishop's Castle,' Kate said. 'It was the annual show, and he bid on an enormous prize ram for Ronnie. We didn't know that he was bidding on it. But at the time you couldn't leave Eric untethered at any time.'

'Eric bought a ram,' Luke said. 'He arrived on the farm and Eric had to try to stop him from escaping. I'll always remember Eric dressed in his suit, trying to wrestle with the ram to stop him escaping.

'Eric also bought Ronnie a gun – well it was a full-on assault rifle. Dad looked pleased and said, "Come on son, we'll go shooting."

'We saw this little bunny on the horizon, he took aim and there was a crack.

'The bunny just turned into a red mist. There was nothing left of him. Just a bit of fur and red mist. Dad picked up the gun and said, "That's no fucking good!" And never used it again. He loved his rabbit stew of course. He liked to take me out with him shooting but I hated it.'

At the beginning of 1977, the Round Table Committee of Cranleigh, a village near Guildford in Surrey, met to discuss their plans for St Valentine's Day. They decided that this year they wanted something different from cheese and wine, raffles, fancy dress and old-time dancing competitions. One of the committee suggested they ask local resident Eric Clapton if he'd like to put on some sort of entertainment, then, bravely, followed it up with a letter.

Eric agreed and brought his old friend Ronnie Lane in to help out. The strict rule was that there would be no publicity and the band would be billed as Eddie Earthquake & His Tremors.

And so it came to be on St Valentine's Day, 1977, the man known to graffiti-ists as 'God', who had, a few months earlier, played to audiences of 15,000 plus in US arenas, was joined by the man formerly known to Small Faces and Faces fans as 'Plonk', to put on a rattling good evening's entertainment for an assembly of 350 at Cranleigh Village Hall – ardent fans at the front, sober-suited Round Tablers with their good lady wives at the back.

Kate and Pattie Boyd (still technically married to George Harrison) turned out too, in their can-can outfits, and gave a leg show. This prompted some of the locals to get up and dance. And to round it all off, God and Plonk gave a wonderful two-part harmony closing-time rendition of 'Goodnight, Irene'.

Apparently, it was all recorded on the Lane Mobile Studio, but the tapes were lost. Or perhaps hidden, mislabelled somewhere, waiting to make a keen archivist's dreams come true.

The Cranleigh gig was the start of something small.

In March, they played a couple of times at a village pub near

Ronnie's, the Drum and Monkey at Bromlow. Before the second gig, the landlord tipped off Dave Bagnoll, a young photographer working on the *Shropshire Star*.

'I was sat on the edge of the stage, which was only a little affair, so I was in their faces and couldn't do the pictures I would have liked to have done. They had Ronnie Lane's band Slim Chance playing, and had their wives dressed as gypsies, dancing almost a can-can dance. I was so close to them that I couldn't photograph them, it was impossible. There were too many people. It was rumoured that some people got in through the toilet window.

'Eric Clapton by then was really famous for 'Layla' and lots of people kept shouting for him to play 'Layla'. ['Layla' had actually been a hit six years earlier]. He responded by saying he couldn't remember the words, which I doubt is very true. All the music they played was Ronnie Lane's music. Strangely enough I liked Ronnie Lane more than Clapton at that time.'

'I remember both shows,' said Charlie Hart, 'as being high-spirited, relaxed and down-home, but with a strong entertainment factor (not least thanks to Katie and Pattie's can-can).'

Alana (who was five at the time) thought that Eric wrote 'Wonderful Tonight' round the fire at the farm one night – although Patti (the inspiration for the song, as well as 'Layla' and George Harrison's 'Something') says she remembers Eric writing it while waiting for her to get ready to go to Paul and Linda McCartney's annual Buddy Holly party. She'd probably know.

Either way, Eric cut the original demo on the Lane Mobile.

For Ronnie's birthday, on 1 April, Eric bought him a green Toyota Land Cruiser (in the region of £5,000 worth of car at the time) and left it outside his house with a big pink bow round it. Around the same time, he asked Ronnie if Slim Chance wanted to tour with him as his support band.

'He knew I needed the dough,' Ronnie said. 'It was just a friendly gesture.'

In May, Ronnie opened for Eric Clapton at the Hammersmith Odeon. Ian Stewart played piano for Ronnie that night and Nick Kent reviewed it for the *NME* (although he admitted missing most of Ronnie's set). 'Rumour had it that Ron himself was not averse to draining a fair few bevvies of an evening, so it came as some surprise to see his slight frame perfectly co-ordinating itself, and commanding what can only be described as yer archetypal good time band.

'Sheesh, he even put the capo on the right fret first time round for his rendition of the old Faces chestnut 'Ooh La La', his final song of the evening. I also noted that the former band's 'Debris' was performed, as well as Lane's solo mini-hit 'How Come?' Anyway, they sounded most melodious to these ears, and I wished I'd arrived earlier to hear more of Mr Lane's pleasingly undemanding toons.'

Again, supporting Eric, the band travelled over to the National Stadium in Dublin. This one didn't go so well. Ronnie couldn't get used to playing support and had trouble getting his head around not being number one. He flew into a rage during the soundcheck because the system had been set up for Eric, and the mixers were unwilling to change things so that, for instance, Charlie Hart's mandolin couldn't be heard through his monitor.

Nevertheless, the show went on, and carried on through Denmark, the Netherlands, Belgium, France, Germany and Switzerland.

The travel arrangements were a world away from the leaky caravans and exploding buses of the Passing Show.

'The whole entourage would travel in their personal train across Europe in luxury carriages,' said Hugh Flint, who was playing with Eric's band, 'including the restaurant car, which had reputedly belonged to Hermann Goering.

'A lot of silliness happened on the tour, including most of the band dressing as tramps and busking on various railway stations they would pull into. The band member who got the most money would have to treat the rest to drinks.'

Back in England in July, Eric and Ronnie recorded some tracks together.

'Eric joined in quite a few recording sessions at Fishpool,' Charlie Hart said. 'The tracks were recorded on the Stones' Mobile Studio [courtesy of Stu], as I think Ronnie's Mobile was not available. Mick McKenna engineered them. I remember putting the tracks down in Ronnie's barn – 'Last Night' with accordion playing the organ line and Eric on acoustic. The tracks were not released at the time as they were not quite enough for an album and Ronnie was not happy to put out an album of predominantly covers.'

They also organised a free open-air show at the Drum and Monkey pub on 15 July.

'At the Drum and Monkey, I think we had Ronnie's Regulars at the time,' Charlie said. 'Hughie Flint, Stu, myself, John Porter, Brian Belshaw, and he were joined by Hughie's friend Tom McGuinness. The small stage was put up in the car park in the open and we had a basic PA. I remember Eric making a joke about the likelihood of one of us crashing into the drum kit!'

The setlist that night included 'Ooh La La', 'How Come?', 'Walk on By' and 'Goodnight, Irene'.

'The gig immediately became part of local folklore and when we were in Shropshire recently, they were still talking about it.'

At the beginning of August, the European tour continued. The whole ensemble flew out to Cannes where Eric had hired two luxury yachts, one for the two bands' members and the other for the two crews, and set sail along the Mediterranean.

'The boat was called *The Liberty*. It hit a rock one night,' Kate said, 'but Charlie Hart kept playing – he called it 'Hell on the High Seas' – the piano was rolling from one end of the room to the other. It all got very fraught, so we docked at Ibiza.'

They were booked to play the Plaza del Toros – the local bull-fighting stadium – in Ibiza.

'Eric's manager said they wouldn't get paid, because they were late,' Kate said. 'So they started busking on the quayside to make some money. When they'd made enough, they went off clubbing. When they came back, Ronnie and Eric decided to change the name of the boat and wrote, "What a fucking" next to the *Liberty* on the side of it.'

Their next stop was an arena just outside Barcelona.

'It was after that show, back in the hotel, that Ronnie gathered the group together and told us that he wasn't well, he had to let the band go and he was going to take a break for a while,' Hugh Flint said. 'He became tearful and excused himself. Despite all the camaraderie and fun, on and off stage, and the wonderful music, Ronnie had had trouble with his right hand. I had taken him to an osteopath friend of mine who couldn't do anything for him except advise rest which, of course, he couldn't do in the middle of a tour and increasingly after only a few drinks he would lose control of his legs, often falling down.'

The announcement came as no surprise to anybody.

'As early as 1976 there were days when Ronnie couldn't button up his waistcoat and would be strumming a guitar [with his fingers] instead of using a pick,' Steve Simpson said. 'These were early signs of what we now know was MS. Of course, it played on his mind.'

Way back when the Small Faces had been re-forming in Joe Brown's studio, Steve Marriott said, 'In the studio, Ronnie kept falling over and I couldn't work it out and got angry with him. I thought he was drunk but now I don't think he was, thinking about it. He was trying to sing and he'd sway and fall over . . . If he told me then I would have been more sympathetic towards why, instead of being annoyed.'

And when they were recording *Rough Mix*, Billy Nicholls remembered that Ronnie was not in a good state. 'I knew even that far back that it wasn't the drink and that there was something seriously wrong with him.'

Pete Townshend had noticed something was amiss, too. 'He could sing OK, but he couldn't play the bass. I got angry with him about halfway through the session because I thought he was just a drunken pig. I was such a hypocrite. I used to drink far more than he did. But he was falling all over the place, and I just got angry and punched him – I punched his right shoulder to emphasise a point – and he went flying down the hall. It was then that I realised he was sick.'

Eric saw it as well, when he was playing guitar on stage. 'He wasn't actually hitting the strings . . . it was sort of just hovering above.'

Glyn Johns remembers, 'Stu [Ian Stewart] and Eric Clapton would often go down to play with Ronnie, both enjoying the solitude of the farm and hanging out with their friend playing music. Stu came round to see me after one of these visits and told me he was becoming increasingly concerned about Ronnie, as he was slurring his words and losing his balance as if he was drunk. At first, no one paid much attention, thinking he probably was. Until one day, when he complained that his arm had pins and needles and had become numb, making it difficult for him to play.'

Outbursts of anger, like the one at the soundcheck in Dublin, were becoming more frequent too. His temper was erratic and often he seemed very drunk after only a glass or two of barley wine. Arguments with Kate became epic. Once after Kate had threatened Ronnie with a knife, Ronnie left and moved in with his friend, a nearby farmer, Dave Phillpot, for two weeks. But after a fortnight of constant drinking and partying, Dave begged Kate to take him back for the sake of his own health.

'There was a time that Ronnie was out in the fields,' Alana said, 'driving a tractor with Luke on his lap and he lost his sight, yeah, went temporarily blind. He told Luke, who was only about four or five, to take the steering wheel.'

'The odd spasm of double vision I didn't take very seriously at first,' Ronnie told the *New York Times*. 'I just put it down to that heavy Saturday night I just had. I had to give up counting sheep on the farm because I always saw more than were actually on the pastures.'

Before the tour, the band had spent some time rehearsing at Ian Stewart's place in Surrey. Stu's wife, Cynthia, became Ronnie's confidante.

'We always liked Ronnie,' Cynthia told *Mojo* magazine in 1985. 'Although he was a naughty little boy, he was also a charming little boy with a twinkle in his eye. He was very demonstrative, very affectionate. He always reminded me of a puppy – you'd get hugs and kisses whenever he came in or went out. Yet he never lost masculinity as a result of that. It was very difficult to be cross with Ronnie.

'He came down one morning and said, "I don't know; Auntie Cyn, I've got something wrong with me. I can't play the guitar properly 'cos my fingers won't work. And my arm has got this funny bit in it like . . . this dead bit." And I said to him, "Well, listen, my love, you must go and see somebody because you can't afford to not be able to play the guitar; that's your livelihood." And I have no idea exactly when he went, but it was quite soon.'

Everyone around Ronnie, then, could see that he was in a terrible state and nagged him to seek a proper diagnosis. In his heart of hearts he must have known what was going on.

'I remember sitting in the Airstream with a guitar and my left hand would not work, the fingers wouldn't grasp, I just could not get them around a riff and some gypsy friends of mine, who lived nearby, took me to a chiropractor and they massaged my back, my neck and limbs and the afflicted hand came back to life, but more signs started coming. My left leg was failing me and return visits to the chiropractor were unsuccessful. Then, right off the blue, the problem mysteriously went. I got on with living for a while and then another sign, this time double vision that never went away.'

Finally, Ronnie went to the Midland Centre for Neurology and Neurosurgery in Birmingham, where he had a myelogram. He was diagnosed with multiple sclerosis.

'They just looked at me with an awful, pitiful, sort of helpless expression,' Ronnie told *Rolling Stone.* 'It was scary — *really* scary. When they look at you like that, you know they can't bleedin' do anything, and oh, do you feel alone. I could have been in a crowded football stadium, but I felt completely alone.

'I never told anybody, except my wife, for a long time. I just bottled it up. MS is an incurable disease of the nervous system and different [people] often display different symptoms and different symptoms arise at different stages of the disease. Because no clinical test yet devised is capable of yielding a foolproof diagnosis, [people with MS] often spend years wondering if they really have the disease.'

Some people associate the onset of MS with emotional traumas – Ronnie thought it was the pain of his father's death the year before.

The doctors prescribed steroids, which helped a little with the condition, and Ronnie went back to Fishpool. 'I got into a self-destructive phase in my life. Which was – an experience. Didn't manage it though. You know why? It's hard to kill vermin.

'I wasn't proud of having MS. As a natural fact, quite the opposite. I was ashamed of it. It didn't fit my personal image of me. So, while I could, I didn't let anybody know. I just started raving, and adventurising. But it got me in the end. I had to own up. If there had been more of an advisory capacity for people who have MS when I first got it, I wouldn't have gone on that self-destruct thing. A bit of revelry is all right. But you have to learn the difference between scratching your arm and tearing it to pieces.'

On 17 September, *Rough Mix*, his collaboration with Pete Townshend, was released on Polydor.

Pete and Ronnie appeared on *The Old Grey Whistle Test* to publicise the album and were interviewed by Bob Harris. The clip, available on YouTube, is uncomfortable viewing if you know what was happening in Ronnie's life.

Ronnie is very quiet, and Pete is running his mouth off constantly – it's hard to tell if it is a chemical-induced mania or just nervousness. When Bob asked how the album came to be, Pete says that Ronnie sent two guys, who were 7ft 6in tall, round to his house and said, 'Do you want to make an album?'

Remembering the days of Don Arden, he said, 'Okay.' When asked if this was going to be the start of future projects, Pete said facetiously that yeah, they were going to issue one a week from now on. Ronnie seemed detached and maybe a little embarrassed when Pete teased him about not answering Bob's questions. When asked what his plans were next he just said that he wanted to get back into his Mobile Studio and write some songs.

The record was well received and made number 44 in an album chart that also included David Bowie's *Heroes*, The Stranglers' *No More Heroes*, Steely Dan's *Aja*, *The Best of Rod Stewart* and *Abba's Greatest Hits*.

Pete's 'Street in the City', backed by Ronnie's 'Annie', was released as a single, but didn't chart.

On the plus side, *the Village Voice* put the album at number 13 in its end of year critics' poll, and *Trouser Press* gave it an honourable mention as one of the finest albums of 1977.

23

As Many Custard Creams as You Can Eat

MS is an unpredictable disease. It's degenerative – over time the symptoms worsen – but it's not a steady decline. The symptoms can go into full or partial remission for days, weeks, months at a time, making it easy for the optimistic to convince themselves that the diagnosis was wrong or that the latest 'cure' they've tried has worked.

Ronnie's initial impulse, according to his brother, on learning the diagnosis, was to beat the disease by drinking himself to death before it got the chance to see him off. Night after night he'd slip away to the Miners Arms, three miles away, and when he came home would inevitably be so drunk he'd fall out of the car.

Russ Schlagbaum, who'd been with Ronnie all through the days of the Faces and the chaos and adventure of the Passing Show, after many years patiently enduring the unpredictability, the irritability and the anger, decided he'd had enough and went home to Ohio.

Ronnie had a go at being a proper farmer and even went to some classes at the agricultural college in Newtown, where his 15-year-old classmates took the piss.

And he started writing for a new album.

'He came back from Eric's tour and somehow got it together,' Charlie Hart said. 'It was truly amazing because suddenly there was a bunch of interesting songs, mostly based on experience. Ronnie tended to write from real experience, either stories people, often travellers, had told him or about things that had happened in his own life.'

With Kate, he came up with a song called 'Kuschty Rye' – Romany for 'a good bloke', 'whose lingo came from God knows where.' With Eric Clapton, still a regular visitor, he worked on 'Barcelona', about the 'shipwreck' they endured when the *Liberty* hit the rock. And with Alun Davies, an old friend who'd been Cat Stevens' guitarist but found himself at a loose end when Cat had converted to Islam and left the music business, he wrote two tracks: 'She's Leaving' and 'One Step', which would eventually be released as a single.

But actually putting the album together was a fraught business. The Mobile Studio, Ronnie's beloved cash cow, had been broken into and vandalised. Some of the equipment had been stolen. The insurance claim was eventually settled but it was a good while before the studio was fully refurbished and up and running again.

Getting backing for an album was a problem too. How good a risk is a man who sometimes can't hold a plectrum steady?

'Ronnie was able to conceal his MS pretty well,' Kate said. 'When he lost his balance he'd say, "I'm just pissed, man." But he wasn't drunk. He needed to conceal it because he wanted an advance for his new album – but no one would finance it if they knew about the MS.'

In November, the weather closed in. The winter of 1977–78 was the coldest since the big freeze of 1962. At Fishpool, blizzards buried the fields in deep snow. RAF helicopters air-lifted 45 stranded families in South Wales in the hills and took food supplies to cut-off rural areas. The cold killed a lot of Ronnie's chickens and most of his sheep. When lambing season came in the new year, the corpses of the new-born piled up in the fields.

'It snowed really badly,' Kate said. 'Eric decided to come down and visit from London and got as far as Lydham about five miles away when he got stuck. He phoned Ronnie from a phone box and asked us to come and get him. Ronnie asked him where he was and he said, "I can't tell, it's all white." Anyway, we worked it out and Ronnie went to get him in his pick-up, but when we got there the door on the phone box was frozen shut. Eric really lost it then. So, Ronnie thought if he pissed up against the side of the phone box that might unfreeze it. He had a bottle of brandy with him too, so he drank more brandy to help it along – but in the end he used the brandy too to get him out. Eric was furious that Ronnie had been pissing on him but we laughed about it later.'

Christmas was notable.

'Ronnie was sitting by the roaring fire on Christmas Eve and decided to clean his gun. He told the children, "If that Father Christmas comes down the chimney, I'll shoot the fat bastard." Alana and Luke burst into tears and ran to their rooms.

He was broke. And he had another mouth to feed. Reuben Jack was born on 2 January 1979. Eric and Pattie were his godparents.

Ronnie sold the bungalow that he had bought for his parents to his brother, Stan. Dad was gone and mum was in a care home with MS. The cash was to tide them over for a while, although Stan maintained that most of it was stolen from Ronnie on his way back to Wales.

On 19 May, the whole family went to Eric Clapton's wedding party in his Italian-style villa, Hurtwood Edge in Surrey. Three of The Beatles (apparently John wasn't invited although he did say he would have gone if he'd been asked) got up on the stage in the garden and played together for the first time since the rooftop concert. Ronnie wandered round, falling over and walking into things. Most people there just thought he was drunk.

Pete Townshend reckoned that Fishpool had become a burden – a lad in Ronnie's condition needed central heating, teaching hospitals and Sainsbury's – and encouraged him to move back to London.

'From the best motives,' Kate said, 'I think Pete thought if Ronnie was nearer to the core of things and got more feedback he'd start feeling happier with himself.'

Ronnie agreed and, in the autumn of 1978 sold the farm for £90,000 and bought 16 Riverdale Road in Twickenham for £85,000. It's an impressive five-bed semi, at the time of writing ranked as the fourth most expensive property in the area and valued at £2,295,000. A big plus for Ronnie was that it was near the boathouse that Pete had bought in 1975 and converted into the Meher Baba Oceanic Centre.

As Pete had predicted, 'nearer to the core of things' Ronnie began to re-emerge as a gigging, recording musician.

Pete's company, Eel Pie Productions, produced a single of 'Kuschty Rye', the song Ronnie had written with Kate. It was eventually released on the Gem label. *Melody Maker* loved it but it failed to chart.

Pete also got Ronnie involved with a benefit concert that Paul McCartney was organising to raise money for the victims of war-torn Cambodia. The distinguished company assembled at the Hammersmith Odeon in what Paul called his 'Rockestra' included, as well as Ronnie, his old bandmate Kenney Jones, John Paul Jones and John Bonham of Led Zeppelin, David Gilmour from Pink Floyd, The Who, Wings and Hank Marvin of The Shadows.

Ronnie even got a new band together, and started gigging. Kate managed the bookings and Ronnie said that she did it as well as any other of his promoters had.

The London music scene had moved on since the days of the Faces. When The Who toured the US in 1973, 20 tons of equipment came with them, carried in three 45ft trailers and manhandled by 12 roadies. For their US tour, Emerson, Lake & Palmer had seven 45ft trailers for the indoor gigs and another three for the outdoor gigs together with three buses for the orchestral musicians and choirs.

Add to this the cost of the artistes' princely demands. By 1973,

Led Zeppelin's rider specified the quality of hi-fi systems that were to be installed in hotel rooms. Their private jet had a waterbed. It was not uncommon for entourages to include personal caterers, physiotherapists, art directors and wardrobe supervisors.

And even when they came off the road and went into the studio, the bloated bands racked up the expenses. The Beatles' first album took a day to record and cost about the same as a used Hillman Imp. Queen's *A Night at the Opera* took four months in three different studios and would've bought a couple of four-bedroom semis in a fashionable part of London.

One reaction to this was pub rock – loud music played by threatening people who hadn't had change for the launderette since 1962 and had never owned an iron. It was mostly a London phenomenon, with notable branches in Essex.

The pub bands did not require a fleet of Edwin Shirley trucks and an army of roadies. No art directors. No fancy wardrobe. The nearest they came to a light show was when the landlord signalled last orders. They made records fast and cheap, knowing a polished product that had the most perfect bass drum sound ever recorded was never a substitute for raw energy. Backstage they needed lager, pills and, if at all possible, a flushing toilet.

The bands proliferated – Dr Feelgood, Kilburn & The High Roads, Ducks Deluxe, the Kursaal Flyers, Chili Willi & The Red Hot Peppers – alongside indie record labels that shoved out their stuff, made so cheaply that you only had to shift a couple of thousand units to start making a profit and mostly recorded in hole-in-the-wall studios run by people called Graham who weren't sure what some of the knobs were supposed to do, so thank God it didn't matter. It was never about records, anyway. It was about the live experience, and along with the bands and labels, a circuit of venues developed, mostly in – the clue's in the name – pubs. Mention the Greyhound, the Half Moon, the Hope and Anchor, Dingwalls, the Dublin Castle to anyone who was half-alive and living in London in the early seventies and a fond smile would light up their face were it not for the fact that they didn't hear what you said, having been permanently deafened by defective PA systems.

The circuit was tailor-made for Ronnie – not quite a circus tent, but close.

Mafalda Hall, the wife of Tony Hall, who owned a promotion and management business, took Ronnie on. His enthusiasm for her wasn't unstinting: he said 'she was as good as anybody I worked with before', but he was happy with the musicians.

'The new band was my best group ever,' he said. 'There was Stu [Ian Stewart], Bruce [Rowland] was back again, Henry McCullough, Chrissie [Stewart] was back again as well, Alun Davies, Charlie Hart and, sometimes, Careless Senior and Careless Junior. There were other floating musician friends about as well: Mick Weaver, Micky Gallagher, Cal Batchelor, Hughie Flint, Brian Knight and Mick Green to name but ten. I did a better job than the Musicians' Union in keeping musicians in employment.'

There was also an album – Ronnie's fourth and final studio album, released at the end of 1979.

It had been through various titles; *True Stories*, *Self Tapper* and *Big Dipper* had all been tried and found wanting. Chrissie Stewart's Glasgow street slang ('See you, Jimmy') provided the final inspiration.

'The songs on *See Me* are basically all about my problems with women,' Ronnie said, 'and also about what has happened to some of us in the business. . . . It can't be too self-indulgent though. It's got to be of interest to everyone. I guess most of the songs are about women though.'

He told journalists that he had been in semi-retirement as a farmer for a couple of years. He had needed a rest from the music industry.

'I'd always wanted to do it, and now I've done it for two years and it's been good. The punk thing was happening with the record companies dragging kids in off the streets. What I did was get out while that was happening, lie low for a couple of years until all the dust settled, and then decide to make a comeback. And here I am!'

And, indeed, there he was, back in London, playing live again. 'I listen to a lot of Cajun music and the accordion is used to play rock'n'roll. Violins and saxophones work together as well. I think we've discovered folk rock from the rock end rather than the folk end.'

The name Slim Chance was history now.★ Sometimes they were billed as Big Dipper, but mostly it was just Ronnie Lane and his Band.

Back in 1979 Charlie Hart was still very much part of the band. 'It was a new incarnation of the band because of Stu, who was absolutely crucial.

'He was a great, underrated pianist and also a very good guy to be around. Ronnie liked the idea we were offering him a gig in his band; not because he'd been with the Stones, he just wanted him in the band, and I think Stu liked that. He was *very* good for Ronnie. Like Ronnie, very into straight R&B, so he fitted in really well, tallying with the musical direction they were going in.

'The only thing Stu didn't like was minor keys. He refused to play in any minor keys, which became a huge standing joke.'

The band played a mixture of covers, like Chuck Berry's 'You Never Can Tell', the calypso song 'Man Smart (Woman Smarter)', Fats Waller's 'The Joint Is Jumpin' and The Midnighters' 'Annie Had a Baby', along with numbers from *See Me* and older Slim Chance hits like 'How Come?' and 'Annie'.

A fan, Kevin Bell, caught them at the Venue in Victoria, a relatively new place owned by Richard Branson, which Ronnie described as,

---

★   Although 'Amazingly enough,' said Steve Bingham, 'Slim Chance re-formed to play Ronnie's songs around 12 years ago (in 2010) and we subsequently recorded four albums on the Fishpool Records Label.'

'a bit like a big hamburger bar. It was a bit too cabaret, it made me feel old.'

'This was 200 miles from where I was living at the time,' Kevin writes on the Ronnie Lane website, 'but word of his illness was beginning to spread and I thought it may get harder to see him. The paying audience was quite small, as there were many invited celebrity guests. The band included Bruce Rowland and Henry McCulloch. The show had a harder edge than previous shows, but it still had the warmth and included my beloved 'Debris'. It was well worth the trip and even getting home at 7 a.m., due to British Rail, did not dampen my enjoyment.'

Ronnie played Dingwalls in Camden Town (with no publicity so only 20 people turned up), the Music Machine at Mornington Crescent, the Greyhound in Fulham, the Bridge House in Canning Town and at least half a dozen times at the Half Moon in Putney.

Sometimes old mates like Mick Taylor and James Honeyman-Scott of The Pretenders turned up to sit in. At the Half Moon, Stu would hump the gear in, help set up and collect all the ticket stubs at the door before slipping behind the piano to play. Ronnie would be drinking downstairs with the locals just before going on stage. They had become the ultimate pub band.

On 19 March they appeared on the German television programme *Rockpalast*. The show went out live and was later released on CD. It's easily accessible on YouTube and probably the last time Ronnie appears on TV as a strong independent showman before his illness starts to compromise his performances

In May they played a free gig in Wormwood Scrubs for the prisoners: 'no rider, just tea and as many custard creams as you could eat.'

Sounds saw them at the Marquee: 'The good time atmosphere and the flow of alcohol doesn't detract from the performance as the boys in Ronnie's band are the sort who've probably got music rather than blood running through their veins. The set ranged from Faces favourites like 'Debris' and 'You're So Rude' through to material from the new album *See Me* to old rock'n'roll classics such as 'The Wanderer'.'

One day, late in the summer of 1980, Ronnie came across three young musicians in a pub on Wardour Street, Soho. They were nursing a single pint between the three of them and had clearly not been having a very nice time.

'We were sleeping in all-night movie theatres in Camden,' one of them said. 'I particularly remember that. I think Friday was The Three Stooges night, which was fine for some shelter. Saturday night was porno, so that was a little more creepy, you know, trying to sleep in there.'

Ronnie was wearing crepe-soled brothel-creepers and a Teddy boy drape coat, which chimed with their dog-eared rockabilly style.

They fell into conversation. The three young men introduced themselves: Brian Setzer, Lee Rocker and Slim Jon Phantom, aka The Stray Cats from Massapequa, New York. They told him they'd spent all their savings getting over to London but were completely broke and couldn't get a gig anywhere.

Ronnie didn't hesitate. He told them they could come and stay with him and that he would help them.

'His wife wasn't too happy about that,' said Lee Rocker. 'We were there for a couple of days.'

Ronnie gave them a few introductions. By the end of August, they were opening for the Fabulous Poodles. By November they were on *Top of the Pops* with their first single 'Runaway Boys'.

'It really turned for us at the first gig, at the Fulham Greyhound,' Setzer recalls. 'We were really just about to turn around and go home.'

The band remained forever grateful to Ronnie and in the next year repaid the favour by letting Ronnie sleep on their sofa.

Because that's how bad things had got with Kate.

24

Oh Mate, Oh Mate

Ronnie was ill. Kate had been suffering depression after the birth of Reuben. And while London seemed to be suiting him, it wasn't doing much for her.

'From the very moment we moved into the Twickenham house,' Ronnie said, 'Katie decided she hated the place and wanted to go back to Wales.

'Now it was quite unbearable. She didn't seem to understand or care that tension and stress made my condition deteriorate and could precipitate attacks. The arguments were fierce and more and more regular and the atmosphere in the home was tense at all times . . . and it all blew up one night. I was working on a song and was recording it and playing it back to myself on a tape machine. It was about 11.30 at night and the children were fast asleep. It may or may not have been playing loudly but without any notice she stormed into the room and turned off the equipment and I completely lost my temper. I decided there and then I would take no more and left the next morning.'

According to Ronnie's brother, Ronnie told Kate that he was just going out to sell his gun to raise some money and didn't come back. Kate rang around their friends, but no one knew where he was.

'I walked out and spent a couple of weeks on friends' sofas (including staying in the Stray Cats' Camden Town flat) before moving in with Boo Oldfield, her two children and her Great Dane called Trampus. I'd only known Boo for about nine months. In that time she'd been working for me in my Mobile Studio.'

Boo had two kids living with her, Christopher, nine, and Kate, seven. She laid down a few ground rules for Ronnie: avoid drink and drugs, and have lots of good food and exercise to try to keep his condition under control. Now and then he had a go at doing as he was told.

That summer Ronnie did Glastonbury. It wasn't quite the accolade it should have been. Judy Tzuke had dropped out at the last minute and Ronnie Lane and Friends happened to be available for the 8 o'clock Sunday evening spot. Tickets were eight quid. They're a bit more than that now (at the time of writing, £335 plus £5 booking fee for the weekend). You got more for your money back then, too, the highlight of that year being a Saturday night onstage fist fight between Roy Harper and Ginger Baker. Roy Harper won. Ginger Baker was taken off to hospital but was well enough to return on Sunday, mad as hell.

His health continued to decline. In July he went over to the US and, while he was in New York, met up with Steve Marriott.

Steve's wife Pam takes up the story in Simon Spence's biography of Steve, *All or Nothing*: 'Ronnie said come on over and Steve was so excited, he couldn't wait . . . and when he opened the door Ronnie was in a wheelchair. Steve burst out crying. It was so emotional, and Ronnie said, "Look, I just didn't want you to know," and Steve just kept saying, "Oh mate, oh mate."'

Back in London, Steve organised a benefit for Ronnie at the Bridge House in Canning Town, with plans to record the show and release it as an album. He assembled a band with Jim Leverton on bass, the legendary Zoot Money on keyboards, Dave Haynes, Mel Colling and Sam Brown, Joe's daughter.

'The crowd was very rough and ready,' Zoot said, 'a seething mass of very drunk Londoners, very spirited. We weren't what you'd call rehearsed, and we were fuelled by various substances.'

Ronnie had to be carried on stage and only managed to stay there for a few numbers before he had to be carried off again.

The show was recorded, as planned, on Ronnie's Mobile Studio, but as often happens with live recordings of lively gigs, the listening experience was not rewarding. You had to be there.

'Ronnie's mind was overactive,' Steve said, 'physically he's knackered . . . but he can still write.'

Accordingly, Steve decided that instead of the live album, they'd put together a studio album. He persuaded Laurie O'Leary – manager, East Ender, mover, shaker, friend of the Krays, the man who made Doris Stokes, medium and clairvoyant, the celebrity she'd accurately predicted she was going to be – to stump up some cash.

They took the Lane Mobile down to the Corbett Theatre in Loughton, east London.

'I had nothing to do,' Ronnie said. 'I'd just had this attack, and, in my mind, I was crawling up the wall, so it gave me something to do.'

'The way the album was intended,' Jim Leverton said, 'was that you'd get a Ronnie song followed by a Steve song followed by a Ronnie song and so on throughout.'

Along with Jim, Mick Green (guitarist formerly with Johnny Kidd & The Pirates), Mick Weaver and Dave Haynes were recruited to play and Steve Fisher and Mick Conroy to engineer.

'I think we achieved something very special indeed,' Steve Fisher said. 'Boo and Pam were around a lot of the time keeping us cheerful. 'Toe Rag' was recorded in the bar. We had very few screens so I piled up all of the soft chairs I could find to get some separation – they looked like gun emplacements! Mostly the musicians were not in a fit state to get home – there was plenty of stuff consumed so I used to drive some of them home in the Toyota Land Cruiser that towed the LMS [Lane Mobile Studio]. It was always very late at night, and we ran a lot of red lights!'

'The whole of the fortnight was really pretty much a drinking situation,' Jim Leverton said, 'and I also remember daily pilgrimages to the local pie and mash shop in Loughton. Ronnie loved the stewed eels and Steve just had to have his daily intake of pie and mash. Then, of course, there would be mercy dashes into Notting Hill to get certain substances! With regards to the recordings what really sticks in my mind is the way Ronnie and I used to work out the bass lines between us. Poignant really, because he was a fantastic bass player, so although he came out with great ideas it was me that actually played bass on all the tracks. He'd hum a line and I'd play it. I was adding ideas as well, so it was a collaboration. I suppose it was a bit sad because of Ronnie's condition at the time that we had to do it like that, but it was also nice in a way.'

On the album, Ronnie's tracks included yet another tribute to his dad, 'The Son of Stanley Lane', which predicted that one day a blue plaque would be put 'outside of my basement' proclaiming, 'Once lived here the son of Stanley Lane'.

When recording was finished, they threw a big wrap party at the Grapes in Islington.

'I remember helping him up a step,' said Jim Leverton, 'and he'd say to me, "Hang on Levertoss, I've just had my application to join the SAS turned down, I can't think why!"'

The album didn't see the light of day until 2000, by which time Steve and Ronnie were both dead. Steve had taken the tapes around to all the usual suspects with no joy.

'I was a no-go as far as the record industry was concerned because of my MS,' Ronnie said. 'And they didn't want Steve either.'

In the US, they drummed up some interest from Clive Davies of Arista Records, but he wouldn't release it without a tour to promote it. Ronnie was in no fit state to tour.

Keith Richards had loaned them about £40,000 to finalise the project. This, according to Ronnie, had been used by Steve to reboot his own career.

Once again Steve and Ronnie were estranged.

Eventually, Ronnie got his decree nisi. His marriage to Kate was over. She moved back to Wales with the children.

'I came back to the Fishpool area – well, about two miles away,' she said. 'We rented a house, but we had to keep moving every six months or so – we even lived in a caravan for a while in an orchard.'

Ronnie had hardly been in a position to fight for custody of the children. But fight he did. He took Kate to court, which Alana remembers as 'horrendous' and which went on for several months. Ronnie tried to seize the boys (and Alana, although she was his step-daughter) and the police had to be involved to stop him taking them illegally out of the country.

By the end of 1981 he was broke, his health was deteriorating, and he was 4,000 miles away in Florida.

What was he doing in Florida?

At this point, Fred Sessler enters the story.

Fred had had a chequered career. He was one of the few members of his family to survive the Nazi extermination camps. In the sixties, he developed the Perma-Weave hairpiece, then went on to head up a company that made amphibious cars. It seems somehow inevitable that such a person would eventually end up connected with the music business, and he became, as he himself described it, 'the world's oldest rock'n'roll groupie.'

By the time Ronnie got to know him he was, using the loosest imaginable definition of the term, a 'business associate' of The Rolling Stones. According to Woody he was a 'sex-fuelled, vodka charged, coke mountain' who supplied Keith Richards with drugs. Keith adored him and looked on him as a father figure.

In the late seventies, Fred encountered Bill 'Snakeman' Haast, proprietor of a 'Serpentarium' in Miami, a place that, mystifyingly, continued to do business even after, in 1977, a six-year-old boy was mauled to death by crocodiles there.

One of the highlights of a visit to the Serpentarium was to see Snakeman Bill milk the snakes then inject himself with their venom, which he insisted brought immense medical benefits.

Either inspired by Bill, or more likely as an entirely unrelated and independent venture, the University of Miami was also conducting clinical trials exploring the efficacy of snake venom in treating various medical conditions. After CBS broadcast an optimistic report on the research, Snakeman Bill and Fred Sessler decided it was time to set up a clinic.

The Miami Venom Institute, Snakeman Bill told the *St. Petersburg Times*, 'will be computerised and fully staffed with specialists to meet all the data gathering requirements of the Food and Drug Administration.' It promised, or at least suggested, that their diluted venom, properly administered, could cure arthritis and a range of other diseases including MS.

Keith Richards' Auntie Joanna, who suffered from MS, had found the treatment beneficial. Ronnie hoped that it would help him too. Fred had known him for years and, keen for celebrity clients to publicise the clinic's miracles, offered to treat him for free.

All the same, money had to be raised for the move to Florida and for living expenses, so Boo sold her furniture and they rented an apartment in Fort Lauderdale.

Four months of treatments followed, the theory being that the venom might 'jolt' Ronnie's bloodstream into battling the MS.

Keith Altham, his friend and sometimes PR man, visited him at the time and reported Ronnie saying: 'I can't say I have noticed any dramatic improvement but there is a beneficial side effect, because if any mosquito bites me it dies instantly.'

In the spring of 1982, despite the clinic's promise to meet all the data gathering requirements, the US Food and Drug Administration closed the place down. Fred Sessler moved his operation to Jamaica. Ronnie returned to London with a year's worth of snake venom in his luggage so that he could carry on with the treatments.

'The illness goes up and down like a pair of trousers,' Ronnie told *Rolling Stone*. 'One day you feel sort of OK. You think you've cracked it. The snake venom is working. You get so excited you can't sleep then the MS hits you and you are back to square one – a bloody useless cripple.

'How can I describe it? Can you imagine the strands of your hair hurting? That's what happens. And when you blink – like that – it's like your eyelids are made of sandpaper. I was quite prepared to feel bad, like with the flu or mumps. But I've never had anything like this. This is like hell itself.

'I wet myself like a baby. I went blind in one eye, but it has come back a bit. Like a camera lens with butter on it.'

Eventually Ronnie accepted that the snake venom was doing him no good and stopped taking it.

Bill 'Snakeman' Haast, incidentally, lived until he was a hundred years old, and survived 173 potentially fatal snakebites.

Ronnie was managing to take a little exercise – but it took him an hour to cover 600 yards. 'I do it three times a day, on Monday I managed five. If I keep trying, I'll make a connection, all the fuses in my body that have blown out will come back together again. That's what I believe. I do a lot of praying that my belief is right.'

In August 1982, he gave an interview to Kurt Loder for *Rolling Stone* in which he reflected on his days with the Small Faces and the Faces.

'I did a lot of really unreasonable things in those days, I'm ashamed of myself for the way I've gone on, very ashamed. I've been there and back, and I know how far it is.'

'I had a bit of money to slide downhill on,' he told the *News of the World*. 'I have been responsible for making millions. I haven't got it now. After I stopped taking junk I became a heavy drinker, I must have been on the edge of being an alcoholic. Boo stopped me from rolling downhill. I didn't have anything worth living for, thinking when it's time to go it's time to go.

'I look at my life and do you know what I see – an illusion. That's all it was – a bloody illusion. It doesn't make you happy. You can be number one and earning lots of money. But it doesn't make you happy. I am happier now than I was when I was number one. You can believe it or not.'

On 14 June, his friend James Honeyman-Scott, guitarist with The Pretenders, died in his sleep from cocaine poisoning. He was 25. Ronnie and Boo, who had seen him only a couple of days before, were heartbroken.

'When I heard that, I started getting depressed again. For years I wanted to pop off like that and particularly since I had MS.

'I didn't grow up until last year. I suppose coping with all this made me decide I wasn't as hopeless as I thought I was. So, I fight, that's why I won't take a wheelchair. I won't give in.'

He'd found more sympathy for his mother too, who was now completely bedridden.

'The pain I feel twists my body; the agony I feel for her gnaws my mind.'

His financial state was dire. He didn't have enough money to hire an accountant to investigate the possibilities of recouping royalties from the sales of old Small Faces albums or even on *Rough Mix*, the one he'd made with Pete Townshend. Then the Lane Mobile was vandalised again and stripped of much of its equipment. He sold what was left of it. He'd had enough.

Encouraged by his brother Stan, he remained convinced that some-where out there he could find something that would ease his suffering.

He'd been in touch with the Rigpa Fellowship, a Tibetan Buddhist Meditation and Study Organisation in Islington. They sent him a Tibetan medicine called Dudtsi – a holy nectar substance for tantric practices and rituals.

A more promising possibility came from a British organisation called Action for Research into Multiple Sclerosis (ARMS), the membership of which consisted primarily of those with MS and their families. ARMS was – in Ronnie and Boo's opinion anyway – more open-minded to new treatments than the larger and more established Multiple Sclerosis Society of Great Britain, who – again in Ronnie and Boo's opinion – concentrated their funds on offering respite care and holidays to people with MS. His mother had been on several holidays funded by them.

'The Society was a great organisation if you want to be a cripple,' Ronnie said. 'You know what I mean? They take you off in a Cripple's Coach . . . to sit by the Crippled Sea . . . to have a cripple party!'

ARMS on the other hand, still offered hopes of, if not cure at least respite and introduced Ronnie to something rather more respectable and high-tech than snake venom. HBOT – Hyperbaric Oxygen Treatment – consists of sitting the patient in a high-pressure chamber filled with nearly pure oxygen. It's been used for the treatment of a range of conditions including gangrene, carbon monoxide poisoning, burns and radiation injuries, and it can relieve some of the symptoms of MS.

25

Arms and the Man

The first time Ronnie tried the treatment it felt like magic.

'Within a week he came alive. He was writing music,' Boo said. 'After 20 sessions he started getting his fingers back, and I started getting excited. He was up until midnight for about two weeks! He was walking without his sticks! He had enough energy and strength to walk without his sticks!'

He started going swimming at the Swiss Cottage baths, splashing around, the water freeing him and lifting him up.

The drawback was price and availability. There was a limited number of hyperbaric chambers in the UK. The treatment was expensive and, after the initial 20, he found he couldn't get any more sessions for four months. The layoff undid many of the benefits.

Boo had an idea. The UK needed more hyperbaric chambers. Ronnie had lots of friends who, as the Concert for Kampuchea had proved, could raise huge sums of money in a single evening. The chambers were about £20,000 a pop. The initial idea was to raise enough to buy just one for the exclusive use of ARMS.

Glyn Johns and Ian Stewart got on the case.

Things began to escalate when the two of them, together with PR man Keith Altham, went to Jeff Beck's birthday party in June 1983.

They pitched the idea of a one-off charity gig at the Hammersmith Odeon to 'raise some money for Ronnie's medical treatment,' Keith Altham said. 'Clapton overheard and promptly volunteered his services.'

Jimmy Page was at the party too. He had barely played since John Bonham's death and the break-up of Led Zeppelin a couple of years earlier, and had become practically a recluse.

The previous summer there had been a Yardbirds reunion. Two of the ex-Yardbirds guitar legends – Eric and Jeff – had played 'and apparently nobody asked Jimmy to play on it, and I think he was a bit pissed off,' Stu said. 'So, at this party while I was discussing the Ronnie Lane benefit with Jeff, Jimmy came up and he said, "Nobody ever asked me to play. Why can't I play on it?" So, we said, "Step this way."'

'Eric . . . turned to me to help him to put a band together,' Glyn Johns said. 'His band was all Americans, so it would have been completely uneconomical to bring them over from the States and put them in a hotel for one charity concert. I got straight on the phone to Stu, Bill Wyman, Charlie Watts and Andy Fairweather Low. By the end of the day, they all agreed to do a show for Ronnie.'

Everybody who knew Ronnie, it seemed, had wanted to do something – anything – to help.

'I remember being around him when he first started to get signs of it,' said Eric. 'I didn't know what it was, nor did he. No one did.'

'I'd heard he wasn't well,' Bill Wyman told *Rolling Stone*, 'but you never really realise how afflicted people are until you actually see them again. I mean, you remember them as they were.'

'I first found out Ronnie was sick when I visited Eric,' Jeff Beck said. 'I just happened to call on him, and the phone rang, and it was Ronnie. They were on the phone for a long time, and I started thinking, "Come on, Eric." But then when he hung up, he told me. He said, "Ronnie's really, really bad."'

Glyn Johns: 'Soon my phone was ringing off the hook with

equipment companies, road managers and the rock'n'roll elite offering their services in droves, responding to the request for help from one of their own.'

Glyn was already arranging Eric Clapton's Command Performance for Prince Charles, so they suggested to the promoter Harvey Goldstein that they should book the Royal Albert Hall for another couple of nights and hold a benefit concert.

'I sold the radio rights in America to raise the cash to pay for our concert to be filmed,' Glyn said in his autobiography *Sound Man*, 'then rang Stanley Dorfman in LA who dropped everything and flew to London at his own expense to come and direct it. He was the only man for the job. He already had a wonderful relationship with everyone on the bill having worked with all of them many times in his days directing *Top of the Pops* and *In Concert* for the BBC.

'Eric invited his old pal Stevie Winwood and added Ray Cooper on percussion to his band. Kenney Jones could not be left out. We rehearsed at my place for a week. They all came from afar and wide. The whole spirit of the event revolved around Ronnie and everyone's affection for him.'

'That shit Rod Stewart announced in the Sunday newspaper that he was going to come over for his "old mate Ronnie Lane,"' Ronnie said. 'He didn't contact anybody to do with the show, just made his big announcement.'

Needless to say, Rod didn't turn up on the night.

Glyn Johns: 'The Stones donated their truck for me to record the radio show and sound for the video that we sold to Laurence Ronson [father of Mark]. It completely sold out, raising more than £1 million from the night.'

The royal seal of approval was added when Charles and Diana – just over a year married – turned up.

The show went on for nearly three hours. Eric opened. Jeff and Jimmy did sets variously supported by Steve Winwood, Andy

Fairweather Low, Bill Wyman, Charlie Watts and Kenney Jones. They were even indulgent enough to do the hits. Jeff did 'Hi Ho Silver Lining', which he's on record as hating. And Jimmy got a huge cheer when he started every beginner guitarist's favourite riff – the intro to 'Stairway to Heaven'.

Then everybody crowded onto the stage for 'Tulsa Time', the Don Williams song that Eric had covered on the double album *Just One Night*, and, the cherry on the cake, 'Layla'. Jeff, Jimmy and Eric all soloed – the first time the three of them had all played together on the same stage.

Some people think that the meeting of Churchill, Roosevelt and Stalin at Yalta was an event of historical importance. They know nothing.

For the finale, Ronnie took to the stage and led the musicians in an emotional rendition of 'Goodnight, Irene'. As Wordsworth put it, 'Bliss it was in that dawn to be alive, but to be young [or maybe in your early thirties] was very heaven.'

'After the Albert Hall,' Bill Wyman said, 'everybody was so knocked out by the fun and the camaraderie of it that they said, "We gotta do this again."'

This seemed an excellent idea so, a few days later, Ian Stewart got in touch with the promoter Bill Graham in the US to see if he would help. Bill agreed to promote the shows for free, although it involved complicated manoeuvring. It was the height of the ice hockey and baseball seasons so most of the more suitable stadia would be unavailable. He persisted, though, and eventually managed to book nine gigs scattered through Dallas, San Francisco and Los Angeles, culminating in two shows at New York's Madison Square Garden.

To prepare for the concerts, Ronnie first went to Fort Lauderdale for a series of 18-hour-long sessions in a hyperbaric chamber.

The all-star line-up flew out to America for three days' rehearsals before the first show in Dallas. Steve Winwood had to drop out, but Joe Cocker stepped in.

'There was a special atmosphere for those ARMS concerts,' Eric said. 'Although all of us had been around for all those years, we were playing together for the first time. I don't think we would have done it for money. That would have been too much aggravation. But because it was for multiple sclerosis and Ronnie Lane, it seemed right. We put down our egos and got on with it. It was a circus and great entertainment.'

Because of the numbers involved and the complexity, it was an expensive show to get on the road, but the first two concerts in Dallas covered the tab. The takings at all the others were pure profit for the charity.

A fan called Bucks Burnett had been sending Ronnie poetry he'd written. While they were in Dallas, Ronnie invited him for lunch at the Las Colinas hotel.

'When he at last limped from the elevator, I was shocked not by his frailty, but by his remarkably elfin qualities,' Bucks said. 'He was like a human flower with a broken stem. We sat at a long table and were soon joined by Bill Wyman and Jeff Beck. They spent the next hour arguing about an obscure jam session at Steve Winwood's house in 1962 [unlikely; Steve Winwood would have been 14 years old]: "Ya were too there," Wyman insisted to Beck. "I've got it on me home computah!" They also made fun of Elton John. Ronnie got the biggest laugh with, "He's a nice bloke . . . when he's asleep."'

'I walked Ronnie up to his room and presented him with an American flag. I told him I'd always wanted to meet Charlie Watts, so he sent me to the room next door. Charlie answered, totally nude and totally asleep.'

Later, Bucks would become one of Ronnie's roster of carers.

Plaudits for Jeff Beck and Eric were loud: less so for Jimmy Page, who seemed to be slowly finding his feet again after his two-year sabbatical.

'This tour has got him moving again,' said Ian Stewart, 'and I hope he can find something to do after this.'

And the climax was always Ronnie's appearance at the end. At Madison Square Garden, he was helped on to the stage by Woody and Kenney and joined everybody in his own composition 'Long Gone' and, again, 'Goodnight, Irene'.

Not a dry eye in the house.

26

Something Can Be Done and You Can Do It

The nine US shows broke box office records in some places and raised a total of around $1 million.

'The following day going home on the plane,' Glyn Johns said, 'it suddenly came to me that I had tricked myself into believing that all that effort and outpouring of affection for Ronnie from so many people over the previous few weeks would, like some kind of fairy story, somehow cure him of this terrible debilitating disease. It was not to be.'

The original aim of the concerts was to raise money for ARMS, a UK organisation. The US money, however, would be donated to an American or worldwide initiative. Ronnie had, however, become disenchanted with the MS Society, the nearest American equivalent to ARMS, and particularly its views about the efficacy of hyperbaric chambers.

'The MS society hired a Dr Fischer, back in the seventies, to prove once and for all, that hyperbaric oxygen is no use, whatsoever, to people with MS,' he said. 'He worked on it for some years, and he couldn't do it. His report came out in favour of the hyperbaric oxygen. They asked him to go back and write his report again. Three times they sent him back to rewrite his report. The last time he finished it was in 1980 while I was still walking about. Ordinarily, I might add.

They didn't rush-release the report at all because it was in favour of HBO. In actual fact, it was only released early last year, 1983. Meanwhile, I've become crippled, you see? They've dismantled his oxygen chamber. It's now in a car park in New York. He could not prove that oxygen was no good. He could only prove that it is of some help. Don't get me wrong, it's not a cure. But it's of great assistance for someone to keep it under control, and to live with it kind of ordinarily, you know? Lead a bit of a life, instead of gradually becoming crippled all of the time. Anyway, that's a story about the MS Society, and it's not a very nice story. Not a very nice story at all, but it happens to be the case.'

Ronnie started to seek out some organisation that he thought might be a more worthy recipient of the money they'd raised.

'I don't know how to find the people. You see, ARMS over here [in the UK] was created by people with MS that got so frustrated at this whole attitude towards MS. You know, this sort of, "Well, you've got an incurable disease now. You're going to get crippled for the rest of your life, but just sit back and accept it. We've got a nice wheelchair for you out in the hall, and everything's going to be rosy. Don't make a panic, you'll upset everyone."

'My idea of starting an Action Research into MS in America has taken a bit of a knocking because I don't know how to put it together properly. I mean, I know how to put one together, but I want to put a very potent one together, an effective one together – not a sham, and not one that's there just to spend the money. So, I've got a little bit more research to do on all that. But it will be done.'

After Christmas, Ronnie had been able to spend a little time with Luke and Reuben. They came to stay at Boo's flat in Kentish Town, London. He told friends that he was worried about the children but realised he wasn't in any state to look after them – his fatigue had eased but he still could not see through his left eye or hold anything with his left hand.

Ronnie's doctor had recommended that he try the Houston Medical Center in Texas, which had a small four-chamber facility, founded by Mae Nacol, a 42-year-old lawyer.

Ronnie arranged to meet Mae and she invited him to stay with her and her sister Barbara while he was having treatments. She owned a 74-acre ranch just outside the city but lived most of the time in her house on Memorial Drive in a very prosperous neighbourhood.

Mae Nacol had had an eventful life. Her mother had been pistol whipped to death ten years before and her father, a wealthy jeweller, had been robbed at gunpoint of half a million dollars' worth of jewellery.

Mae met Ronnie off the plane.

She told him that she had MS, too, but, thanks to HBO treatments, was pretty much free of all of the symptoms. Six years earlier she couldn't walk, was practically blind, going deaf and could barely feed herself. She'd flown to Florida. After 20 treatments she could walk again and was well enough to return to Houston, rebuild her legal practice and start work on establishing the facility at the Medical Center, which was now managed by her sister Barbara.

To Ronnie, Mae Nacol sounded the ideal person to head up the charity he wanted to found in the States to help people with MS. Initially, though, she was reluctant: she told Ronnie that she didn't need the extra work. 'With this disease,' she said, 'you can't handle stress.'

But Ronnie, ever the charmer, persuaded her to help, and in the autumn Mae and Barbara flew to England for three weeks to meet all the main players at UK ARMS. They went home with a cheque for $1 million to set up the new organisation, to be called ARMS of America. In Houston, in order to be able to devote herself full-time to the charity, Mae wound up her law practice.

ARMS of America was to be run by a general membership of people with MS and their relatives and was to be directed by a board of six, including Ronnie and a British authority on HBO, Dr Philip James. The purpose of the new organisation, its literature proclaimed, was to further research into the cause, the treatments and cures for multiple sclerosis.

Ronnie flew to Texas. On the plane over he got extremely pissed and had a big fight with Boo, who'd just about managed to keep him reasonably sober for two years. The row was such that, as soon as they landed in the US, she left him there and took the next flight home.

On 11 December, the board of the new organisation met in Houston and took some decisions that should have started alarm bells ringing. It abolished the general membership's voting rights, instead appointing an executive committee charged with managing the day-to-day affairs of the charity. So, although only Mae Nacol, who had MS, should technically have been eligible for membership, Barbara, Mae's sister, became president, Carol Kent, an attorney who'd worked for Mae for 15 years, became vice-president and Beverley Ashley, the wife of one of Mae's first law clients, became the organisation's treasurer. All four were put on the payroll.

Ronnie was not a member of the executive committee.

Gradually, worrying revelations began to seep out.

Mae Nacol's brother had had his medical license revoked for administrating dodgy hormone treatments to his patients; Mae herself had been taken to the bankruptcy court in 1978, at which time irregularities had turned up in her accounting. The financial records she had filed weren't complete. She alleged that some of them had been stolen by a former law firm associate. Some of her unsecured creditors who had loaned her money without acquiring collateral took significant losses. One of them was her then partner Linda Hudson, who had loaned Mae $42,000. During the six months following the end of her relationship with Hudson, Mae had found a new source of unsecured loans – her legal secretary Barbara Leigh

Hunt, the same woman who had been introduced to Ronnie as her sister. Twice in the next few years Mae would state under oath that she and Barbara were sisters. In October 1977, by means of a legal document drafted by Mae's office, Barbara had in fact changed her name to Barbara Nacol.

Ronnie moved into a modest apartment in the suburbs of Houston, next to the freeway. Mae had arranged everything for him, getting a carer, Ron Chandler, to look after him full time. But Ron quit quite soon after, saying it was too much for him.

Bucks Burnett, the fan who had come to one of the ARMS concerts in Dallas and had had lunch with Ronnie afterwards, told the *Dallas Observer* in 1997: 'In February 1985, I visited Ronnie at his Houston apartment and ended up moving in with him a week later, signing on as his personal assistant. We spent our days swimming at the Y, going to physical therapy, shopping, and eating steaks at Dirty's Steakhouse. Through it all, Lane's humour remained intact. By that time, the disease had robbed Ronnie of any sphincter control – requiring frequent clean-ups – he would break the tension by moaning in mock supplication, "Kill 'im again, 'e's not dead yet."'

Ronnie went into the ARMS office in downtown Houston most weekdays to answer calls on the organisation's 800 number for people with MS. With Bucks' help (Ronnie always called him his butler) he did his best to rebuild his health, going into the HBO chamber two or three times a week to get free treatments. He met the press, appeared at rock shows in his wheelchair and lobbied musicians to stage benefit concerts.

'In March 1985, The Firm featuring Jimmy Page and Paul Rodgers played a show in Austin,' Bucks said, 'and Jimmy invited us both along, with transport laid on, best seats in the house and two hotel suites in a very posh block and a couple of hours of socialising thrown in as well . . . Ronnie's health was very up and down, I got to see it very up close and personal during this time. One day he'd be physically, horrifically bad, or he would have a really dark mood swing, and the very next day he's walking unaided and calling me "Darling". He told me from the outset that I had to be prepared to see the bad side of him and the bad side of the disease. He'd say, "I'm a puppet and it's the hand on the puppet that responds, there's no Ronnie Lane left," and he was right . . . the disorder would make him a jerk. It was all part of the package; I knew what I was getting into.'

Ronnie often talked to Bucks about his children and how he missed them. He thought he was protecting them by not contacting them. He remembered what a detrimental effect his mother had on his childhood and didn't want the same for them.

'Occasionally we would entertain out-of-town guests,' Bucks said. 'I remember watching Ronnie and Ian McLagan sing 'Ooh La La' – my favourite Faces song – at the kitchen table. I was now butler to two Faces. It was like butlering for an army of monkeys. They were hilarious together . . . Later that night, the three of us crawled drunkenly to our bedrooms, Ronnie being the only one with a good excuse for not walking upright.'

Ronnie got friendly with a healer called Don Shoffner in Houston: he told Ronnie that he was a car with a dead battery and that he, Don, would act as a jump lead and battery to get him started again. In a series of healing sessions, he laid his hands on Ronnie while breathing deeply and meditated on filling Ronnie with the spark of life. Nothing really happened, but as he didn't charge anything for the treatment and it didn't harm Ronnie, they remained friends.

Mark Bowman, a rock photographer who had met Ronnie (and Ian McLagan) backstage in February, remembered going around to Ronnie's flat in Houston in August for a dinner party with Heart's Ann and Nancy Wilson, DJ Dayna Steele and Cameron Crowe.

'This was the first time I ever started trying to play a guitar . . . It was at Ronnie Lane's, and I would plink around on his Gibson Les Paul and Ronnie would play his Faces-era 70s tortoise shell bass guitar from Zemaitis. He told me to keep the Les Paul at my place and practice on it. Just another way Ronnie Lane had a profound impact on my life . . . I had it in my possession until I handed it to Mary Elena Holly [Buddy Holly's wife], when she won it in a charity auction in December 1985.'

When he could, Ronnie was still trying to work.

He later told Jody Denberg, a well-known disc jockey in Austin: 'I recorded a song called 'Spiritual Babe', which is the most recent thing I've written. I've got these "Canadian canes", which is a polite way of saying crutches, and I'd been learning to walk on them. I got this idea for a song called 'Stay with Me Lord', but then I thought no one would buy it; "C'mon, leave it off, Ronnie." So, I changed 'Stay with Me Babe' and it became 'Spiritual Babe'. It was recorded in Houston on to cassette, not even reel-to-reel.'

Ronnie didn't ever make a proper recording of the song, but Ian McLagan did after Ronnie's death.

Pete Townshend suggested to Ronnie during one of their long transatlantic phone calls that he should write his autobiography and Ronnie asked Bucks Burnett if he would like to help him (they even had a working title – *I Can Take It*).

When Ronnie talked it over with Mae she said absolutely not (apparently Ronnie had signed a contract with her to allow her to manage Ronnie's affairs). She chose another writer, but nothing ever came of it.

Ronnie had run out of money by the summer and ARMS was paying for everything, even Buck's wages. Mae and Ronnie sometimes discussed his expenses but not the wider financial ARMS expenditures because, Ronnie said, 'that was mainly, you know, beyond my understanding.'

His brother Stan visited him in Houston and had a tour of the ARMS offices. He told Ronnie he didn't trust Mae and thought the set-up seemed fishy, but Ronnie couldn't see any problems with her.

He had enough on his plate with his own health worries and didn't want to get too involved. He stayed on the edge of the daily life of ARMS and out of the seemingly ordinary tiffs that developed between the office workers there.

But by the summer of 1985, the problems were becoming more obvious. Mark Bowman, the official photographer for ARMS, quit going there because 'the vibes were too bad'.

The relationship between Mae and her lover/pretend sister and colleague Barbara Nacol was breaking down.

In October, it was reported in *Texas Monthly*, when the six members of the ARMS board met – for the first time that year – that Barbara Nacol opened the session's business by offering her resignation as president. It was accepted. Explaining that 'Barbara's concerns are not the best interests of ARMS but revenge on me', Mae Nacol then proposed that Barbara be removed from the board of directors too. Barbara protested but the motion passed: Barbara was purged. Philip James, the Scottish doctor who had worked closely with Ronnie, proposed that Mae should be removed from the board as well. His motion was defeated.

Mae Nacol ordered the locks to be changed on the doors, apparently to bar Barbara's re-entry, and then at the opening of the board's second meeting that year in November, she submitted her own resignation.

Ronnie says he didn't really understand what was going on at ARMS during the feud. Until late October, when Barbara reverted to the name Leigh Hunt, he believed the two were really sisters. He cast his support with Mae, almost on the basis of instinct. Mae in all her dealings with him had been perfectly amicable.

At a benefit at Fitzgerald's, a Houston club, Ronnie met JoRae Di Menno. JoRae was working as publicist for the club at the time and interviewed Ronnie. Ronnie made her laugh and the two of them

269

became friends. She said she could tell right away Lane wasn't doing so well.

'He was really pretty bad off when I met him. His complexion was white and pasty. He didn't look healthy at all – one of his eyes was turned in. He didn't seem to be able to do a lot.'

JoRae knew two people with MS who had been receiving treatment from a doctor in Iowa called Robert Soll. It had bought them a lot of relief, but when they had tried to contact Ronnie at the ARMS office the messages didn't get through. JoRae suspected that Mae Nacol was too wedded to promoting the HBO treatment to want to investigate any alternatives. She gave Ronnie a book called *MS: Something Can Be Done, and You Can Do It*, that explained it all.

Robert Soll believed that allergic reactions could possibly be a cause of MS. Enthused, Ronnie flew off to Iowa to start the treatment. By this time, Bucks Burnett had left his job as Ronnie's carer when Mae Nacol halved his wages unexpectedly. JoRae stepped up to look after him.

For the first part of the treatment, Ronnie had to observe a distilled water diet for four days. The hunger was especially hard to bear, Ronnie said, because one of their fasting days was Thanksgiving. During the four days both Ronnie and JoRae took daily doses of niacin, a vitamin that causes flushing of the face and neck. By the time they had finished their fast, niacin (used liked dental disclosing tablets in Robert Soll's treatment) no longer caused them to flush.

Then under the doctor's supervision they began rebuilding their usual diets, food by food, taking 100 milligrams of niacin before each meal. Ronnie's pulse rate got faster, and he flushed badly after eating several foods, eggs and avocado among them. So, he eliminated them from his diet.

After about two weeks, he surprised JoRae (and himself) by standing up in front of the mirror to shave. By Christmas he was back in Houston, where he amazed everyone by walking up the stairs to his second-floor apartment.

Once again Ronnie felt some hope for his future.

He had the energy now to look around and see what was happening in the ARMS organisation. As he was on the board, he asked to see the financial records but was deflected at every turn.

'At one point I remember a guy on the ARMS board yelled at me at one of the hearings,' Ronnie said. "Who are you? King Lane? King Lane, is it? King Lane, are you?" What an arsehole. All I wanted to do was get out of it all.'

He was told that during the feud between Mae Nacol and Barbara lots of the records went missing, presumably stolen to hide any mismanagement. Ronnie, through various friends, found an attorney, Larry Hysinger (he was a massive *Ogdens' Nut Gone Flake* fan), who volunteered to represent Ronnie for free. Larry obtained bank statements and documents from the archives which, he believed, clearly showed that there had been an abuse of trust. The members of the ARMS board responded to these allegations by voting Ronnie off the board, but Larry Hysinger took the financial information to the Texas Attorney's office and asked for an investigation.

On 31 March it all came to a head. A state district judge appointed a receiver, Ron Sommers, who found that 'the affairs of ARMS had been mismanaged', that there had been 'a pattern of self-dealing between the board of directors, executive committee and officers' and that 'various expenditures authorised by the executive committee and officers were inappropriate'.

He also found that ARMS was nearly broke. Only one of the Houston benefits had shown a profit. During its less than 18-month existence, US ARMS had an income of $1.2 million including the founding check of $1 million. Only $90,000 was left.

Almost everyone had got a generous slice of the pie. Mae had managed to cream off almost $200,000 a year one way or the other, while Barbara Nacol, who was the titular president before she was booted out, was paid an annual salary of $72,000. Carol Kent was paid a salary of $40,000 to handle Mae's private legal work and to serve as vice-president of the organisation. Three public relations firms hired by ARMS were paid $123,000 in retainers and fees.

In their mission statement issued when they started the organisation, they promised that ARMS would spend some $450,000 on research grants during its first year of operation. It actually spent $67,000 – just 5.6 per cent of its budget.

In court Mae tried to defend herself. She implied that things weren't that bad and 'additional fundraisers were anticipated in the near future'.

Unfortunately, because Ronnie had been a director of ARMS and the organisation had been paying for his apartment and a carer for a while, the court filed a suit against him for fraud and negligence. To make matters worse, Mae Nacol decided to sue Ronnie in June for $10 million for libel, slander and defamation of character.

★ ★ ★

Around this time, Rod Stewart called round all the ex-Faces to try to get them to come and play at his upcoming show at Wembley in July. Ticket sales had apparently been sluggish until Rod announced in the *Evening Standard* on 14 May that a reunion was on the cards, and then things picked up.

Ronnie and JoRae Di Menno decided to fly to London from Texas and were in England for four months. They stayed at Stan's, Ronnie's brother's place, during the week and would go to visit friends at the weekends – sometimes Pete Townshend and once at Pattie and Eric Clapton's huge country pile, Hurtwood Edge in Ewhurst.

'We had a great time, and we hung out as I do with my friends in Austin,' JoRae remembered. 'We bought Indian food, brought it back to their house, and watched the British show *Spitting Image* on television in a small, comfy kitchen. It was so much fun, and we had so many laughs.'

It was on this trip that Reuben, Ronnie's youngest son, saw his father for the first time in years. It would also be the last time.

'He was in a wheelchair then. He came to see my last sports day at school. They were closing the village school down because it only had 15 pupils back then. We used to talk a bit on the phone, and he sent me books about animals sometimes.'

Rod Stewart took Stan, JoRae and Ronnie out to dinner in a ritzy restaurant in Buckhurst Hill in Essex. He also got his cheque book out and wrote Ronnie a cheque for £5,000. Ronnie wasn't bowled over by Rod's magnanimity, though – according to Stan, he growled, 'That's a drop in the ocean to what that cunt owes me.'

On 5 July, Rod (and his 'very special guests') took to the stage at Wembley. Mac was there, with Woody, guitarist Robin Le Mesurier (Hattie Jacques' son – who knew?) and Bill Wyman standing in for Ronnie. The band looked markedly different from their peacock heyday. Rod was stocky and ordinary with his football shirt and short hair and the others looked like weekending chartered accountants. But Rod was in good voice and for the encore Ronnie shuffled onto to the stage on the arm of JoRae, and was positioned on a stool with a microphone. Deafening yells of admiration and sympathy came from the crowd as he sat down, and the Faces bumped and ground easily into their old party routine, cranking out '(I Know) I'm Losing You', 'Twisting the Night Away' and 'Stay with Me'.

Ronnie had hoped to sing some of his old songs, and had even rehearsed some of them, but nothing came of it. He hummed along with 'I'm Losing You' and Rod rather embarrassingly sat on the floor next to Ronnie's chair, resting his head on Ronnie's leg during 'Twisting'.

Afterwards, Ronnie told Mac: 'I felt stupid really, a token cripple on the stage. I didn't feel as though I was really necessary. It was more like people were taking pity on me. I didn't want to step on stage again unless I felt that I deserved to be there.'

Before returning to the US, he had all his mercury tooth fillings removed and replaced as it was thought that some people with MS had contracted mercury poisoning from them. On his return he told a Texan newspaper. 'It's unbelievable. When I had all my fillings changed to plastic the effects were remarkable. I'm left now with the weakness of someone who has had MS, but I don't have it anymore. I'm not slurring my speech and I'm not as easily fatigued. It's all pretty much gone because my fillings were changed, and I stopped eating food that I was allergic to.'

But once again the hope and optimism eventually turned to disillusion and disappointment.

JoRae and Ronnie decided that they would leave Houston for good and move to Austin. His new attorney, William Gage (Larry Hysinger was up to his neck in litigation against ARMS), managed to get Ronnie's case settled out of court

'The terms of Ronnie's settlement with the state,' Gage said, 'were that he would pay a fairly small amount only in the event that they recovered less than a certain amount of money from Mae Nacol. Ronnie didn't want to be involved in this anymore. His health had reached the point where it was an incredible burden on him.'

According to Glyn Johns: 'Ronnie wrote to the president [Ronnie Reagan – history doesn't record if he was a fan of the Faces] for assistance and he was completely absolved of any responsibility, but for a man who was seriously ill to begin with it must have been extremely straining.'

Chelsey Milliken, a manager and music business character who Ronnie knew from a European tour with the Small Faces in the Immediate Records years, helped Ronnie and JoRae relocate. 'I told him he'd be a lot better off in Austin than that godawful Houston,' Milliken told the *Austin Chronicle* in 2000. 'They came up and stayed in my house, then they got their own place.'

Austin was much less humid than Houston and that helped to ease his symptoms. But even more than that, Austin had had a thriving music scene ever since the 19th century, when the German community had made sure there was an oom-pah band in every beer garden.

By the fifties and sixties, a proliferation of jazz and blues clubs, mostly on the east side of town – Big Mary's, Ernie's Chicken Shack, Victory Grill, Charlie's Playhouse – were regularly playing host to the top acts of the day, like Ray Charles, Ike & Tina Turner, Chuck Berry, Janis Joplin.

The big kick came in 1970 when local entrepreneur Eddie Wilson stumbled upon an abandoned National Guard armoury on 525½ Barton Springs Road. It was huge, had the worst acoustics imaginable and was difficult to find – half-hidden behind a skating rink. Nevertheless, Eddie decided it would be a wonderful location for a music venue and his enthusiasm was further stoked when he discovered it was ridiculously cheap and realised that, if the punters had difficulty finding the place, the police wouldn't stand a chance so it would never be busted.

It was named, for reasons we need not go into, the Armadillo World Headquarters, and for ten years became a haven for those seeking all that is good and true in the world. Everybody worth knowing played the Armadillo – from AC/DC to ZZ Top. In 1974, Mr Springsteen did three nights there. Commander Cody & His Lost Planet Airmen recorded a live album there. The Austin Ballet Theatre played there once a month for eight years. And the 25c cups of beer and shrimp enchiladas were the stuff of legend.

'It takes,' Eddie Wilson said, 'good nutrition and good rich calories from food, to turn that alcohol buzz into a productive sort of thing. We were probably the most energetic people that have ever been accused of smoking too much pot or drinking too much beer, and as a result we converted a lot of rednecks. If they're having so much fun and the hippie chicks are that pretty, there must be something in it for us. All the guys with cowboy hats started growing their hair and all the guys with long hair got cowboy hats.'

A second kick came in 1972 when Willy Nelson abandoned the rednecks of Nashville and moved to Austin. Others followed, including Steve Earle and Waylon Jennings. A sloppy historian might date Willie's move to Austin as the birth of 'new country', 'cosmic country', 'country rock', 'progressive country', call it what you like. It had been going ages before 1972, anyway, but it's nice to have these historical watersheds.

By the time Ronnie moved there, Austin had a club on every corner and a radio station on every other block, all pumping out rock, R&B and jazz, and the loose federation of musicians, DJs and punters that had grown up in the place were only too glad to take Ronnie Lane into the bosom of their community.

'Chelsey Milliken introduced me to the Austin music scene, and I was soon doing lots of local radio interviews.'

He shared a two-bedroom house with JoRae Di Menno in Austin's tree-shaded Clarkesville neighbourhood, a quiet place far removed from his bitter memories of Houston. He spent some of his evenings hanging out with his new friends and sitting in on sessions with Austin musicians.

He also set up the Ronnie Lane Foundation, a new organisation for taking care of his needs and probing into new treatments for MS. But his strength started to wane again, and he was soon back in a wheelchair.

'We split fairly soon after returning from England,' JoRae said. 'I needed a "normal relationship", but we stayed in touch. He was trying to find out how he could stay in the States, and I researched it for him. I told him the only way to do it is to get married, that's the standard way to obtain a green card.

'Ronnie was a dear, sweet, naive (in an endearing way – he trusted just about everybody), feisty, funny, stubborn, and lovely man. I feel lucky to have known him.'

27

An Uncommon Amount of Courage

One day, Ed Mayberry, a DJ with Austin's rock'n'roll radio station KLBJ-FM (which had once been owned by the family of President Lyndon Baines Johnson, hence the call sign), was mooching around backstage at a rehearsal complex in Austin, looking for Jimmie Vaughan. He poked his head inside a trailer and saw a guy sitting alone. He asked him whether he'd seen Jimmie Vaughan and, when he said he hadn't, withdrew, thinking '"Man, that sure looked like Ronnie Lane." So, I opened the door again, and asked him. He confirmed who he was, and we arranged to do an interview at a later date. I was blown away by running into him – I had no idea he was in Austin.

'I think it ended up that my colleague, Jody Denberg, got him in the studio for the first interview and then, later, I produced a Valentine's Day broadcast with Ronnie for KLBJ-FM.'

That show was very special. It featured Ronnie calling up his celebrity friends on their home phones and asking them if they had any requests they wanted playing for Valentine's Day.

They caught Eric Clapton, eating fish and chips on the sofa at home in Surrey. He requested 'Wonderful Tonight', presumably for Patti.

Jeff Beck, just back from recording with Mick Jagger in Barbados, chatted amicably on air, as did Bill Wyman (who they woke from an afternoon nap), Jimmy Page and Pete Townshend, who was in the studio that day.

Woody had just come back from picking up his kids from school. He wanted to hear 'Young Blood' by The Coasters. Ronnie and Mac read out the weather report. For a local radio show it was an incredible coup.

'I remember thinking,' Ed said, 'that it's not just name-dropping for people on his radio special – they're his friends.'

Ed's colleague Jody Denberg had a band, the Seven Samurai, and talked Ronnie into guesting with them at the Continental Club. In the band was the Mexican guitarist/singer Alejandro Escovedo. By coincidence, Escovedo's previous band, the True Believers, had sometimes featured Ronnie's songs – 'Debris' and 'Oh La La' – in their sets. And here was the man himself.

'If you can imagine playing on your favourite baseball team, that's what it was like,' Escovedo said. 'He always made me feel good about life in general.'

The *Austin Chronicle* proclaimed that night at the Continental one of the year's highlights. After that, Austin bands were queuing up to recruit Ronnie. He rehearsed for a while with a band called The Tremors, and felt he was on good form.

'I don't have the dexterity back in my hands to play the guitar yet. And when I started, my voice was so rusty, it was like something that had been left out in the yard for 11 years. But all the rehearsing that I've been doing has improved that.'

Chelsey Milliken, the man in whose house Ronnie had stayed when he first arrived in Austin, took on the role of Ronnie's manager and started to line up gigs.

'I will probably play with The Tremors as well as with other bands. There are a lot of musicians in the Austin area that are really good.'

With The Tremors and sax legend Bobby Keys (who'd played with Eric, George Harrison, John Lennon and wailed wonderfully on, among many other tracks, the Stones' 'Brown Sugar'), Ronnie performed a few numbers at the Austin Music Awards Banquet. The set included The Kinks' 'Tired of Waiting', the Faces' 'You're So Rude', Ronnie's recent composition 'Spiritual Babe' and Johnny Kidd & The Pirates' 'Shakin' All Over'. The irony of a guy with MS playing 'Shakin' All Over' with a band called The Tremors was not lost.

Chelsey lined up a mini-tour, and over the next few months, The Tremors, featuring Ronnie and Bobby, played the Steamboat in Austin, the Mason Jar in Phoenix and a few small clubs in San Francisco and New York.

'The end of the show is always the hardest part of the day for me,' Ronnie told the *LA Times*. 'You sing your heart out for an hour and it takes a lot more energy than you realise. So, you're just drained at the end.

'This [tour] has probably been harder than I imagined, but my spirit is pretty good. The hour on stage is wonderful, just wonderful. I'm quite proud because I am doing something that I've never known anyone to do: go on the road with MS.'

The reporter then had the nerve to ask Bobby Keys if he was playing with Ronnie as a favour.

'Hell, no. If I just wanted to be a nice guy, I could sit out in the audience and yell, "Atta boy, Ron" and shake his hand after the show. The bottom line is I wouldn't be on stage if the music wasn't good.

'Places like this are a long way from the Forum and Madison Square Garden, but it's still fun because the music is valid. To me, the man has an uncommon amount of courage. You see how hard it is for him to walk onto the stage, but once he gets to the microphone, it's a different story. That's probably the best medicine in the world for him.'

In New York they played a special Easter Sunday show at the Limelight club. The last time Ronnie had played the city was at Madison Square Garden, when he had sung 'April Fool' and 'Goodnight, Irene' at the end of the ARMS concert. At the end of this show, he realised he didn't have the energy to get down off his stool, walk off stage, then walk back on again for an encore, so he just told the lighting crew to turn off the lights, then turn them back on again, at which point he said, 'Since I'm still here, we might as well do an encore.'

The audience loved him.

'I'm still a cripple,' he told the *New York Times*, 'which in the dictionary definition means somebody who can't walk unaided. But I'm a lot better than I was at Madison Square Garden. I feel that I have found the answer to this lousy disease. I have a lot more energy, and I don't have that terrible fatigue, so I can take on something like a show.

'I had spent the last 11 years thinking that my life was over, and I was just left here to think about it, but now, if I knew how to stage it, I could work pretty regularly. I know my limitations now, and I don't see why I couldn't carry on for years.'

Old pals and industry well-wishers turned out in droves. One night, he spotted Andrew Loog Oldham in the audience.

'I asked Andrew very nicely when I was on stage via the microphone, "Hey Andrew, where's my million dollars?" I think he sneaked out through the toilet window."

In San Francisco, he gave an interview to the *Globe and Mail*, lying on the bed in his 'matchbox-sized hotel room answering questions in a soft, weak voice.'

'It's fantastic to be on stage again, I never thought I'd be able to do it. Perhaps I shouldn't be doing it. But I want to. So that's that.

'I don't want to do anything like that ARMS benefit again. I want to help people who've been suddenly told they've got MS. I don't want people to be in the same situation as I was in when they told me. They told me, "Don't do anything." That's all they said. I was not encouraged to exercise. I was not encouraged to do anything.'

Michael Jackson had just revealed to the press that he had an HBO chamber that he used to prevent the ageing process.

'Good stuff,' Ronnie said, 'pure oxygen under pressure. It helps indeed. I go in and take a dive once in a blue moon when I've got the money. Before I had the HBO I couldn't talk. I was slurring my speech like a drunkard. I wasn't drinking, but I couldn't get my mouth around the words. My health is not that good, although it's not as bad as it was. And it's hard to kill vermin. I'm here to prove that.'

From San Francisco the band flew off to stay in Ronnie Wood's mansion in Malibu for a few weeks.

Back in Austin, he moved into a new apartment and lived on his own for the first time in ages.

His association with The Tremors fizzled out, but he kept playing with friends like Alejandro Escovedo, his bandmate from the True Believers; guitarist J. D. Foster; accordion player Randy Banks; bassist Ronnie Johnson; and a singer called Susan Voelz.

'I chopped and changed the musicians on a regular basis though, that was governed by the "prosperity" of the band.'

At the time there were over 60 clubs in Austin and most of them had a live band playing every night. Most working musicians would find themselves gigging with bands under several different names, so that became the norm for whatever group Ronnie assembled: sometimes called Slim Chance, sometimes the Ronnie Lane Band, they'd get together, rehearse, do a few shows, then go off their separate ways.

'Ronnie seemed to love having people drop in at his various Austin homes, for a smoke and for conversation,' Ed Mayberry said. 'And not just to talk about music. Or I'd drop by to pick him up for a dinner at Katz's Deli or one of the other Austin restaurants. Sometimes his MS was so bad that I'd have to lift him from his wheelchair into the car seat, and the trip would tire him out.'

At the end of October at the Black Cat Lounge in Austin when a band called Alamo Choir were playing, Ronnie met Susan Gallegos. In her early thirties, with two young daughters to bring up, she was

281

half-Mexican, half-Native American – possibly the granddaughter of an Apache chief. When they were first introduced, she had no idea who Ronnie was.

'We sat for a long time talking like we'd always known each other,' she said. 'We both had very surprised looks on our faces. Especially Mr Lane. He was out of his arena.'

In the spring of 1988, Ian McLagan found himself in Austin to record an album with The Georgia Satellites and took Ronnie, Susan and a bunch of their friends out for dinner.

He noticed that Ronnie and Susan were wearing identical rings.

'We're married,' Ronnie said.

The wedding had taken place at a friend's house. Jody Denberg from KLBJ was best man.

They moved into Susan's apartment in north Austin, part of a complex (now seemingly demolished) mostly filled with students and minimum-wage employees. But it was next door to a golf course and on sunny days Ronnie liked to sit in his wheelchair on the edge of the rough, dodging the misplaced drives.

He was still performing. At the Austin Music Awards he and his band did a short set consisting of 'Debris' and 'Oh La La'.

'Ronnie's gigs in Austin ALWAYS brought tears to my eyes,' Jody Denberg said. 'Few singers strike me that way. 'Ooh La La' was like the story of his life, in a way, with lines like "I wish that I knew what I know now when I was stronger." He always sang with soul, and he had a voice – live or on record – that sends chills through me with its honesty. I'll always remember seeing him onstage performing as all the musicians looked at him with such love and reverence.'

In July he did a set for KLBJ, 'April Fool', 'Kuschty Rye', 'Under the April Skies'.

It was after this show that Susan fired Alejandro for being drunk which, as somebody remarked, was like 'being booted out by Willie Nelson for smoking too much pot.'

But money was always short. Ronnie did not have a health plan and US medicine is expensive. Chelsey Milliken contacted former bandmates for help.

'All the boys contributed to his medical bills,' Kenney Jones said, 'with Rod and Woody taking the lead in that, while I fought hard to wrestle back royalties owed to the Small Faces, which would eventually achieve a degree of success and some income for Ronnie.'

There were still good days, but the overall trajectory was down.

In the September of 1988, he did a live set for another Austin radio station, KUT. The voice is weak. The high notes flutter and falter, but still, there's that layer of vulnerability that messes with your emotions.

A month later, he appeared again at the Continental Club. 'Lane's soulful vocal moans, that display a quirky folksy quality, lifted the sprightly music to a more resonant powerful plateau,' the *Austin Chronicle* said.

His mum died on 20 October in her care home in Havering. She was 78 and had outlived his father by many years. Ronnie hadn't seen her for a while and wasn't well enough to go to the funeral. One time when he had been to see her, she'd told him he'd never walk again. That had stiffened his resolve for a while, but these days the condition was getting the upper hand.

In January 1989 he went into Arlyn Studios in south Austin, to record four tracks. He wanted to get a good take of his song 'Spiritual Babe' that he'd written a few years before. But the session had to be abandoned and they decided they'd come back to it when and if his health improved.

He managed another gig at the Continental, with the audience throughout buoying him up with their enthusiasm.

'After the set,' Michael MacCambridge wrote in the *Austin Statesman*, 'Lane was about to be lifted off the stage when another round of cheering went up for a final song. The band played a new one – 'Sally

Ann' – which might match 'Ooh La La' in tragic irony ("By and by . . . nothing is sweeter than to die").

'Austin is blessed to have him.'

Though England hadn't entirely forgotten him.

The *News of the World* ran a piece describing the squalor the 'tragic rock star' was living in now. They reported that Ronnie was in a cockroach-infested home with his wife and her daughters and that while she worked full time at a beauty salon, he waited at home, incontinent and unable to clean himself, smoking marijuana to relieve his pain.

'My wife sorts everything out. She gets depressed but she manages to pay the bills and keep our heads above water. I don't have any income except for royalties. When 'Itchychoo Park' gets played on the radio I get about 2 cents. That's it.'

Susan told the reporter: 'We get up at 5.30 just to have some time together before my two young daughters wake. Then I work 10 hours a day five days a week just to pay the bills. And I still have to cook and look after everyone.'

Susan slammed Ronnie's old rock pals for not helping him out. 'It wouldn't hurt them to give some money, but they are never round when you need them.'

Ronnie remembered the primary interest of *News of the World* readers and obliged. 'We have sex of a sort,' he said. 'At least . . . it's like it was like when I was a boy and wouldn't go all the way in case I got a girl pregnant.'

The paper also reported that Mae Nacol had agreed to drop her libel/slander/defamation case against Ronnie after finding out his living circumstances.

'It's a big relief as I haven't any money to give her anyway,' he said.

In July 1989, Ronnie and Susan travelled to Dallas to see Ringo Starr & His All Starr Band play the Park Amphitheatre. Afterwards, Ringo treated him and the rest of his (genuinely all-star) band to a slap-up dinner at the Four Seasons.

Mark Bowman, the photographer, was there too.

'It's amazing the things that happened with Ronnie if you were around him. I looked around and there was a four-star catered dinner and a room filled with Clarence Clemons, Ringo Starr, Barbara Bach, Joe Walsh, Billy Preston, Rick Danko, Levon Helm, Jim Keltner, Dr. John and Nils Lofgren. It was almost too much to process.

'I kept my camera out of the way for the most part and just snapped a couple of quick ones of Rick Danko and Billy Preston with Ronnie because they both wanted a shot with Mr Lane.'

At the other end of the glamour spectrum, a couple of months later, a fan, Nigel Jones, while waiting for his washing to dry at an Austin laundrette, wandered into a beer garden next door and happened upon a Ronnie gig.

It was not the most auspicious of venues and the sound was terrible but within minutes, 'I was surrounded by cheering and whooping and silliness, which Ronnie actively encouraged.

'Ronnie Lane was not MEANT to be heard in some sanitised and clinical perfect audio environment. It's not who/what he and his music represented. He was RIGHT about the travelling circus, right about the vaudeville aspects of his music. It's good time music, in the strictest sense. And this particular environment was his chosen place to be and the spirit in his music was perfectly framed in the looseness of a laundromat beer garden in the Texas sunshine. He played for over an hour, gave two encores and would have done a third but the band was tired . . . go figger, eh?'

Ronnie took time out during the beer garden concert to mention that his mate Pete Townshend was playing a big concert that night at the Cotton Bowl in Dallas with The Who.

And Ronnie was there. Pete arranged for him to watch from the wings in his wheelchair. His old mate Billy Nicholls was there, too, singing backing vocals with The Who.

'He grasped my hand with a vice-like grip,' Billy said, 'and just

285

wouldn't let go.' Then Billy went on stage. By the time the show was finished, and the encores had faded away, Ronnie had left.

That handshake turned out to be Billy's last goodbye.

In 1990, John Pidgeon, the rock writer who had once become a Faces roadie to get the inside story, visited Ronnie in Austin.

'I'd wanted to record them both for my Radio 1 series, *Classic Albums*, for which the Small Faces' *Ogdens' Nut Gone Flake* was an overdue candidate, and figured that, with Mac at his side, Ronnie would be a livelier interviewee than on his own. I was right. The interview, recorded at Ronnie's house between rehearsals, was punctuated with laughter and impromptu repartee, hilarity I hadn't heard from them since 1973.'

Ronnie surprised John by telling him the two of them would be going off to tour in Japan in late March. 'It was a bold undertaking for someone whose central nervous system was under daily attack,' John wrote. 'Having recruited a band of Austin musicians, he twisted Ian McLagan's arm to play keyboards.'

Ronnie had been convinced by David Lindley's manager, Ray Woodbury, that he could make a lot of money touring over there.

'Ronnie asked me if I'd tour,' Mac said, 'and I said, "fucking right I will. I won't play 'Itchycoo Park', though." "Aw, fuck, man. I *wrote* that." I said, "I don't care. I hate it. Sorry, but it ain't 'all too beautiful"'.'

Mac got his way.

At the end of March, after a warm-up gig at the Continental, the band – Rich Brotherton, guitar, Scott Garber, bass, Danny Castro, guitar, Don Harvey, drums, Ian McLagan, keyboards, Ronnie Lane, vocals – flew off to Japan.

It did not go well.

'Ronnie was in bad shape physically,' Mac said, 'and was taken to and from some shows in an ambulance. The tour wasn't a pleasurable experience. Ronnie wasn't at all happy and wasn't singing well. His microphone kept falling away from his mouth without him realising, hence nobody could hear his vocals.'

The tour exhausted Ronnie and he had to have a couple of months' complete rest. But he was antsy.

'The trip to Japan kind of got me wanting to work again because I wanted to keep this band together,' Ronnie said. 'All that I have learned in my life is that if you want something, you've got to keep it together.'

So, in October 1990, the Keep It Together tour, with a different line-up – no Mac, but including Ponty Bone on accordion – set off for Chicago, Atlanta, Boston and Minneapolis.

He was a trier.

'We didn't do anything important,' he told the *Chicago Tribune*, looking back over his work with the Small Faces and Faces. 'And when I come to think of it, what importance do any of us have? . . . I've just been looking at the whole thing about existence and everything really hard. What good do we really do to this earth? I can't really see the reason for our existing. It's quite a fair view, I think. You think about it. There is no answer – apart from the fact that God must be a very compassionate fellow.'

In April 1991, Kenney phoned to say Steve Marriott had died or 'Ciggie Blaze Kills Rock Legend', as the *News of the World* put it.

Steve had died in the night in a fire at his 16th-century cottage in Arkesden, Essex. Most reports came to the conclusion that Steve, drunk and possibly stoned, fell asleep with a cigarette in his hand. Some thought it was an act of arson carried out by the mob, although which mob remains unspecified – one or other of them.

All Ronnie said was, 'I'm jealous.'

But like the Dude, he abided.

Bucks Burnett, Ronnie's friend and ex-butler, still kept in touch.

'Susan was taking good care of him. Physically she seemed to do a good job of keeping him alive: keeping him clean, keeping him fed, keeping him laughing. I saw them quite happy together.'

But there were moments.

'It was in America while I was on tour,' Eric Clapton said, 'this was a 1992 tour. He came to see me in Dallas I think, or it might have been Houston. He was pretty angry, I mean he was funny, but he was fed up. He really wanted to see the show, but it was a very frustrating experience for him. I think it was the predicament of being backstage with all the normal things that he would have been very much a part of. He was in a lot of conflict, you know. He was very angry about his own condition, and it was sad and very hard to be around him 'cause you could feel his pain.'

He did some more recording, a demo of a song he'd written with Brad Brobisky, 'King of the Lazy World', but it had to be done in spurts. A single line or phrase was all he could manage in one go.

Later, Brad asked Ronnie if he could finish the track off himself and it ended up on a 1995 album by Brad's band The Keepers, *Looking for a Sign*, along with another Lane/Brobisky track 'The Boulevardier'.

'In '92 there was a Ron Wood show here and a party the night before,' Joe Denberg said. The show was at the Terrace in Austin – part of Woody's Slide on This tour. 'I wound up at a table with Woody, Mac and Ronnie. It was boisterous fun.'

At the gig, Ronnie was invited on stage in his wheelchair. He managed a chorus or two of 'Ooh La La'. It was his last ever performance.

A couple of years later, at another event, Jody found himself back-stage with: 'Rod Stewart, Ronnie and Mac. In other words, three-fifths of the Faces. The difference in atmosphere between those two gatherings was quite apparent. Rod Stewart and Ronnie Lane didn't quite know what to say. I think Rod's looking at Ronnie thinking, "There but for the grace of God go I". Ronnie's looking at Rod going, "Well, I appreciate him taking care of my medical bills, but it's hard to come out and just say thank you." It was an awkward situation."

Susan became increasingly protective of her husband, causing some of his Austin buddies to feel like they were being eased out of his life. But the endless flow of late-night visitors, hangers on and drug dealers were putting a strain on their family. While Susan was out at work things had been stolen from the apartment, including one of Ronnie's guitars.

Then they decided to move to Trinidad – not the Caribbean island but a tiny town (pop. 7,000) in Colorado.

'We sensed a spiritual pull to this beautiful small town which lies in the shadow of Fishers Peak. We needed the kind of people who lived there. We were attracted to the old-time, solid values which it had. We had to be where the soul is free, and this town didn't let us down. It had emotional freedom. There was a lack of big city complications. It was Ronnie's father's dream to come out here and live in the Rocky Mountains. He lived his father's dream. Ronnie told me many times that his father, Stanley, was also his very best friend, he absolutely worshipped him.'

The move came as a bit of a shock to some of Ronnie's friends. Mac had just made the move from LA to Austin with his wife, Kim. But a month after they arrived, Ronnie, Susan and her two daughters upped sticks and left.

'Perhaps Susan didn't relish the idea of having us as neighbours,' Mac said.

In some people's eyes, Trinidad didn't seem the best choice. Although it was cooler than Texas, the medical care available in the town was limited but not entirely absent because Trinidad was a leading centre for gender reassignment surgery, with its own specialised hospital.

The roads in and out of the town go over passes, through valleys and historic mountain villages. But Ronnie didn't see much of that and spent most of his time in bed, looking out of his picture window at a single aspen tree and the street outside.

'I talked to Ronnie when he was bedridden,' said Kenney. 'I spoke to him more or less every day. When he was lying down towards the end he couldn't speak much because his lungs were collapsing so I

289

would do the talking for him. I would crack jokes and his wife would say he's smiling and laughing down the phone. I used to talk to myself basically . . . We'd just been kids together at the birth of the thing that had made us all.

'I knew he was going to die.'

Susan told *Mojo* magazine that Ronnie loved watching westerns on the telly and listening to music. 'Van Gogh prints hung on the wall, as did a Small Faces calendar sent to Ronnie by *The Darlings of Wapping Wharf Launderette*, a British fanzine. A picture of eight-year-old Ronnie dressed in a pirate's costume sat on a shelf, while a framed letter from Ronald Reagan thanking Ronnie for his efforts during the ARMS concerts hung by the front door. Ronnie had just enough mobility left in one hand to lightly stroke a cat or touch the hand of a visitor indicating he had something to say.'

Susan told friends that Ronnie's favourite game at that time was 'playing dead'. He'd go limp and lie motionless until people started to panic around him and then he'd open his eyes and laugh.

Ronnie still had pictures of Meher Baba on the wall, too: hopefully they bought him solace.

'I have no fear or apprehension whatsoever about dying and have contemplated suicide on more than one occasion. I've seen more in my life than many people see in three of theirs. I've taken chances and that's what it's all about.'

In April 1997, Susan phoned Mac and told him that if he wanted to see Ronnie for the last time, he should hurry to Trinidad where he was in hospital.

'I saw him a month before he passed,' Mac said. 'I went up to Trinidad to visit. They had thought even many years before that he wouldn't survive long. He had this big moustache. I said, 'Ronnie, don't shave the moustache. I think it's the only thing keeping you together.' He laughed at me. He always had a sense of humour. It couldn't have been easy most of the time, but he never showed it.'

But within days of Mac's visit Ronnie was out of hospital and back home with his family. The Lanes' financial problems had eased in the previous year. Thanks to Kenney Jones' efforts they'd managed to claw back some of the money owed by Decca and Immediate.

In 1996, Kenney had also produced and released a tribute album called *Long Ago and Worlds Apart*, featuring artists like Paul Weller, Primal Scream, Buzzcocks and Ocean Colour Scene covering Small Faces hits. All proceeds went to Ronnie and MS research.

He'd been ill for 21 years. Finally, he contracted pneumonia and died on 4 June 1997 in Mount Raphael Hospital.

In accordance with Susan's Native American traditions, he was interred just a few hours later, dressed in his favourite cowboy shirt. He was buried near a statue of Kit Carson, famous hunter and adventurer of the Wild West, a 'hardy explorer of the trackless wilderness', in Trinidad, Colorado. Susan would have a headstone made to mark the grave inscribed simply.

Lane

'God Bless Us All'

'He was a musician who could no longer play, a singer who could no longer sing,' Wayne Pernu wrote movingly in *Mojo*, 'an exquisitely gifted songwriter who doubtless had melodies running through his head but no longer possessed the means of bestowing on the world.'

'His widow called me up a few days after he died,' Kenney said, 'and said, 'Trinidad and Tobago post office just called me from the Caribbean, and they had a letter for him.'

The letter contained a huge royalty cheque.

Selected Bibliography

Books

Arden, Don, *Mr Big*, Robson, 2004

Altham, Keith, *The PR Strikes Back*, Blake Publishing Ltd, 2001

Baba, Meher, *The Path of Love*, Sheriar Foundation, 2000

Brooks, Elkie, *Finding My Voice*, Robson 2012

Browne, Phil, *Are We Still Rolling?* Tape Op, 2011

Coleman, Ray, *Survivor: The Authorized Biography of Eric Clapton*, Sidgwick & Jackson, 1985

Garner, Ken, *The Peel Sessions*, Ebury Press, 20007

Hellier, John and Hewitt, Paolo *Ronnie Lane: Can You Show Me a Dream?*, Griffiths Publishing, 2017

Hewitt, Paolo, *The Soul Stylist*, Mainstream Publishing, 2001

Johns, Glyn, *Sound Man*, Penguin Random House, 2014

Jones, Kenney, *Let the Good Times Roll*, Blink Publishing, 2018

Johnson, Eddie, *Tales from the Two Puddings*, 51st State Press, 2012

Marsh, Dave, *Before I Get Old: The Story of The Who*, Plexus Publishing Ltd, 1989

McClagan, Ian, *All the Rage*, Sidgwick & Jackson, 1989

Neill, Andy, *Faces*, Omnibus Press, 2011

Oldham, Andrew Loog, *Stoned*, Vintage Publishing, 2001

Oldham, Andrew Loog, *2Stoned*, Vintage Publishing, 2003

Peel, John, and Ravencroft, Sheila, *Margave of the Marshes*, Corgi reprint, 2006

Pidgeon, John, *Rod Stewart and the Changing Faces*, Granada Publishing Limited, 1976

Power, Martin, *Jeff Beck: Hot Wired Guitar: The Life of Jeff Beck*, Omnibus Press, 2014

Rawlings, Terry, Hellier, John and Sharp, Ken, *Quite Naturally, the Small Faces*, Complete Music Publications Ltd, 1997

Rawlings, Terry, *Rock on Wood*, Pan Macmillan, 1999

Spence, Simon, *All or Nothing*, Omnibus Press, 2020

Spence, Simon, *Immediate Records: Lets You In*, Better Publishing, 2008

Stringfellow, Peter, *King of Clubs*, Little, Brown, 1997

Weight, Richard, *Mod, a Very British Style*, Bodley Head, 2013

Wood, Ronnie, *Ronnie*, Macmillan, 2007

Wright, Tom and Vanhecke, Susan, *Raising Hell on the Rock'n'Roll Highway*, Omnibus Press, 2007

Publications

Austin Chronicle

Austin Statesman

Beat International

Dallas Observer

Disc Magazine

Disc and Music Echo

Melody Maker

New Musical Express

New Statesman

New York Times

Phonograph

Rave

Record Hunter

Record Mirror

Rolling Stone

Sounds

Stratford Express

Texas Monthly

Uncut

Village Voice

Documentaries

On the Music Moguls: Masters of Pop – Money Makers, BBC documentary, 2016
The Passing Show, DVD made by Rupert Williams and James Mackie, released 2008

Websites

https://www.fishtailparkas.com
https://www.furious.com/perfect/ronnielane
http://www.makingtime.co.uk
https://mikemcinerney.com
https://nostalgiacentral.com
https://petetownshend.net
https://powerpop.blog/2020/01/11/ronnie-lane-how-come
https://www.ronnielane.com
https://www.slim-chance.co.uk
https://vintagerock.com
https://vinylmemories.wordpress.com
http://www.wappingwharf.com
https://www.whereseric.com/the-vault/websites-official/
    ericclaptoncom
https://www.youtube.com/channel/UCoSq2rEcRyYI-ki625mJqpQ

UK Discography

Singles with the Small Faces

'Whatcha Gonna Do About It'/'What's a Matter Baby', Decca 1965
'I've Got Mine'/'It's Too Late', Decca 1965
'Sha-La-La-La-Lee'/'Grow Your Own', Decca 1966
'Hey Girl'/'Almost Grown', Decca 1966
'All or Nothing'/'Understanding', Decca 1966
'My Mind's Eye'/'I Can't Dance with You', Decca 1966
'I Can't Make It'/'Just Passing', Decca 1967
'Patterns'/'E Too D', Decca 1967
'Here Come the Nice'/'Talk to You', Immediate 1967
'Itchycoo Park'/'I'm Only Dreaming', Immediate 1967
'Tin Soldier'/'I Feel Much Better', Immediate 1967
'Lazy Sunday'/'Rollin' Over', Immediate 1968
'The Universal'/'Donkey Rides a Penny a Glass', Immediate 1968
'Afterglow'/'Wham Bam Thank You Mam', Immediate 1969

Albums with the Small Faces

Small Faces, Decca 1966
From the Beginning, Decca 1967

Small Faces, Immediate 1967
Ogdens' Nut Gone Flake, Immediate 1967
The Autumn Stone, Immediate 1970

Singles with the Faces

'Flying'/'Three Button Hand Me Down', Warner Bros. 1970
'Had Me a Real Good Time'/'Real Wheel Skid', Warner Bros. 1971
'Stay with Me'/'Debris', Warner Bros. 1971
'Cindy Incidentally'/'Skewiff (Mend the Fuse)', Warner Bros. 1973

Albums

The First Step, Warner Bros. 1970
Long Player, Warner Bros. 1971
A Nod Is as Good as a Wink, Warner Bros. 1971
Ooh La La, Warner Bros. 1973

Singles as Ronnie Lane/Slim Chance

'How Come?'/'Tell Everyone', GM Records 1974
'The Poacher'/'Bye and Bye (Gonna See the King)', GM Records 1974
'Anymore for Anymore'/'Roll on Babe', GM Records 1974
'What Went Down (That Night with You)'/'Lovely', Island Records 1974
'Brother, Can You Spare a Dime?'/'Ain't No Lady', Island Records 1975
'Don't Try 'N' Change My Mind'/'Well Well Hello (The Party)', Island
    Records 1976
'Street in the City'/'Annie (with Pete Townshend)', Polydor Records 1977
'Kuschty Rye'/'You're So Right', Gem Records 1979
'One Step'/'Lad's Got Money', Gem Records 1979

Albums as Ronnie Lane/Slim Chance

Anymore for Anymore, GM Records 1974
Ronnie Lane and Slim Chance, GM Records 1975
One for the Road, Island Records 1976
See Me, Gem Records 1979

Collaborative albums

Mahoney's Last Stand (with Ronnie Wood), Atlantic Records 1976
Rough Mix (with Pete Townshend), Polydor 1977

A selection of posthumous releases

Ronnie Lane, *Kuschty Rye – The Singles*, NMC Records 1997
Ronnie Lane with Slim Chance, *You Never Can Tell – The BBC Sessions*, NMC Records 1997
Ronnie Lane, *Tin and Tambourine*, NMC Records 1998
Ronnie Lane, *April Fool 1967–1981*, NMC Records 1999
Ronnie Lane, *Live in Austin*, Sideburn Records 2000
Ronnie Lane Band, *Rocket 69/Rockpalast*, NMC Records 2001
Faces, *Five Guys Walk into a Bar* (box set), Warner Bros. 2004
Ronnie Lane and Steve Marriott, *The Legendary Majik Mijits*, Wapping Wharf Records 2014
Ronnie Lane Band, *Just for a Moment (Music 1973–1997)*, UMC 2019

Acknowledgements

Keith Altham
David Barraclough
Steve Bingham
Mark Bowman
Bucks Burnett
Billy Bragg
Claire Browne
Chris Charlesworth
George Chiantz
Ron Chimes
Eric Clapton
Colin Davey
Alun Davies
Jody Denberg
JoRae Di Menno
Ron Fawcus
Steve Fisher
Hughie Flint
Benny Gallagher
Charlie Hart
John Hellier

Paolo Hewitt
Des Horsfall
Glyn Johns
Casey Jones
Kenney Jones
Nigel Jones
Nicola Joss
Alana Lane
Charlie Lane (for the wonderful
    Rock Behind the Roll
    Interviews, posted on
    YouTube)
Kate Lane
Lisa Lane
Luke Lane
Reuben Lane
Stan Lane
Susan Lane
Jim Leverton
Bill Livsey
Graham Lyle

Ed Mayberry

Drew McCulloch

Ron Nevison

Billy Nicholls

Bill Puplett

Terry Rawlings

Carol Reyes

Russ Schlagbaum

Warren Sherman

Steve Simpson

Keith Smart

Pete Townshend

The doctors, nurses and all the
staff at University College
Hospital London

And special thanks to the re-formed Slim Chance band (currently Charlie Hart, Steve Simpson, Steve Bingham, Brendan O'Neill, Geraint Watkins and Billy Nicholls) for keeping the flame alight.

Picture Credits

Ronnie at age 5 Margate ©Alamy
Ronnie in Outcasts, from the personal collection of Ron Chimes
Don Arden ©Getty
Small Faces on Ladder ©Mirrorpix
Small Faces in room with Victorianna ©Alamy
Small Faces in hotel room with guitars ©Mirrorpix
Small Faces walking alligators ©Mirrorpix
Small Faces with PVC macs ©Alamy
Tin Soldiers with PP Arnold ©Alamy
Small faces looking groovy ©Getty
Ronnie with a cigarette ©Shuttershock
Gorgeous small faces ©Alamy
Cover of Ogdens ©Alamy
Ronnie and his first wife ©Alamy
Faces ©Alamy
Faces in bathroom ©Getty
Faces at the Oval ©Getty
Rod and Ronnie ©Getty
The launch of 'Ooh La La' ©Getty
Caravan ©Getty
LMS, courtesy of Keith Smart

Fire eaters, courtesy of Drew McCulloch
Ronnie Passing Show ©Getty
Slim Chance at the table ©Getty
Ronnie and Pete Townshend ©Getty
Ronnie and Eric Clapton ©Alamy
ARMS Concert ©Getty
Andrew Loog Oldham ©Getty
Faces and Bill Wyman ©Getty
Ronnie and Susan ©Mirrorpix

Index

A Nod Is As Good As A Wink . . . To A Blind Horse 159–62
Acquaye, Speedy 88
African-American music 26
Alberto Y Los Trios Paranoias 153
Ali, Muhammad 144
'All Or Nothing' 61–2
Altham, Keith 68, 99, 102–3, 197, 252, 256–7
Ambrose, Dave 128
Animals, The 41, 42
Anymore For Anymore 191–2, 206
Apostolic Intervention, The 86
'April Fool' 226
Arden, David 41
Arden, Don: Faces interest 136; management style 40, 41, 70–1; singing career 40; Small Faces compilation 92; Small Faces, early interest 37, 41–2; Small Faces management 42–6, 50–1, 52–4, 58–9, 63–4, 69–70; Tony Calder, opinion on 77–8
ARMS (Advancing Research in Multiple Sclerosis) 255, 256, 263
ARMS of America 263, 264–5, 268–9, 271–2
Arnold, P.P. 101–2
Artwoods, The 131
Ashley, Beverley 265

Austin music scene 274–6
Autry, Gene 6, 7

Bad Company 207
Bad Finger 217
Bagnoll, Dave 230
Baker, Ginger 248
Baldry, Long John 128
Baldwin, Alan 15–16
Banks, Randy 281
Barclay, Billy 197
Bart, Lionel 75
Batchelor, Cal 243
BBC, banned songs 80, 91–2
Beach Boys 72
Beatles, The 51, 60, 62, 72, 85, 91–2, 97, 240
Beck, Jeff 74, 128, 134, 257, 258–9, 260, 277
Bell, Kevin 244–5
Belshaw, Brain 207, 232
Benjamin, Keith 214
Bennet, Kenny 12
Bingham, Steve 189–91, 193, 200, 203
Birch, Martin 137
Birds, The 35, 128
Blackwell, Chris 208
Blake, Adam 152
blues music 26

Bobbin, John 83
Bolan, Marc 152–3
Bone, Ponty 287
Bonham, John 188, 241
Boucher, Caroline 150–1
Bowman, Mark 267–8, 269, 285
Boyd, Pattie 229, 230
Bragg, Billy 209
Brinsley Schwarz 182
Brobisky, Brad 288
Bronco (TV Western) 9
Brooks, Elkie 32
'Brother, Can You Spare A Dime?' 212
Brotherton, Rich 286
Broughton, Edgar 145
Brown, Joe 40, 44, 222
Brown, Pete 116
Brown, Sam 248–9
Browne, Phil 109–10
Buckley, Lord 28–9, 91
Burdon, Eric 42
Burnett, Bucks 260, 266–7, 270, 287
Burns, Tito 71
Burrows, Steve 9–10
Buzzcocks 291
Byrds, The 72, 85

Calder, Tony 19, 76, 77–9, 89, 97, 105,
    126, 218
Cambridge, George 14, 21, 22
Caravelles 49
Careless, Snr & Jnr 243
Castro, Danny 286
Caulfield, Les 214
Cavern (London club) 36–7
Charlesworth, Chris 176
Chkiantz, George 89, 97, 215
Chili Willi & The Red Hot Peppers 242
Chimes, Ron 9, 12, 14
'Cindy Incidentally' 174
Clapton, Eric 192, 224, 225–6, 228–33,
    234, 239–40, 257, 258, 259–60, 272,
    277, 288
Clarke, Steve 210–11

Clayman, Barry 31–2
Cochran, Eddie 40–1
Cocker, Joe 259
Colling, Mel 248–9
Collins, Phil 18
Colour Me Pop (TV) 117–18
Complete Book of Self-sufficiency (Seymour)
    187
Conroy, Mick 249
Cooper, Alice 143
Cooper, Ray 258
Corbet, Bill 56
Corcoran, Pauline 58–9, 95
Costello, Pat 165
cowboys, film and TV heroes 6–8, 9
Crackerjack! (TV) 64–5, 102
Cream 135
Cristo, Bobby 19
Crowther, Leslie 64–5

Danko, Rick 285
Davey, Colin 212, 221
David, Mack 9
Davies, Alun 239, 243
Davies, Clive 250
Davis, Miles 24, 25, 26
Davison, Harold 71, 74
Dee, Kiki 49
Denberg, Jody 268, 277, 278, 282, 288
Di Menno, JoRae 269–71, 272–3, 274,
    276
Diderot, Denis 82
Disco2 (TV) 150–1
Dodo (psychic) 184
Donovan 127
'Don't Talk To Me Of Love' 15
Dorfman, Stanley 258
Dr Feelgood 242
drugs use, post-war 26–7
Ducks Deluxe 242
Dylan, Bob 84

Eagle, Roger 32
Edge, Graeme 68

Eel Pie Productions 241
EG Management 207–8, 221, 224
Eggs Over Easy 182
Emerson, Lake & Palmer 241
Enthoven, David 207–8
Entwhistle, John 224
Epstein, Brian 68
Escovedo, Alejandro 278, 281, 282

Faces: band tensions 172–3, 174, 177,
    179–80; benefit concert for Bangladesh
    155–6; Billy Gaff's deal 135–7; Canada/
    US tour 1970 143–4; 'drink first,
    playing second' 134–5, 142, 147, 159;
    drug use 169–70; early gigs 137, 139;
    festival appearances 145–6, 152–3,
    168–9; first releases 140–1; hotel
    wrecking reputation 153–4, 163, 165,
    168; John Peel collaborations 141–2;
    'Lead Vocalist Syndrome' 154–5, 165–6;
    Marquee gig 1970 147; Rock'n'roll
    Circus tour 1972 163–6, 192–3; Rod
    Stewart joins 134–5; Ronnie Lane's
    departure 180–1; Ronnie Wood's
    instigation 128–32; songwriting 140,
    148; stage gimmicks 163; Sundown, last
    gigs 181; *Too Drunk For The BBC*
    session 174–5; TV & radio appearances
    140, 142, 150–1, 156–7, 163, 174,
    175–6; UK gigs 1970 145; US tours
    146, 150, 153–5, 158–9, 163–6, 169–70,
    178–80
Faithfull, Marianne 91
Farlowe, Chris 77, 85–6
Fawcus, Ron 214, 215
Fingers, The 83
Firm, The 266
Fisher, Steve 249
Fisher, Tony 97
Five Guys Walked Into A Bar 163
Flint, Hugh 231–2, 233, 243
'Flying' 140
Foster, J.D, 281
Frampton, Peter 105, 122, 125

Franks, Jim 212
Fraser, Andy 166
Free 164, 166

Gaff, Billy 135–7, 158, 161, 168, 180–1,
    184, 195, 206
Gage, William 274
Gallagher, Benny 183, 190, 191, 195, 224
Gallagher, Micky 243
Gallagher, Rory 207
Gallegos, Susan 281–2, 284, 287, 288–90
Garber, Scott 286
Gardener, Kim 131
Gaydon, John 207
Gersten, Victor 71
Gilmour, David 241
Goldstein, Harvey 258
Grade Organisation 71
Graham, Bill 259
Green, Mick 243, 249

Haast, Bill 'Snakeman' 251–2
'Had Me A Real Good Time' 147
Hall, Mafalda 243
Hallyday, Johnny 122–3
Harper, Roy 188, 248
Harris, Bob 237
Harrison, George 17, 85, 99
Hart, Charlie 207, 210, 211, 213, 215,
    216–17, 224, 230, 232, 238–9, 243, 244
Harvey, Don 286
Haynes, Dave 248–9
Hazell, Irving 221
Hellier, John 14, 50, 93
Hellman, Francine 85
Helm, Levon 285
Hendrix, Jimi 73, 96, 146
Herd, The 122, 135
'Here Come The Nice' 91
'Hey Girl' 60–1
High Numbers, The 16
Hill, Captain Peter 1, 200
'hippie' culture 82–3
Hirst, Michael 195

Hollies, The 111
Honeyman-Scott, James 245, 254
Horn, Jim 167
'How Come?' 185, 189
Hudson, Linda 265
Humble Pie 134
Hunt, Susan 66, 86, 99, 114
Hutch, Brian 184
Hutton, Alan 12, 14, 21, 22
Hysinger, Larry 271

'I Can't Make It' 79–80
'I Got Mine' 48, 49
In Memoriam 133
Ingham, John 158–9
Intergalactic Elephant Band 188
'Itchycoo Park' 96–8, 99
'Itchycoo Park' (re-release) 218

Jagger, Mick 4–5, 44, 77, 79, 101, 130
James, Philip, Dr 265, 269
jazz music 24–5
Jeff Beck Group 128
Jethro Tull 192
Jewell, Jimmy 2, 190, 202
John, Dr. 285
Johns, Glyn: ARMS benefit concert
    256–9; house share 129; Immediate
    recording 77; Lane, Gallagher & Lyle
    introduction 183; Lane/Townshend
    project 224, 225; production
    contributions 87, 109, 137, 159, 166,
    169; Ronnie's MS 234, 262; Ronnie's
    Reagan letter 274; Small Faces,
    Hallyday album 122–3; Small Faces,
    Oldham introduction 79; Small Faces,
    work exhaustion 57–8
Johns, Jasper 26
Johnson, Ronnie 281
Jones, Brian 4–5, 130
Jones, Davy 18
Jones, John Paul 241
Jones, Kenney: Andrew Loog Oldham
    meeting 79; ARMS benefit concert
258, 259; benefit concert act 241; Don
    Arden's management 42, 43, 52; early
    bands & gigs 14–15, 21–2; Faces, band
    relations 174; Faces, Canada/US tour
    144; film soundtrack 167, 223; 'Itchycoo
    Park' 96; Lane/Marriot, music shop sale
    19–20; management rip-offs 133;
    Rock'n'roll Circus tour 1972 192–3;
    Ronnie, final conversations 289–90;
    Ronnie, financial support 283, 291;
    Ronnie, first meetings 9–10, 13;
    Ronnie, post-Faces 182; Ronnie/Steve
    relations 86; Selmer job 16; Small Faces,
    mini-tour 1965 33; Small Faces, reunion
    idea 219, 220–1, 222; songwriting 48,
    87; tribute album 291
Jones, Nick 88
Jones, Nigel 285
Juke Box Jury 61–2

Kanner, Alexis 166
Keltner, Jim 285
Kent, Carol 265, 271–2
Kent, Nick 231
Keyes, Bobby 167
Keys, Bobby 278–9
Kilburn & The High Roads 182, 242
King, Maurice 31–2
King, Ron 44–5
Kirke, Simon 166
Knight, Andy 195
Knight, Brian 243
Korner, Alexis 123–4
Kursaal Flyers 242
'Kuschty Rye' 239, 241

Lambert, Paul 194
Lamont, Norman 201–2
Lane, Elsie (née May) 3–4, 5, 8, 12, 100,
    217, 254, 283
Lane, Kate: Eric Clapton's gifts 228; Lane/
    Clapton's village gigs 229–30; London
    return 241; medical tips 227; Passing
    Show project 1–2; Ronnie, divorce and

custody fight 251; Ronnie, MS related tensions 234, 239–40, 247–8; songwriting 224. *See also* McInnerney, Kate

Lane, Lisa 213, 227

Lane, Luke Kito 183, 228–9, 234, 240, 263

Lane, Ronnie: Andrew Loog Oldham, opinion on 79; ARMS benefit concert 256–9; ARMS of America project 263, 264–6, 268–9, 271–2, 274; Austin, music collaborations 278–80, 281, 282, 283–4, 285; Austin radio special 277–8; Austin relocation/residency 274–5, 276, 281; Australia/NZ tour tensions 1968 104, 105–6; bass playing 17, 89; benefit concert act 241; Billy Gaff's deal 135–6; biography idea 268; birth 5; childhood 5–6; children, post-divorce relations 263, 267, 273; Don Arden's management 47, 53, 64, 69–70; drug use 68, 143; early bands & gigs 12–15, 21–2; EG Management 207; Eric Clapton collaborations 231–3; Eric Clapton, friendship 228–30; Faces, critical view 150; Faces promotion 139; Faces reunion gig & UK visit 272–4; fan mania problems 74, 95, 113; fatherhood 183; final weeks and death 290–1; financial problems 254, 268, 272, 283, 291; Fishpool farm, country living 187–8, 212–14, 228–9, 239; Glastonbury appearance 248; high life, hidden woes 162–3; house moves, UK 125–6, 132, 157–8, 185–6; Island Records deal 208; Japan tour 1990 286–7; Jimmy Winston conflicts 49–50; JoRae Di Menno, friendship 269–71; Kate, divorce and custody fight 251; Kate McInnerney, friendship/ relationship 118, 132, 141, 170–3, 178, 180; Kate McInnerney, wedding 214; Kate, MS related tensions 234, 239–40, 247–8; Lane/Clapton's village gigs

229–30; Lane's Mobile Studio (LMS) 167–8, 174; London return 240–1; *Mahoney's Last Stand* (soundtrack) 166–7; management mistrust 39–40; Meher Baba, interest in 104–5, 118, 132, 144–5; mini-US tour 1990 287; MS benefit tour, US 259–61, 262; MS, early signs and diagnosis 233–6; MS, living and working with 238–40, 250, 253, 266–8, 279–81, 283–4, 288; MS, search for treatments 252–3, 254–6, 264, 270–1; MS Society, dislike of 255, 262–3; music career, reflections on 219–20, 253–4; musical beginnings 8, 11; musical circus project 184–5; musical influences 16, 28, 94; *NME* interviews 68, 99–100, 103, 119, 219–20; *Old Grey Whistle Test* 236–7; parties and police 154; Passing Show project 1–2, 193–204, 210, 215; Pete Townshend, friendship 118–19, 132–3, 226–7, 285; Plonk nickname 44; pop comic parody 53–4; quits Faces 180–2; Ringo Starr gathering 284–5; *Rockplast* appearance 245; Rod Stewart, relations with 154–5, 180, 181, 272, 273, 288; Ronnie Lane and his Band 243–6; Ronnie Lane Foundation 276; Ronnie Wood, Faces instigator 128–32; *Rough Mix* collaboration 223–6; school days 8–9; Selmer job 15–16, 28; shared homes 67, 119, 120; Slim Chance, recruitment 183–4; Slim Chance tour 210–11; Small Faces, mini-tour 1965 32–3; Small Faces, origins of 27–30; Small Faces, regroup problems 126–7, 133–4; Small Faces, reunion idea 220–1, 222–3; solo collaborations 188; songwriting 85–6, 93–4, 96, 107–9, 115–16, 149, 192, 212, 215; spiritual happenings 184; Steve Marriot, music shop sale 19–20; Steve Marriot, support projects 248–51; Steve Marriot, tense relations 86–7, 125–6; Steve Marriot's gig hijacking 210–11; Susan Gallegos, relationship/marriage 281–2, 284, 287, 288–9; Susan Hunt, relationship/ marriage 66, 86, 99, 114, 171–2; teenage jobs and girls 9–11; tour exhaustion 57–8; The Tremors, joins 278–80; Trinidad, Colorado relocation 289; TV billing arguments 61

Lane, Rueben Jack 240, 263, 273

Lane, Sandra 213

Lane, Stanley, Jnr.: birth 3–4; childhood 6; marriage 13, 213; Ronnie & JoRae's visit 272; Ronnie, Houston visit 268; Ronnie quits Faces 180, 181; Ronnie's career, contributions to 13, 15, 29, 69; Ronnie's Merc gift 162

Lane, Stanley, Snr.: death 217; family man 5–6; Fishpool farm visit 192; marriage 3–4; Ronnie, supportive relationship 8, 12, 17, 20, 172; society, reflections on 99–100

Lane, Susan 125–6, 132, 158, 170, 171–2; *see also* Hunt, Susan

Lane's Mobile Studio (LMS) 167–8, 174, 185, 192, 207, 214, 217, 225, 230, 239, 249, 254

'Lazy Sunday' 110–12

Le Fleur, Glen 212

Le Mesurier, Robin 273

Led Zeppelin 217, 241–2

Lennon, John 68, 99, 192

Leverton, Jim 248–50

Livsey, Billy 183, 190, 191, 198, 206

Livsey, Josie 197

Loder, Kurt 253

Lofgren, Nils 285

Lollobrigida, Gina 25

Long Player 148–50

Low, Andy Fairweather 257, 258–9

Lucas, Robin 195–6, 197

Lucas, Terry 32, 33–4

Lucken, Wally 194–5, 200

Lyle, Graham 183, 185, 190, 191, 195, 224

Lynch, Kenny 53, 60, 92

MacCambridge, Michael 283–4

McCartney, Paul 80, 85, 241

McCoys, The 77

McCulloch, Drew 195–6, 197–8

McCullough, Henry 243

McGuinness, Tom 232

McInnerney, Alana 170, 171, 190, 213, 230, 234, 240, 251

McInnerney, Kate: Fishpool farm, country living 190, 191, 213–14; Fishpool farm purchase 187–8; Passing Show project 193–5, 196, 197, 200–1, 203; Ronnie Lane, friendship/relationship 118, 132, 141, 170–2, 178, 180; Ronnie Lane, marriage 214–15; songwriting 192, 209

McInnerney, Mike 104–5, 118, 132, 141, 163, 170–1, 172

Mckenna, Mick 232

McLagan, Ian: album title 116; Austin relocation 289–90; Billy Gaff's deal 135; Don Arden, first meeting 50–1; Don Arden's management 63–4, 70; drugs bust 103; early bands 14; Faces, band relations 151–2, 169; Faces, Canada/US tour 143; Faces, early gigs 139; Faces reunion gig 273; film soundtrack 167, 223; 'Itchycoo Park' 96; Japan tour with Ronnie 286–7; money problems 133; Rod Stewart's talent 131; Rod's unfair criticisms 177; Ronnie, US visits 267, 282, 290; Ronnie Wood/ Stones sessions 129; Ronnie's radio special 278; royalties exclusion 121; Sandy Sergeant, relationship/marriage 66, 102, 170; shared homes 67, 119; Small Faces, band relations 86; Small Faces, new member 51–2; Small Faces, reunion idea 222; Steve Marriot's departure 123, 126; Sue Lane affair 172; tour experiences 56–7, 58

Magee, Chuch 173

'Maggie May' 155, 156–7

Mahoney's Last Stand (soundtrack) 166–7, 223

Mansfield, Mike 181
Markee, Dave 224, 226
Marriott, Pam 248–9
Marriott, Steve: Australia/NZ tour
    tensions 1968 104, 105–6; death 287;
    Don Arden, first meeting 42;
    girlfriends 68, 80; girls and sex 65;
    Hollies argument 111; Humble Pie
    career 134; Jenny Rylance,
    relationship/marriage 101; The
    Moments 15, 19; musical beginnings
    18–19; Outcasts gig 21–2; Peter
    Frampton poach 105, 122, 125; P.P.
    Arnold affair 101; psychedelia dismissal
    85; Ronnie Lane, music shop sale
    19–20; Ronnie Lane, tense relations
    86–7, 125–6; Ronnie, support projects
    248–51; Ronnie's MS symptoms 233;
    shared homes 119, 120; Slim Chance,
    gig hijacking 210–11; Small Faces
    image 92; Small Faces, mini-tour 1965
    33–4; Small Faces, origins of 27–30;
    Small Faces, reunion idea 222–3;
    songwriting 85–6, 93–4, 101–2, 107–8,
    110–11, 119–20; tour exhaustion 57;
    TV billing arguments 61
Marsh, Dave 164–5
Marvin, Hank B. 8, 241
Mason, Sue 73
Mayberry, Ed 277–8, 281
Meehan, Pat 37
Meek, Joe 76
Meher Baba 104–5, 118–19, 125, 188
Melly, George 46
Metzger, Gustav 72
Miller, Jean 95
Milligan, Spike 114
Milliken, Chelsey 274, 276, 278, 279, 283
Mods 24–5, 26, 27
Mojo, The (Sheffield club) 34–6, 46
Moments, The 15, 19
Money, Zoot 248–9
Monkees, The 103
Moon, Keith 16, 106

Morice, Barbara 178, 197
Mott The Hoople 217
Move, The 72, 98
MS (Multiple Sclerosis) Society 255, 262
Muleskinners, The 12, 21
Murdoch, Rupert 103
*Music Moguls: Masters of Pop – Money
    Makers* (documentary) 45
musician/artiste, management relations
    38–9
'My Mind's Eye' 64, 65

Nacol, Barbara (Leigh Hunt) 264–6, 269,
    271
Nacol, Mae 264–6, 268–9, 270, 271–2,
    274, 284
Napier Bell, Simon 71
Nash, Graham 83
Nashville Teens, The 41, 48
Nelson, Willie 276
Nevison, Ron 167–8
Newman, Kenny 14, 15
Nicholls, Billy 86, 144–5, 162, 171, 233–4,
    285–6
Nightingale, Annie 44

Ocean Colour Scene 291
Ogdens' Nut Gone Flake 109–10, 114,
    115–17
Oldfield, Boo 248, 252, 254, 256, 265
Oldham, Andrew Loog: hustling skills 75;
    music industry enterprises 75–7; P.P.
    Arnold signing 101; Ronnie's rebuke
    280; Small Faces image 92; Small Faces
    management 79, 81, 87, 89–90, 92, 107,
    116, 126, 133, 136
O'Leary, Laurie 249
Oliver, Sue 68
O'Lochlainn, Ruan 207
One For The Road 215–17
Ooh La La 169, 176–7
Orbison, Roy 74
Osbourne, Jan 135
Osbourne, Sharon 71

O'Sullivan, Mick 91
Outcasts, The 14–15, 21

Page, Jimmy 45, 188, 257, 258–9, 260, 266, 278
Parkinson, Dale 4
Passing Show 1–2
'Patterns' 80
Peel, John 92, 141–2, 156–7, 163, 174–5, 177
Pernu, Wayne 291
phasing (flanging) 96–7
Phillpot, Dave 234
Pidgeon, John 173, 205, 286
Pink Floyd 72, 85
Pioneers, The 21
Playmates 223
Police, The 153
'Pool Hall Richard' 189
popular culture, post-war influences 24–7
Porter, John 232
Potter, Brian 42–3
Powsenby, Clive 214
Preston, Billy 285
Pretenders, The 214
Primal Scream 291
Prioe, Les 153
psychedelia 72, 83–5, 98
pub rock 182–3, 242–3
Pumus, Doc 52–3

Queen 242
Quiet Melon 132

Randall, Jennifer 73
Rave (magazine) 53–4
Ready, Steady, Go! 45, 62, 64, 66
Reagan, Ronald 274
Reid, Taylor, Jenkins 23
Reynolds, Anthony 32
Richards, Keith 44, 77, 251
Rigpa Fellowship 255
Rimbaud, Arthur 84
Robinson, Tony 18

Rocker, Lee 246
Rodgers, Paul 266
Rogers, Roy 6, 7
Rolling Stones 4–5, 51, 75–6, 85, 89, 98, 130, 258
Rolling Stones Rock and Roll Circus, The 192
Ronnie Lane 208–9
Ronnie Lane and his Band 243–6
Ronnie Lane Foundation 276
Ronson, Laurence 258
Rough Mix collaboration 223–6, 236–7
Rousseau, Jean Jacques 82
Rowland, Bruce 1, 183, 185, 190, 194, 203, 243
Rylance, Jenny 101, 107

Salewicz, Chris 219–20
Samwell, Ian 42–3, 92, 136–7
Saturday Club (Radio show) 44
Savage, John 83
Scene at 6.30 (TV show) 63
Schlagbaum, Russ 170, 172, 178, 179, 194, 195, 199, 221, 238
Schuman, Mort 52–3, 92
See Me 243
Sergeant, Sandy 66, 102, 170
Sessler, Fred 251–3
Setzer, Brian 246
Seven Samurai 278
Sex Pistols 217
'Sha-La-La-La-Lee' 53
Shampan, Harold 48–9
Sheeley, Sharon 40–1
Shoffner, Don 267
Shrimpton, Chrissie 80
Simpson, Steve 183, 207, 211–12, 221, 233
Skinner, David 90
Slaven, Kenny 195–6, 197–8, 200, 201
Slim Chance: album releases 208–9; band recruitment 183–4, 189–90, 195–6, 207; Eric Clapton, support band 231–3; Fishpool farm experiences 190–1;

members departure 206; musical circus project 185; poor sales and sackings 219, 221; single releases 205–6; TV & radio appearances 185, 189, 209; UK tour 210–11

Small Faces: Arden's complication album 92; Australia/NZ tour tensions 1968 103–6; band tensions 49–50, 96; constant touring, screaming fans 55–8; *Dateline Diamonds*, film parts 48–9; Decca deal 42; departures and rethink 126–7; Don Arden, first meeting 41–2; Don Arden's management 42–6, 44–6, 50–4, 58–9, 63–4, 69–70; drug use 52, 56, 67–8, 79, 91, 110; European tour 1967 89–90; fan club formed 58–9; fan mania problems 56–7, 113–14, 121–2; fanbase 73, 95; festival appearances 121; first gigs & mini tour 31–7; George Melly interview 46; girls and sex 65–6; Harold Davison's management 74; hotel wrecking reputation 106; Johnny Hallyday collaboration 122–3; Maurice King's management 32, 35; money problems 133; new member 223; *NME* interview 102–3; Oldham/Calder's management 79, 81, 87, 89–90, 92, 107, 120–1, 126, 136; Oldham's unauthorised releases 133; origins of 27–30; Peter Frampton poach 105, 122; Pimlico shared home 54, 67–8; pop comic parody 53–4; promotional film 98; reunion idea 218–19, 220–1, 222–3; Roy Orbison support 74; songwriting 48, 52, 60, 91, 93, 107–9; Steve Marriot's departure 123–4; TV & radio appearances 44, 45, 46, 61, 62, 63, 64, 80, 102, 112, 117–18; Upper Cut gig 1967 73; US tours non-starters 63–4, 96, 98–9, 107, 117

Small Faces (Decca) 60

Small Faces (Immediate Records) 87–8, 92–4

Smith, David 195
Soll, Robert 270
Sommers, Ron 271
Sonny & Cher 44
Sounds 212, 223
Spence, Simon 71, 77
St James Gate 207
Stafford, Caroline 155, 156
Stanshall, Vivian 2, 197–8
Starr, Ringo 284–5
Stewart, Chris 183–4, 189
Stewart, Chrissie 243
Stewart, Cynthia 235
Stewart, Ian 129, 167, 224, 231, 232, 234, 243, 244, 245, 256–7, 259
Stewart, Rod: early career 128; ex-girlfriends 101; Faces albums, criticisms 141, 177; Faces, Canada/US tour 144; Faces new member 134–5; Faces reunion gig 272, 273; house buying 157; music awards 156; record deal perks 133; Ronnie Lane, financial support 283; Ronnie Lane, relations with 154–5, 180, 181, 258, 272, 273, 288; Small Faces, potential member 129–30, 131–2; solo releases 139, 146–7, 155; songwriting 158–9; stage persona 151–2
Stigwood, Robert 70, 135, 218
Stray Cats 214, 246
Stringfellow, Peter 34–6, 46
Symes, Phil 151

T-Rex 152–3
Taylor, Mick 130, 245
Taylor, Rod 63
Taylor, Steve 12, 14
Thank Your Lucky Stars (TV) 44, 61
The Autumn Stone 133
The First Step 140–1
'The Poacher' 205–6
'The Universal' 119–20
Thomas, Chris 215
Thompson, Dave 134

Thornton, Eddie 'Tan Tan' 88, 121

'Tin Soldier' 101–2

Tonks, Hilary 95

Top Gear (radio show) 112, 142

Top of the Pops 45, 46, 61, 62, 64, 98, 102, 112, 140, 151, 174

Townshend, Pete: art student 26; biography idea 268; Faces, praise for 138; film soundtrack 167, 223; Lane's London move 240–1; Ronnie & JoRae's visit 272; Ronnie Lane, friendship 118–19, 132–3, , 226–7, 285; Ronnie Lane's *Rough Mix* album 224–6, 236–7; Ronnie's MS symptoms 234; Ronnie's radio special 278; Small Faces revamp 127; stage antics 16, 72; Steve Marriot, tense relations 104, 106

Trads 24

Traffic 85, 98

Tremors, The 278–9

Tuck, Stuart 31

Tweddell, Nick 116

Twice As Much 86, 90

Twisted Wheel, The (club) 32, 33

Uhse, Beate 146

Unwin, Stanley 114–15, 118

Upper Cut (club) 73, 95

Valentine, Hilton 17

Velvet Underground 91

Vincent, Gene 40–1

Voelz, Susan 281

Wakeman, Rick 207, 217

Walker, Scott 32

Waller, Mickey 129, 167

Walsh, Joe 285

Watson, John 153

Watts, Charlie 224, 257, 260

Weaver, Mick 243, 249

Weedon, Val 50

Welch, Chris 74, 196, 226–7

Weller, Paul 93, 291

Westlake, Kevin 183, 190, 192, 198, 205

'What Went Down (That Night With You),' 208

'Whatcha Gonna Do About It' 42–4, 45, 47

Whitehead, Peter 77

Who, The 16–17, 72, 104, 156, 185, 192, 217, 241

Whole Earth Catalog, The 187

Wickham, Vicki 44

Williams, Tiger 144

Williamson, Sonny Boy 35–6

Wills, Rick 223

Wilson, Eddie 275

Wings 241

Winston (Langwith), Jimmy 28, 30, 35, 37, 42, 49–50, 60, 92

Winwood, Steve 258

Wood, Art 131–2, 133

Wood, Ronnie: art student 26, 127, 128; Austin gig with Ronnie 288; The Birds 35, 128; Faces, Canada/US tour 144; Faces formation 128–31; Faces, Lane's departure 180; Faces reunion gig 273; Fred Sessler, opinion 251; house buying 157–8; Jeff Beck Group 128; *Mahoney's Last Stand* (soundtrack) 166–7, 223; Rod's songwriting 158–9; Ronnie, financial support 283; Ronnie's radio special 278; stage persona 152; studio complaints 150

Woodbury, Ray 286

Wright, Tom 159–60, 165–6

Wyman, Bill 4–5, 257, 259, 260, 273, 277–8

Wyndham, Francis 75

Yamauchi, Tetsu 189

Yardbirds, The 85